MWN

VEGETARIAN
INDIAN
FOOD & COOKING

CONTENTS

Introduction

Indian dishes are adored throughout the world and vegetarianism has long been a significant part of this popular cuisine. Vegetarian Indian food offers so many combinations of tastes and aromas that it never becomes bland or predictable. Fresh vegetables in rich fragrant sauces; nutty lentils, beans and peas; and of course an incredible array of spices: these characterize exciting recipes that warm the body and soothe the soul. Besides offering fabulous flavours, the dishes are also extremely fresh and healthy.

The vast and vibrant land of India conjures up images of mystery, magic and romance. It is a land steeped in heritage and history, one that has witnessed great empires rise and crumble.

Exotic spices have been grown in India for centuries, and it is the carefully prepared blends of these ingredients that provide the mouthwatering tastes and aromas of countless vegetarian dishes eaten throughout the entire country.

India has long been known as the spice bowl of the world. The use of premium quality aromatics in this sun-drenched, monsoon-fed land was an established way of life long before the traders arrived.

Among those lured to the country by valuable spices were Arabs, English, Dutch, Portuguese and Spanish traders.

RELIGIOUS INFLUENCES

India is a land of many religions: Muslim, Hindu, Christian, Sikh, Buddhist and Jain. The impact of these on Indian food has been profound. Muslims and Hindus predominate overall, and they have certain restrictions: for example, Muslims abstain from eating pork or consuming alcohol, and Hindus as well as Sikhs do not eat beef.

Hinduism is the major religion of the country and around 30 per cent of Hindus are vegetarian. The members of the highest caste within the Hindu community, known as the Brahmins, are the most stringent followers of vegetarianism. They do not eat eggs, and avoid strong-smelling ingredients, such as onion and garlic, as these are generally associated with cooking meat, poultry and fish. However, some Hindus do include fish and shellfish in their diet. Buddhists are similarly split, with some adhering to vegetarianism and others eating meat and fish. Jains, however, are strict vegetarians, with many followers taking it to the next level and embracing veganism.

A RICH AND VARIED CUISINE

Foreign immigrants introduced cooking techniques to India that are still practised today. The north continues to be dominated by Mughal cuisine, while the east has tribal and Anglo-Indian influences. In the south, Syrian Jews and French traders passed on their cooking methods, and western India came under the influence of the Portuguese and the Persians (Parsis). The result is a rich, multi-dimensional cuisine with a colourful repertoire of world-famous recipes.

Spectacular scenery, fascinating ancient customs and glorious foods all continue to draw foreigners to this magical land. Just like the breathtakingly beautiful scenery, culinary traditions have been influenced by geographical and climatic conditions. With vast distances to be travelled, and no means of transporting fresh produce efficiently, cooks have made the best use of the ingredients available to them locally.

The beauty of Indian cooking is in its variety. Different areas and traditions have developed their own regional specialities, and recipes have been handed down through the generations. Although many

Left *Barbecued corn on the cob is a popular snack sold by street vendors all over India, filling the air with its appetizing aroma.*

dishes are fiery with chillies, there are others that are mellow. Many of the most familiar regional dishes come from northern India. These include koftas, mild kormas and tandoori recipes. The cuisine of North West Province, which is now in Pakistan, is aromatic but does not use chillies excessively, so it is not as hot as many of the tongue-tingling dishes found elsewhere.

The most fiery spice blends, such as the famous *vindaloo*, originate from western India. The recipes of this region tend to favour the use of dairy products including yogurt and buttermilk, and the meals are typically accompanied by all kinds of unusual pickles. Coconuts are favourite ingredients of eastern and southern India, and are used for making both sweet and savoury dishes, including deliciously creamy sauces. As south Indian cuisine is predominantly vegetarian, there is no shortage of delectable meat-free recipes to choose from, which utilize nuts, beans, peas and lentils, making hearty and nutritious meals to appeal to both vegetarians and meat-eaters alike.

Above *A stunning mountainside tea estate in Kerala, south India. Tea, along with rice and wheat, is one of the staple crops in India.*

VEGETARIANISM FOR HEALTH

Indian vegetarian cooking aims to produce a balanced, healthy and appetizing meal. A vegetarian diet consists of good-quality protein and high-fibre foods with all the essential vitamins and nutrients. The main sources of protein for vegetarians are beans, peas, lentils, grains and dairy products. Indian cooks use these in numerous ways to make delicious and varied meals. Fresh vegetables and fruits provide all the vitamins and minerals that the body needs. Rice, the staple accompaniment in many parts of the country, is a good source of carbohydrate, which is also believed to steady blood sugar levels. Even the bread, chapati, is made of wholemeal (whole-wheat) flour, which has a high percentage of bran and wheatgerm, and this provides the necessary intake of fibre and protein.

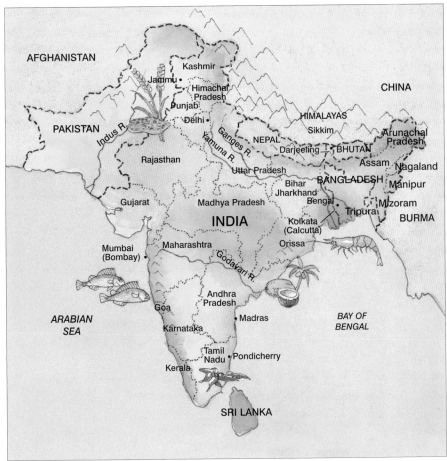

Left *India is a vast country boasting diverse landscapes and climates, which produce different ingredients and cooking styles.*

Vegetarian meals are on the whole inexpensive and quick to make, and the numerous different ways in which the dishes can be cooked stops the diet from becoming too monotonous. These cooking processes mainly use light oils such as sunflower or vegetable oils, which are important in maintaining good health. Fat is a wonderful flavour enhancer as well as a great source of energy, and we all need small amounts of it for the repair and growth of cells, although excessive amounts have well-known negative effects on our bodies.

Many of the popular ingredients used in Indian vegetarian cooking claim to have medicinal powers. For example, garlic has antiseptic properties that aid the digestive system and is excellent for lowering the blood cholesterol levels and reducing the risk of heart disease. Onions have antioxidant and probiotic properties that help the body fight diseases. Fresh ginger reduces stomach acidity and combats the risk of ulcers, while cinnamon, cardamom and cloves are good for fighting the symptoms of coughs and colds.

PLANNING AN INDIAN VEGETARIAN MEAL

Rice and bread are the staples of an Indian vegetarian diet, accompanying a main dish that is often served with a platter of inviting little side dishes, such as pickles, chutneys and salads flavoured with fresh herbs, chillies or yogurt.

Traditionally, Indian dishes are not strictly categorized into appetizers and main courses. Several dishes are cooked and served at the same time and the diners simply help themselves to everything. What is more, people generally have second helpings of everything on offer! It is, however, customary to start the meal with bread and follow with rice, accompanied by spicy dishes. In the classic style, all the food is served on a *thali* (large platter) traditionally made of stainless steel. Rice and bread are placed in the centre, with bowls containing various curries, pickles, chutneys and raitas around the edge.

Above *A thali meal is a well-balanced selection of small dishes served on a platter with some bread and rice.*

A meal will usually end with fresh fruit, rather than elaborate or cooked desserts. Fruits can be served with flair, however, and are often combined with other ingredients to create imaginative and exciting flavours. Choose one or two exotic fruits, such as papaya, pomegranate or star fruit (carambola), and combine them with everyday fruits for a zingy salad, then serve with Greek (US strained plain) yogurt flavoured with rose water and ground cardamom. Indian sweetmeats tend to be quite rich so are more commonly served as a snack with tea and coffee.

Until recent years alcoholic drinks did not accompany an Indian meal. This is because most Indians prefer to drink only refreshing water or a cooling yogurt drink (lassi) with their meal. This is a practice that is now changing since beer, lager and wine are becoming more popular and readily available accompaniments to food. India now produces very good quality wines, which complement spicy food, and there are also plenty of light white wines or low-tannin reds from other countries. Fiery dishes are best accompanied by a really

Left *Spices, on sale here in an open-air market in Goa, India, are the building blocks of the wonderful flavours found in Indian dishes.*

HOW TO USE THIS BOOK

This recipe book is divided into types of dish that represent the best of the different vegetarian cuisines of India, from soups, snacks and appetizers to main dishes, desserts and sweetmeats. It also includes a variety of side dishes, salads, chutneys and relishes, as well as breads, rices and drinks – in fact, everything you need to create the perfect meal, whether it be a light supper or a more elaborate dinner party for friends and family.

Many recipes are quick to prepare with the simplest of spice combinations, whereas others call for a more varied store of spices and flavourings, including some lesser-known ingredients such as mango powder (amchur) and compressed tamarind. Today, most of these special ingredients are readily available from supermarkets. Fresh herbs such as coriander (cilantro) are sold cheaply in large bunches in Asian stores and markets. These stores also sell large bags of whole spices, which will provide you with a plentiful supply for flavouring all your favourite Indian dishes and are ideal if you enjoy preparing spicy food regularly.

Featuring traditional recipes from around India, this book will whet your appetite and equip you with the skills to create a magnificent repertoire of Indian classics.

Above *Tea is often served after a meal, as well as being enjoyed throughout the day both at home and on the street.*

well-chilled and full-bodied white wine. Tea and coffee are traditionally enjoyed after a meal, and hot or chilled spiced tea is a particular favourite throughout India.

If planning a party, it is a good idea to cook the main dishes a day ahead, storing them in the refrigerator until you are ready to reheat them. You could also make them several weeks in advance and then freeze. Frozen dishes must be defrosted and then reheated thoroughly. Accompaniments can also be prepared 24 hours in advance, although the seasonings should not be added until just before serving. You can prepare vegetables the day before, but do not cook them more than a few hours ahead. Likewise, you can prepare ingredients for raitas a day ahead, but do not assemble them until a few hours before they are needed, as the yogurt should always be fresh.

Below *Aubergines (eggplants) are grown in India and are used in many dishes.*

Below *Coconut is a key south-Indian ingredient, particularly in Kerala, where it grows in abundance.*

Below *Red-hot chillies grow well in the spice fields of Andhra Pradesh, southern India.*

North India

The Himalayas dominate the states of north India, from Kashmir in the north west to Uttar Pradesh in the south east of the region. All of the 14 highest peaks in the world can be found here, including Mount Everest, and with precipitous slopes and changeable weather it is no wonder that the food in the northern region is very different from that of the hot, ocean-bathed south. Main dishes often use meat, poultry or delicate river fish such as rainbow trout, but there is also an abundance of fruit and vegetables.

JAMMU AND KASHMIR

In this stunning, northernmost region of India, the brightly dressed women tend gardens full of vegetables and fruit, which flourish around the lakes in the pleasant warmth of summer, selling the fresh produce at the many floating markets that attract thousands of shoppers. In the autumn, trees are laden with plums, peaches, cherries, almonds and walnuts, and these are dried and stored for the bitterly cold winter months. Saffron, arguably the most important ingredient grown in Kashmir, is also produced here – the crocus flower from which it is made grows in large quantities in the cool northern fields.

Kashmiri cuisine offers some of the most exquisite-tasting vegetable dishes. It uses ingredients such as the delectable morel mushroom, the roots of locally grown lotus flowers, walnuts and an array of fresh and dried fruits. The rich supply of good quality ingredients leads to all sorts of splendid traditions, including that of the Kashmiri banquet. These enormous feasts consist of many courses, most of them containing meat, although there are many vegetarian delicacies too. The dishes are skilfully

prepared by chefs known as *wazwans*, who carefully blend generous amounts of spices to produce delectable vegetarian treats, such as Lotus Root Kebabs and Stuffed Sweet Peppers, nutritious desserts such as Ground Rice in Saffron-scented Milk and warming drinks, such as Spice-infused Kashmiri Tea.

Kashmiri chefs have a unique tradition of shaping ground spices into discs, from which small amounts can be broken off and added to dishes as required. The spicing is different in Hindu and Muslim cooking, with Hindus favouring Asafoetida, fenugreek, ginger and fennel and Muslims favouring onion and garlic. Both groups, however, use Kashmiri chillies, which lend an intense colour without being overly pungent.

Left Many crops, including (bell) peppers, grow in the mountain state of Himachal Pradesh.

Above *Oxen are used on the terraced Himalayan rice paddies in Himachal Pradesh.*

HIMACHAL PRADESH

Just south of Kashmir, Himachal Pradesh, 'the mountain state', is a stunning mosaic of dense forests, snow-clad peaks and lush, green valleys. Spiky pines and verdant, broad-leafed trees cling to the lower slopes of the precipitous mountains, while gently meandering rivers and serene lakes create a beautiful panorama.

Agriculture is the main source of income in Himachal Pradesh and wheat, maize, barley and rice are grown in abundance where the terrain flattens out below the Himalayan foothills.

The food in this state is not dissimilar to that found in other parts of north India. Meat features strongly on most menus, and spices such as cardamom, cloves, chillies

Above *Fruit and vegetables abound on the shores of the Kashmiri lakes in the Himalayas.*

and cinnamon are used liberally to add flavour and character to the dishes. A typical meal in many households will often, as elsewhere in north India, consist of *dal-chawal-subzi-roti*, a lentil broth served with rice, a vegetable curry and bread.

PUNJAB

Situated at the foot of the Himalayas, Punjab is home to Delhi, which was the heart of the Mughal empire and remains one of the most important cities in India. The name 'Punjab' is derived from two Persian words *panj* and *aab*, the former meaning 'five' and the latter 'water' or 'river'; the state is rich in natural resources as well as in superb architecture. Primarily an agrarian state, agriculture is the focal point of the economy. The main crops are wheat and maize, and the state is known as the 'granary of the nation'.

As elsewhere in northern India, the region has long been influenced by invaders, pilgrims and traders from north of the mountains, who made their way across the Himalayas centuries ago, aiming to subdue and rule the native people and to make use of their agricultural land. They brought some of their own traditions of farming and cooking with them. The most succesful of the invaders were the Mughal lords who rode through the Khyber Pass in 1526 and

imposed their rule on almost the whole of India for 200 years. Their legacy is the popular tradition of Mughal cuisine, with its silky sauces and the fragrance of saffron, as well as many monuments and tombs.

Punjab is also famous for its tandoori cooking. The *tandoor* is a barrel-shaped clay oven that it is believed to have originated in Egypt. Charcoal is used to fuel the *tandoor* and the food is usually cooked on a spit as a kebab. The combination of clay and charcoal produces a fierce heat – usually around 400°C/750°F – which seals the outer surface of the marinated meat or vegetables instantly, locking in flavour and keeping the inside moist and succulent. The temperature is then lowered for the remainder of the cooking time, and the result is meltingly tender and flavoursome kebabs. Naans are also cooked in the *tandoor*, and these breads make the ideal accompaniment to any number of kebabs and spicy curries.

As elsewhere in the north, Mughal food features prominently on the menus, especially in Delhi, which is often called the gastronomic heart of India as it is such an eclectic mixture of cultures and cuisines. Among the many dishes on offer are kormas, pasandas, pulaos and biryanis and, of course, kebabs cooked in the *tandoor*. Mughal-influenced rich *shorbas* (soups) and *kulfi*, the popular Indian iced dessert, are also of Mughal origin.

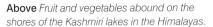

Above *Wheat, along with maize, is the primary crop grown in Uttar Pradesh.*

UTTAR PRADESH

Lying in close proximity to Nepal, Uttar Pradesh is home to the oldest city in the world, Benares (or Varanasi), through which flows the Ganges, India's holy river. The land is very fertile and the state is India's largest producer of oil seeds and food grains, including wheat, barley, maize and sugarcane, as well as some of the best basmati rice in the country. As such it is an important area in economic terms, and agriculture is the primary source of income for the region.

Over the centuries the state has been influenced by many religions, such as Hinduism, Islam, Jainism and Buddhism, and these have all had an impact on the cuisine. Today, the diet of the local population is rich and varied, with lamb and chicken being the most popular meats for those who are permitted to eat it, usually accompanied by rice or bread and a large pot of locally grown vegetables, including mustard greens, corn, spinach and tomatoes, and split peas or lentils.

Dairy products, such as milk, ghee, paneer (Indian cheese) and yogurt supply much of the protein in the diet, which is especially important for the vegetarians, and these also feature in the many delicious desserts on offer.

North-East India

Seven states make up the region of north-east India. This is a picturesque, hilly country, bordering the eastern edge of the Himalayan mountains where they tower over Nepal, Bhutan and China. These states are all landlocked – the only access to the sea is via Bangladesh or Myanmar (Burma) – and so the main focus of regional cuisine is on meat and dairy products rather than fish, along with a huge range of vegetables and fruits and the staple accompaniments of rice and bread.

ASSAM

Perhaps the best known of the north-eastern states, because of the association with its tea crop, is Assam. Peoples of distinctly different cultures and trends of civilization settled here – the Dravidians, Indo-Mongols, Tibetans and Burmese are among those who contributed to the creation of this unique community. The soil is very fertile and the climate benign, making it perfect for growing the main food crops of tea, rice and turmeric. There are over 700 tea plantations in the state and more than half of the crop is exported to other states in India and to the rest of the world. Assam is also famous for its exquisite silk.

The food in the state is simple and nutritious, with fish and rice forming the major part of the daily diet, but vegetables are also very important. This is probably the only state in India where healthy eating is a way of life – very little fat is used in cooking and the emphasis is on fresh vegetables, plenty of greens, and pulses tempered with garlic, mustard oil and chillies. Dishes such as banana flower curry and a tomato and

Above *Lush green tea gardens are a common sight in Assam, which produces much of the world's tea.*

Left *The ridge of high mountains in Cherapunji, Meghalaya, is one of the wettest places on earth.*

lemon curry known as *tenga* are among the delicacies that the people of Assam have made their own. Another distinctive Assamese dish is *khar*, which is typically made with raw papaya, raw banana or a mixture of peas, beans and a vegetable such as marrow (large zucchini). *Khar* is believed to aid the digestion, as it includes *kharoni*, an ingredient made from burnt banana ash.

ARUNACHAL PRADESH

The smaller, more remote states that cluster around the foothills of the Himalayas include Arunachal Pradesh which, owing to its easternmost position in this region, is popularly known as 'the land of the rising sun'. It is situated directly in the shadow of the high snow-clad peaks, and its thick evergreen forests and meandering rivers make beautiful vistas.

The majority of the population here have Tibetan and Burmese ancestors, and they have maintained the culinary traditions of these countries. Meat – often lamb, goat or yak – forms the basis of many dishes, and cooks in Arunachal Pradesh do not use many spices – only garlic, ginger, chillies and aromatic herbs. A popular locally brewed drink called *apong* is made from fermented rice or millet.

MEGHALAYA

Meaning 'abode of the clouds', Meghalaya is a small, hilly state with the highest rainfall levels in the world. Together with Arunachal Pradesh, it is considered to be the most stunning of the north-eastern states. The warm, very wet climate is perfect for growing a large variety of fruit, vegetables, medicinal plants and spices, including rice, maize,

wheat and oilseeds such as mustard and rapeseed, and Meghalaya turmeric is one of India's most prized spices. Despite this bounty of fruit and vegetables, many of the local dishes are meat-based, with pork being the first choice.

MANIPUR

Once part of British India, Manipur is a culturally rich state, and its temple dance, known as the 'Manipuri Dance', is renowned all over India. The food in Manipur is an eclectic mixture of fish, meat, poultry and vegetables with some pulses. Fish cooked with bamboo shoots is one of the most popular dishes, and rice is the staple here.

TRIPURA

The majority of the population in the hilly landlocked state of Tripura is Bengali, and the Bengali influence is evident in the food of the region. The area produces oil seeds, sugar cane, potatoes and pulses, although rice is the staple crop and forms the basis of the diet, along with fish cooked in mustard oil. Tripura is also well known for hand-woven cotton and intricate wooden carvings.

Right *Villagers till the earth in Arunachal Pradesh to produce the few crops that will grow there.*

NAGALAND

Bordering the states of Assam and Arunachal Pradesh and the country of Myanmar (Burma), Nagaland is a hilly state with a tribal population that is mainly Christian. Most of the hills consist of tropical and sub-tropical evergreen forests that are important for the timber trade, and local farmers produce a few staple crops in cleared areas which, together with meat, form the basis of the simple daily diet.

Above *Tripura is known for its wood carvings, some of which can be seen at Ujjayanta Palace.*

MIZORAM

Strategically positioned between Myanmar and Bangladesh, Mizoram is a beautiful state with rolling hills and huge rivers and lakes. The diet consists of meat and the few crops that can be grown locally, and the preference is for smoked, stewed and steamed meat without the addition of any spices.

East India

The eastern states comprise Bengal, Bihar, Jharkhand and Orissa, with the former dominating the region and being home to the capital city Kolkata (formerly Calcutta). It is an area of contrasts, with the topography ranging from the precipitous uplands of the Himalayas to the verdant flood plains of the Ganges, where approximately 30 per cent of the nation's rice crops are produced. Tea is another important commodity in the region, and the beautiful town of Darjeeling produces some of the best leaves in the world.

Above *Tea plantations abound on the slopes of the Himalayas in Darjeeling, western Bengal.*

Dairy products such as yogurt, paneer (Indian cheese) and ghee are used imaginatively to create fabulous sweet and savoury recipes. But perhaps Bengal's greatest contribution to the food heritage of India is its magnificent spectrum of desserts, which are famous all over the nation. Sweets such as *gulab jamoon* (fried milk puffs in sugar syrup), *sandesh* (a kind of soft fudge made of fresh cheese), and milky cardamom- and cinnamon-scented rice pudding are among the classics that have made the reputation of Bengali cooks.

BENGAL

The influence of Anglo-Indian food can still be found in Bengal, many years after the end of British rule. The Bengali people are proud of their own rich cultural heritage – the poet Rabindranath Tagore is one of their most famous celebrities – and Bengali cuisine is part of this artistic tradition. The use of spices was fairly minimal here until medieval times, and so the Bengalis have developed a subtle cuisine using ingredients available in their own region. Locally grown spices include the major crop of the region, tea, especially in Darjeeling, as well as fresh ginger, turmeric and mustard, and the five-spice mix known as *panchforon* that was invented by Bengali cooks.

Plenty of fish and shellfish are caught in the Bay of Bengal, and this helped the Bengalis to create a stunning range of fish recipes, which are renowned all over India.

BIHAR

The wide fields of Bihar in the north of the region are dominated by the eastern sweep of the Himalayas, and by the magnificent Ganges River, which meanders slowly down from the mountains to emerge in Bangladesh (the independent Muslim state that was once part of Bengal). In landlocked Bihar, the climate is very hot in the summer and very cold in the winter, but wheat is grown here and bread is as popular as rice as a staple accompaniment to dishes.

Below left Sandesh, *a dessert made from soft cheese that is moulded into decorative shapes, is a Bengali speciality.*
Below right *Jharkhand has a number of protected areas, including a tiger reserve.*

ORISSA

The state of Orissa lies in the tropical zone and enjoys equable temperatures. Rice predominates in these lower, wetter areas of east India, where the climate is ideal for its cultivation. Sugar cane, coconuts and turmeric are the other main crops. However, the state is frequently hit by calamities such as cyclones, floods and droughts, which badly affect people's livelihoods as well as threatening their lives, since the population relies heavily on agriculture.

The long coastline at the northern edge of the Bay of Bengal means that fish and shellfish are a major part of the diet, often cooked in fragrant coconut-based sauces. During the heat of the summer, a delicious cool dish consisting of fermented rice and yogurt is a great favourite as it helps to lower the body temperature.

Below *Rice is the primary crop grown in Orissa, and lush green paddies are a common sight.*

The daily diet in Bihar consists of rice, flat bread stuffed with spicy vegetables, lentils, raw vegetables and pickles. Thick and creamy yogurt is made by boiling buffalo's milk and then cooking it until it reduces to half its quantity, and as a result, the yogurt has a low water content and is smooth, delicious and very nutritious. The people of Bihar are very fond of ghee and tend to use it freely in cooking instead of oil. They also maintain the thrifty tradition of preserving fresh food for future use, and this is usually done by drying summer vegetables in the fierce sun or preserving them as pickles.

JHARKHAND

This relatively new state was created from the southern area of Bihar in 2000. Meaning 'land of the forests', the region is primarily situated on the Chhota Nagpur Plateau, and is rich in minerals, including iron ore, copper, graphite and limestone, among others. The abundant forests are home to a wide range of flora and fauna, and there are a number of protected areas, including a tiger reserve, which provides sanctuary for all kinds of wildlife as well as the famous endangered mammals.

With a population that traces its roots to diverse regions of India, Jharkhand does not have a particularly strong culinary footprint. Native inhabitants base their diet primarily on rice, and there is a huge number of rice dishes, including *dhuska*, which is made with mashed rice and pulses and served as an accompaniment to *aloo dum* or mutton curry. Flowers and leaves (*sag*) are notably used as vegetables to add variety to the food; the blooms plucked from the drumstick, august and jhirool plants are the most popular.

South India

The four states of Andhra Pradesh, Tamil Nadu, Karnataka and Kerala make up the region of south India. Foreign traders and explorers have often landed on these shores over the centuries, attracted by the promise of a lucrative trade in exotic and costly items such as spices and silks. They inevitably brought outside influences with them, which have had an impact on all aspects of life in the area, including food. The result is a varied and exotic cuisine that reflects the wealth of ingredients on offer to local cooks.

KARNATAKA

The name of this state is derived from the word *karunadu*, which means 'lofty land'. Much of Karnataka is on the high plateau that lies between the western and eastern Ghats, precipitous mountains that run along the western and eastern coasts of peninsular India. The rest of the state lies along a 300km (186-mile) stretch of coastline with smooth, sandy beaches that are popular with tourists.

Numerous crops grow in this diverse landscape, including tea and coffee, which are produced in huge, lush plantations on the western coast. Rice, millet, groundnut and sesame, along with other agricultural crops, are also abundant. Farther inland, deep forests of much sought-after ebony, cedar and sandalwood trees cover the slopes of the western Ghats, providing timber that is perfect for furniture-making.

Above *Coffee and rice are two of the staple crops grown on lush plantations in the Kodagu (Coorg) region of Karnataka.*

Above *A wide range of fresh vegetables is on offer at colourful street markets in Andhra Pradesh, such as this one in Puttaparthi.*

Sandalwood, used for incense, is perhaps the most valuable commodity, although the area also produces more than 85 per cent of the country's raw silk.

A mainly vegetarian state, Karnataka offers a wealth of exciting dishes based on rice, lentils, vegetables and dairy products. Typical ingredients include raw bananas, green mangoes, colcosia leaves and red-hot chilies, as well as the exceptionally fresh fish and shellfish that is eaten in abundance in the coastal towns and villages. Vegetable curries are often served with rice drizzled with ghee, and the famous sweetmeat of this state is *mysore pak*, a delicacy made with generous quantities of ghee, sugar and chickpea (gram) flour (*besan*).

ANDHRA PRADESH

Situated on the eastern seaboard, Andhra Pradesh has quite a different climate from Karnataka, with the humidity of the monsoon making it ideally suited to rice production, earning it the nickname the 'granary of the south'. Cotton, tobacco and pulses are also grown in huge quantities and exported all over the world.

The twin cities of Hyderabad and Secunderabad make up the municipality of Hyderabad, which is one of the largest metropolises in India. It is a beautiful place, with stately architecture and shops displaying colourful uncut precious stones, softly glistening pearls of different shades and delicate filigree work on pure silver.

The cuisine of Andhra Pradesh owes much of its unique nature among the southern states to the influence of both Muslim and Mughal cooking, dating back to the invaders who fought over this land from the 14th century onward. Unlike the other southern states, Andhra Pradesh has

Right *The stunning palm-fringed coastline of Kerala is famous both for its beaches and its many spice plantations.*

more meat-eaters than vegetarians. Mouthwatering kebabs and biryanis are a speciality in this part of the country and are famous all over India. Chillies – including the famed Guntur red chillies, which are known for their pungency – are one of the main crops of this region, and hot mixtures such as lime pickle are a favourite side dish.

KERALA

Representing only 1.8 per cent of the total area of India, Kerala is the smallest state of south India. This strip of land along the Arabian Sea leads right to the southernmost tip of India, and has a beautiful coastline that stretches 590km (367 miles). Kerala's most prized possession, along with its beautiful sandy beaches, is its fabulous spice plantations, where crops of cardamom, cinnamon, cloves, chillies and peppercorns, among others, are grown in abundance. As a producer of such valuable spices, the area has long been visited by traders, including the Romans, Chinese, Syrians and Arabs.

The cuisine of Kerala is very light and refreshing, using locally grown coconut and exotic spices. Every part of this nut is

Above Idlis, *served on a green banana leaf, are very popular in Tamil Nadu. Traditionally, the banana leaf would be fed to cows after the meal.*

used, from the milk to the flesh, and not forgetting the husk, which makes a good, tough building material. The fine, delicate flavour of the pure white flesh and the coconut cream permeates both sweet and savoury Keralan recipes.

Although this is not a vegetarian state, with fish and shellfish being key ingredients, Kerala does have a special vegetarian banquet known as *sadya*, which consists of rice and an array of vegetables, lentils, peas, pickles and chutneys. Most dishes are healthy, with minimum use of fat and maximum use of fresh ingredients, including the many tropical fruits, such as cashews, mangoes, bananas and jackfruit, which thrive in the area.

TAMIL NADU

The history of the picturesque state of Tamil Nadu, on the south-eastern coast of India, is one of occupation by the Dravidian people, who are supposedly the descendants of the ancient Indus Valley civilization.

Indications of people farming in this warm, wet land go back 6,000 years, and the Dravidian Tamil language is at least 2,000 years old. In later centuries Tamil Nadu became part of the European trade routes and a focus for the East India Trading Company.

The food in Tamil Nadu is almost all vegetarian, partly for the purely practical reason that meat deteriorates faster than vegetarian food in the muggy heat, and partly for religious reasons, as the majority of the population are Hindu or Jainist. Soft, fluffy *idlis* (rice dumplings), crispy, paper-thin *dosas* (rice pancakes) filled with spicy potatoes, and colourful vegetable and lentil dishes are all presented on emerald-green banana leaves. The food tends to contain a lot of fiery chillies; perhaps because this is where these now ubiquitous fruits were first introduced to the country by the traders from the New World. Locally grown spices such as curry leaves, tamarind, coriander, cumin and nutmeg also have a strong presence.

Central India

Central India is made up of one large state, Madhya Pradesh. This area is completely landlocked, with the Arabian Sea bordering the state of Gujarat to the west, and the Bay of Bengal bordering the state of Orissa to the east. The countryside is made up of beautiful rolling hills rising to 600m (2,000ft) – where primeval forests flourish and ancient temples and palaces still stand – and fertile valleys containing lakes and rivers that teem with freshwater fish and provide water for the many crops that are grown.

Madhya Pradesh sits at the northern edge of the Deccan plateau, a huge area of volcanic basalt that stretches across the whole central and southern part of India. This rock was laid down in thick layers and the subsequent nutrient-rich volcanic soil has enabled the state to establish a hugely successful agricultural economy.

The region has been a witness to the major external and internal influences that have been instrumental in shaping the country's culture and cuisine over the centuries. The state is a typical example of the diverse nature of Indian culture: beautiful Hindu and Sikh temples and Muslim mosques grace the region, with all the different religions and races now coexisting in relative harmony after the major upheavals of the 20th century.

The economy of central India relies mainly on agriculture. This fertile state is blessed by regular weather patterns – a hot

Above *Cotton grows extremely well in the predictable climate of Madhya Pradesh, and it is one of the major exports of the region.*

summer from April to June, followed by the relief of torrential monsoon rains in July and August – which enable the farmers to plan which crops to grow and when to plant and harvest them. The main food crops are rice, wheat, sorghum and coarse millet, usually grown for the local markets. The typical flat bread of the region, made of sorghum, has become popular all over India. Oilseeds, cotton, sugar cane and soya beans are the main commercial crops, all of which are exported all over the world as well as being eaten locally. Although rice is a common ingredient in central Indian cooking, wheat is the preferred staple in the drier western areas, and is used to make a range of delicious breads.

Left *The area around the state capital, Bohar, is surrounded by forest-covered hills and there are numerous lakes in the valleys.*

Right *One of many temples in the region, the Vishvanatha temple in Khajuraho dates back to 1002CE and is dedicated to the god Shiva.*

The main cities are Bhopal, Indore and Gwalior. Bhopal, the state capital, is situated in a beautiful area surrounded by lakes and hills, and is home to the third largest mosque in the world, Taj-ul-Masjid. In the days of British domination, the state was ruled by various Indian princes, all of whom maintained strong loyalty to the British. Even now, in the 21st century, all three of the major cities still have Indian princes and princesses living in their palaces, and the traditions of an exotic royal cuisine are maintained among the wealthy.

The cuisine of Madhya Pradesh owes much to the nearby states of Gujarat, Rajasthan and Bihar, with their emphasis on the kind of dishes that best suit hot, dry areas. The luxurious dishes served for royal banquets, with edible gold and silver decorations, are not part of most people's everyday diet, of course. However, the daily food of central India does include plenty of variety in terms of the different spices, nuts and seeds that are added to the basic meat, fish and vegetables. The people also love snacks, often dainty morsels of vegetables deep-fried to perfection in a spicy batter, or tasty sweet cakes flavoured with cashew nuts.

Left *Wheat is one of the staple crops, and the lush green fields are often overlooked by ancient temples, such as this one in Orchha.*

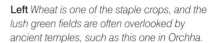

Above *Street food, especially deep-fried snacks such as patties and samosas, is extremely popular in the towns and cities.*

West India

Four states make up the region of west India: Goa, a tiny enclave perched on the west coast; Maharashtra, a large state stretching from the Arabian Sea across almost the whole width of India; Gujarat, another coastal state that proudly claims to be the birthplace of many of India's political leaders, including Gandhi; and Rajasthan, a vast landlocked desert region bordering Pakistan. The food in all of these is fragrant and flavoursome, packed with spices and influenced by the settlers and traders who visited the region.

GOA

The tiny state of Goa, popularly known as 'Golden Goa' and 'Pearl of the Orient', lies on the southern edge of west India. A rich tapestry of cultures, it was ruled, in turn, by Hindus, Muslims, Portuguese Christians and the British. The lure of Indian spices and silks brought the Portuguese explorer Vasco da Gama to this part of India, and the Portuguese established an eastern empire for themselves with Goa as the central state.

Although local ingredients such as fish and coconut predominate, Goa's cuisine also reflects the influence of European culture, with dishes such as Portuguese Pullao and the now ubiquitous *vindaloo*, a term for a spicy pork dish that originally derived from the Portuguese words for 'vinegar' and 'garlic'.

MAHARASHTRA

The food of the large state of Maharashtra is fiery, as both chillies and black pepper are used with great relish. Peanuts and cashew nuts are another distinctive feature of Maharashtrian cooking, and peanut oil forms the basis for many dishes. Pulses, sugarcane and wheat are also plentiful.

The people here have a sweet tooth, and use a lot of palm sugar (jaggery) and kokum, a purple berry-like fruit with a pleasant sweet-and-sour taste. Mumbai

Above *Central Gujarat produces many grain crops, such as wheat.*

(Bombay), the capital of Maharashtra, is a historic and cosmopolitan city, also known as the 'Gateway of India'. Here, all sorts of dishes have been created by the different communities that have made Mumbai their home – it is a real food-lover's paradise and is probably the only city in India where you can sample food from almost anywhere in the country, as well as recipes that owe much to foreign influences. The newest arrival in Mumbai is the Bollywood film industry, helping to maintain a high level of excitement and artistic passion in the city.

GUJARAT

Within the colourful diversity of Indian regional cuisine, Gujarat merits a special position of pride as the state that has perfected the true art of vegetarian cooking. This is mainly due to the influence of the Jain religion, which prescribes an attitude of non-violence to all things and therefore

Left *Coconuts grow in abundance in Goa, and their flesh and milk appear in most local dishes.*

Far left *The array of foods on offer in Gujarat will be transformed into vegetarian dishes.*
Left *Fresh red chillies are dried in the sun in Rajasthan to help preserve them.*

RAJASTHAN

This is the ancient land of Indian emperors and princes, where an elaborate cuisine was developed, often using the game caught during a day's hunting. Despite the royal culinary tradition, which is evident in the number of game dishes that are still enjoyed today, there are many vegetarians in this state, including most members of the Marwari community, the main controllers of business whose influence has spread throughout India.

This is, perhaps, surprising, given the desert climate, and the fact that only a small variety of vegetables can be grown in regions that are slightly less dry or where farmers can afford irrigation systems. The little produce harvested then tends to be sun-dried. Most dishes are cooked in ghee and flavoured with spices, yogurt and dried fruits, and curries tend to be based on pulses or gram flour (*besan*).

forbids the consumption of any food where production may involve the harming of animals. This means that meat, fish, eggs and, for some, dairy products are not permitted. Despite these limitations, Gujarati cooks have created a dazzling array of delicious and nutritious dishes that have become famous across the whole of India.

In addition to the influences of Jainism on the dishes of the region, Persian cuisine has also played its part in shaping the local diet. Situated on the banks of the Arabian Sea, the region attracted and absorbed a variety of immigrants throughout the centuries, including Persians, and over time the native Parsis integrated the distinctive flavour of Persian food with their own traditional dishes, creating exotic and colourful treats, such as the world-famous *dhansak*.

The three main regions of Gujarat have distinct climatic differences, which has led to a very varied cuisine. Western Gujarat is an arid area where there is a scarcity of fresh vegetables, but it is rich in dairy produce, and there is a strong tradition of making delicious sweetmeats and desserts based on milk and yogurt. Central Gujarat is known as the 'granary of Gujarat' because of its abundance of grain crops. The south of the state, with a much wetter climate, is covered with lush green vegetation, and here a fantastic variety of fresh vegetables grow.

The concept of a *thali* (a meal served on a steel platter), which is popular in India as well as in the Indian restaurants in the West,

originated in Gujarat. Roti, an unleavened flat wheat bread, is a speciality not to be missed, as is cool, cumin-flavoured lassi, a diluted natural (plain) yogurt drink for the long, hot summer. Gujaratis are also very partial to *farsan* (snacks) and an exotic variety is made and used to welcome guests, to pack in children's lunchboxes or just to enjoy with a cup of afternoon tea.

Right *Lentils, such as those sold at this market in Jaisalmer, are widely used in Rajasthani food.*

Indian festivals and celebrations

India is a spiritual land comprised of many religions: Hindu, Muslim, Christian, Sikh, Jain and Buddhist. It is, therefore, not too surprising that Indian culture is rich with numerous vibrant and joyful festivals and celebrations. However, the vast majority of the religious holidays celebrated in the 21st century are Hindu in origin. Most of these events have elaborate stories and rituals associated with them, not to mention fantastic food to accompany each celebration.

The sheer number of different religious affiliations in India has given rise to a huge variety of special foods for both family events, such as weddings, births and deaths, and national celebrations.

Festivals are very important and there are 13 major ones in the country every year. Each has its own distinct style of food, with religious traditions dictating what is to be cooked. However, it is not just the religious aspect that determines celebratory cuisine: secular festivals associated with the season and the crops that are growing or have been harvested are also of significance, and are marked with bountiful feasts.

RELIGIOUS FOOD CULTURE

The influence of religion on Indian food has been profound. The two main religions, Hinduism and Islam, have certain taboos: for example, Hindus do not eat beef as the cow was the sacred companion of Lord Krishna, and Muslims are prohibited from eating pork or drinking alcohol according to their holy book, the Koran. Sikhs, Jains and Buddhists have certain food rules in common with Hindus, but also have distinctive food cultures of their own.

There is a stunning variety of festival foods in India to accompany the many major festivals held every year. In the Hindu religion, more than one god and goddess is worshipped, and each one is believed to be the patron of a particular profession or trade. A farmer may offer the gods of sun and rain their favourite dishes, for example, so that they will bless him with a fruitful harvest.

Rice, ghee, sugar, milk, yogurt and honey are considered to be the purest foods. They are also thought to have spiritual qualities, hence the practice of cooking sweet dishes and offering them at the altar before distributing them to family and friends. Throughout the country rice pudding is given as a holy offering, embellished and enrichened with nuts, cardamom and saffron.

HARVEST FESTIVALS

At the beginning of the year, the two Hindu harvest festivals, known as Lohri and Baisakhi, are celebrated in northern India. Lohri is celebrated by the people of the Punjab in January and Baisakhi follows in April. It is customary to serve dried fruits, sweetmeats and spicy savoury snacks similar to Bombay mix, as well as a spicy dish of mustard greens (*sarson ka saag*) and flat breads made of cornmeal (*makki ki roti*).

The people of Tamil Nadu in south India celebrate their harvest festival, Pongal, for four days each year, starting on 13 January. 'Pongal' in the Tamil language means 'boiling over', which signifies prosperity due to a bountiful crop. The food cooked during Pongal is totally vegetarian. The special dish of the day is *khichri*, which is a sweet and creamy combination of rice, milk and palm sugar (jaggery). It is cooked in a pot called a *Pongal panai*.

January sees another harvest festival in the north-eastern state of Assam. This is known as Bihu, when a good harvest is celebrated with family and friends by lighting an early morning bonfire and cooking yams in the burning ashes.

SEASONAL FESTIVALS

Holi, the festival of colours, brings a special feast for the entire family and friends in the spring. Sweetmeats, savoury snacks such as *vadai* (lentil fritters) and *papri* (a crisp bread) are made. It is also a tradition for parents to present new clothes in bright colours to a daughter and her children.

In the autumn, Durga Puja is a major Hindu festival celebrated all over India. The goddess Durga is believed to be the defeater of evil, and the festival commemorates her triumph over the wicked demon Mahisasur. Food such as deep-fried puffed bread, spiced potatoes, fragrant lentils and

Above *Creamy Indian rice pudding scented with spices is given as a holy offering before being shared among family and friends.*

Above Khichri *is boiled in a special pot called a* Pongal panai *at a village harvest festival in Tamil Nadu.*

Above *A mixed selection of sweets (candies) ready to share at a Diwali celebration.*

Above *A colourful plateful of soft fudge-like sweetmeats known as* burfi.

Above *Young folk dancers celebrate a Pongal festival in a village in Tamil Nadu.*

different kinds of sweetmeats are offered at the altar and then shared between everyone present.

Onam is a festival mainly celebrated in Kerala, south India. It marks the end of the monsoon season, but legends and myths have a strong influence in India and Onam also celebrates the life of King Mahabali, a past ruler of Kerala. The Onam feast is traditionally served on banana leaves, and consists of fish and seafood cooked in spicy coconut broth, chutneys made with coconut, as well as spicy vegetables and rice.

Diwali, the biggest Hindu festival, is also celebrated over five days in the autumn. It commemorates the return of the Hindu prince Rama from 14 years of exile. Rama was supposed to have returned in the evening and oil lamps are lit everywhere to welcome him, hence the name Diwali, meaning 'festival of lights'. During the festival, sweets (candies) are the most important foods; in keeping with the Hindu belief that exchanging sweets among family and friends represents inner goodness, many varieties of sweetmeats made of coconut are made and distributed.

Right *Coloured rice powder is used during many different festivals to create decorative patterns on the streets.*

Raksha Bandhan is another major festival in India that is mainly celebrated in the north and west. On this day, a sacred thread is tied to a brother's wrist by his sister to signify her love for him, and she offers special prayers for her brother's welfare. The brother in turn pledges to love and protect his sister in any circumstances, strengthening the bond between them. The brother also gives gifts to his sister and she cooks an elaborate

meal, which the entire family shares. Such delights as fruit and vegetable patties, soft fudge (*burfi*), sweet dumplings (*malpua*) and cardamom-scented vermicelli pudding are part of the feast.

Whatever the festival, sweetmeats always feature prominently, as Indians believe that they spread love and goodwill, and there is a tremendous range of traditional treats on offer across the country.

Tools and equipment

Throughout India, different types of equipment and cooking techniques are used to produce the dishes that are characteristic of each region. Pans tend to be heavy, with lids that provide a tight seal and keep moisture locked inside, and they come in various shapes and sizes. No traditional Indian kitchen would be complete without a mortar and pestle and grinding stones, but in a modern kitchen a coffee grinder and a food processor can provide excellent results in a very short space of time.

There is a vast array of favourite cooking utensils in India. All along the southern coastal regions, terracotta cooking pots are preferred. These tend to be unglazed as aeration is easier; this means that the food does not need immediate refrigeration in spite of the extreme heat in the south. In the north, the emphasis is more on sealing cooking pots well so that the flavour of the food is concentrated inside – a method of cooking known as dum. Most traditional Indian cooking is done in heavy cast-iron, steel or copper cooking pots and pans. These help to distribute the heat evenly, cooking the food without losing any of the natural moisture and allowing the spices to be pre-fried without sticking to the bottom.

HANDI

A handi is used to cook many steamed dishes. It is a heavy copper pot with a neck that is narrower than the base, a somewhat bigger version of a degchi. Decorated ovenproof handis are now available and they have become a favourite in the modern Indian kitchen.

KADHAI/KARAHI

Fried puffed breads (*puri* and *luchi*) are deep-fried in a round-bottomed pan, similar to a wok, known as a *kadhai* or *karahi*. A *kadhai* is also needed to produce all types of bhuna (stir-fried) dishes – an amazing range of mouthwatering treats have been created using this humble cooking utensil. The *kadhai* is thought to be one of the oldest kinds of cooking pans used in India – archaeologists have discovered the ancient remains of a pan that closely resembles the *kadhai*. Today this pan is a common sight in most domestic and restaurant kitchens and in every street-side eatery in northern India and Pakistan.

PATILA

A heavy steel pan with a lid, known as a *patila*, is used for making stock, kormas and bhuna dishes. Kormas need heavy cooking pots with tight-fitting lids, as very little liquid is used during the cooking process. Korma, which means 'braising', is essentially a technique of cooking rather than a particular dish.

LAGAN

A shallow copper utensil known as a *lagan* is used for cooking certain dum dishes in Lucknow, northern India. The *lagan* has a slightly rounded bottom and a heavy, tight-fitting lid. The temperature must be kept quite gentle, and indirect heat is created by placing burning charcoal on the lid. This method can easily be replicated using a casserole dish in a low oven, as long as the dish is sealed well.

DEGCHI

Pilaus and biryanis require a special shape of cooking pot, as the food is cooked entirely in steam, producing fabulous flavours. This pot, known as a *degchi*, is pear-shaped and can be made of either brass or copper. The narrow neck helps to keep all the steam inside, and a strip of sticky dough made of flour is laid around the neck of the pot in order to hold the lid in place and to ensure that no steam can escape. It is, however, possible to cook biryanis successfully in a standard cooking pot, preferably one made of heavy steel or

Above Handi *pots, often made of copper, are narrower at the neck than at the base.*

Above *The wok-like* kadhai *is used to make stir-fried curries and fried puffed bread.*

Above *A* patila *is a heavy pan with a lid, often used for making stocks and kormas.*

Above *In coastal regions of southern India, terracotta pots are favoured over metal pans.*

Above *The chapati rolling pin is available in many different sizes.*

Above *The tawa is a flat hot griddle pan traditionally used to cook chapatis on.*

copper. To seal the pot, well-moistened baking parchment can be used to cover the top layer of the rice, with a damp dish towel on top, and then a double thickness of foil.

TAWA

Most unleavened breads such as chapatis are cooked on a cast-iron griddle known as a *tawa*. A bigger and heavier version of the domestic *tawa* is used by the street vendors in India to make tasty griddled snacks, the aromas of which fill the air, drawing people towards the *tawa* like a magnet.

TAPELI

Used for cooking rice, a *tapeli* is a useful pan made of heavy stainless steel or copper. A *tapeli* is shaped like a normal pan, but has a very tight-fitting lid that is ideal for cooking rice by the preferred absorption method, which gives the best results.

TANDOOR

Leavened breads such as naans of various kinds are cooked in the *tandoor*, a barrel-shaped clay oven. This was originally only used for cooking bread, but has now been adapted for all sorts of other dishes.

CHAPATI ROLLING BOARD

This round wooden board on short stubby legs is used to mould breads into shape. The extra height provided by the legs helps to disperse excess dry flour. A wooden pastry board placed on a flat surface makes an appropriate substitute.

CHAPATI SPOON

The square, flat-headed chapati spoon is used for turning roasting breads on the hot chapati griddle. A fish slice (spatula) or wooden spatula may also be used, or a pair of kitchen tongs.

COLANDER AND SIEVE (STRAINER)

These are used for washing rice, vegetables and fruit before preparation, draining boiled rice and vegetables, and for straining other cooked ingredients. A sieve (strainer) can also be used to produce a smooth purée when a paste is pushed through it. Choose long-handled, sturdy varieties made from stainless steel, as these allow you to stand back to pour steaming rice out of a pan, and will not discolour like plastic ones.

SLOTTED SPOON

Stirring cooked, drained rice with a slotted spoon will make the rice soft and fluffy by allowing air to circulate between the grains. A slotted spoon is also useful for removing food from hot liquids.

FOOD PROCESSOR

Traditional grinding stones make the best chutneys and spice pastes, but a food processor is the answer for today's busy cooks. It can be used to chop onions and make ginger and garlic purées, which are essential ingredients in Indian cooking. The purées can then be frozen in small quantities and used as and when required.

MASALA DANI

A spice box, known as a *masala dani*, is the pride and joy of many an Indian cook. It is very often handed down from mother to daughter or grandmother to granddaughter. Small steel containers shaped like miniature cups are neatly arranged inside a large, usually airtight box with a lid, also made of stainless steel. The containers are used to store a selection of whole spices, such as mustard seeds, cumin seeds, dried red chillies, nigella seeds and black pepper, which are used in everyday cooking.

SPICE GRINDERS

In an ideal world, freshly ground spices are the only way to achieve full flavours, but modern life is so hectic that it is hard to find time to cook at all, never mind to grind the spices! However, whole spices do have a longer shelf-life than ground ones, and can be ground in small quantities as and when required with the right equipment. In India, many households still use the traditional grinding stone (*sil-batta*), made of two stones: a flat platform on which the spices are placed, and a small cylindrical roller, rather like a rolling pin, used to grind spice pastes.

A mortar and pestle (*haman-dasta*) is also traditionally used to grind dry spices. These methods do produce fabulous flavours, but electric gadgets such as coffee grinders are fast becoming the popular choice and will produce finely ground spices in seconds.

Cooking techniques

Different methods are used to create the distinctive types of dishes in Indian cuisine. Dum cooking, for instance, involves braising the ingredients in a tightly sealed pan, which traps the steam and produces succulent and well-flavoured food. Tandoori cooking, on the other hand, relies on the kebabs or breads being cooked quickly at a very high temperature, lending them a uniquely smoky flavour. Other techniques call for spices to be fried in different ways and added to the food at a strategic point in the cooking time.

The unique character of Indian cooking comes from the ingenious and skilful art of combining spices, aromatics and other flavourings in various ways. Coupled with this are several basic techniques that let the cook create different flavours from the same range of ingredients, allowing greater flexibilty and inventiveness in the kitchen and resulting in truly memorable dishes.

BHUNA

This is a method that involves frying the spices at a high temperature, with a small amount of water being added at regular intervals to stop them burning and sticking to the bottom of the pan. This enables the cook to scrape up the spices and mix them into the dish. It is this technique of scraping, stirring and mixing the spices without letting them burn that makes a perfect bhuna dish. Salt is added at the start of the cooking process to enable the food to release its natural juices, keeping the dish moist.

DUM

This method of cooking is relatively easy. After the initial cooking process, the food is put into a heavy pan with a tight-fitting lid, and the pan is sealed completely so that no steam can escape. Traditionally, dum cooking is done over charcoal and live coals are placed on top of the lid after sealing it with a sticky dough made with plain (all-purpose) flour and water. It is crucial to follow the given cooking time because the pot should be opened only when the food is fully cooked.

KORMA

The term korma is commonly misunderstood as meaning a dish, but it is in fact one of the most important techniques in Indian cooking. It simply means 'braising'. There are different types of kormas around the country. Northern ones tend to be mild, rich and creamy with subtle flavours and smooth, velvety sauces; nut pastes made

from ingredients such as cashew and almond are used as well as cream and saffron. Kormas from south India, on the other hand, are enriched with coconut milk and can be quite fiery.

The size of the pan is very important in cooking a successful korma. If the pan is too big the food will dry out quickly; if too small it will produce too much juice. The pan should be just big enough to hold the main ingredients comfortably.

TADKA OR BAGHAR

A heavy pan shaped like a miniature wok is used to heat up small amounts of oil, and the whole spices are then thrown into the hot oil, where they release their amazing aroma. Both the oil and the spices are then folded into the cooked dish. This technique is known as tadka, meaning 'seasoning'. In a Western kitchen a steel ladle or a small pan is a perfect substitute utensil for preparing hot oil seasonings.

Above *A bhuna dish is made from a carefully fried combination of spices.*

Above *A small wok-like utensil is used for the seasoning technique called tadka.*

Above *Kormas are braised dishes that often include ground nut pastes or cream.*

Above *A tandoor is ideal for cooking naan to perfection, producing fluffy, aromatic bread.*

TALANA

This is a method of deep-frying that produces an exciting range of mouthwatering snacks. In India, a *kadhai*, which is shaped like a wok, is generally used for deep-frying. It is made of heavy cast iron and because of its shape, a small quantity of oil can be used. A few simple rules will ensure light and crispy deep-fried food. Firstly, it is essential to use a light cooking oil such as sunflower oil. Secondly, the oil needs to be at the right temperature, usually about 180°C/350°F/Gas 4. A food thermometer is perfect for this, but a good way to judge the temperature without a thermometer is to drop in a small piece of bread as soon as the surface of the oil has a faint shimmer of rising smoke. The bread should rise to the surface in a few seconds without browning, and then turn brown in a minute or so.

TANDOORI

This is an age-old technique that is believed to have found its way into India with the ancient Persians. A *tandoor* is a barrel-shaped clay oven that is capable of grilling (broiling), roasting and baking food simultaneously. It is mainly used for cooking meat, poultry and leavened bread, although delectable vegetarian tandoori recipes have evolved with time. However, a domestic oven, grill (broiler) or barbecue can also produce tandoori-style food.

COOKING WITH SALT AND SPICES

Using freshly ground spices for each meal is still common practice in India. However, it is possible to cook delicious food with pre-ground spices so long as they are stored away from direct light and used up quickly.

Using the correct amount of salt is vital. It is always added at the beginning or during the cooking process, which ensures the proper blending of flavours. To some people, the quantity used may seem excessive, but salt is treated almost as a spice, to balance all the flavours. In dry spiced vegetable recipes, salt is added at the very start, to help release the vegetable juices and preserve all the nutrients.

Above *Salt is always added during the cooking process rather than at the table.*

USING SPICES

Mastering the art of maintaining a delicate balance of spices comes with practice and care. To produce a really great dish, bear the following important points in mind:

• Using freshly ground spices for each recipe produces the very best flavours, although pre-ground ones can also be used.
• The sequence in which the chosen spices are added affects the final taste of the dish.
• Cooking the spices correctly is the most important step in creating a good curry.
• It is essential to fry the spices at different temperatures in order to achieve a rounded flavour, so follow the timings and temperatures specified in a recipe.

Above *Fresh spices have the best flavours.*

• Dry spices, ground or whole, should be gently sizzled over a very low heat so that they do not burn.
• Wet spices such as onion, ginger and garlic should be fried over a gentle heat and allowed to become soft and translucent before adding the other ingredients.

Vegetables

With such a large percentage of the population being vegetarian, and with such a wealth of produce on offer, it is little surprise that Indian cooking specializes in truly stunning vegetable dishes. From deep-fried snacks through to curries, the recipes make wonderful use of everything from cauliflower, potatoes and peas to more exotic and unusual varieties, such as okra, bottle gourds and aubergines (eggplants). When it comes to Indian cooking, vegetables are simply indispensable.

Most of the vegetables used in Indian cooking are commonplace and widely available, while others, such as bottle gourds, may be a little harder to track down. Asian and African stores and markets are often a good place to look.

CUCUMBERS, COURGETTES (ZUCCHINI) AND MARROWS (LARGE ZUCCHINI)

Belonging to the same family, the cucurbitaceae, these vegetables appear in many guises in Indian cooking. Cooling and crunchy, cucumber is usually served raw, often finely diced in raitas. Tender and flavoursome, the whole of a courgette can be eaten raw or cooked, with or without its skin. Marrows are essentially big courgettes, and have a thicker, more bitter skin than their smaller cousins, and this is not eaten. The pulp and seeds of marrows should be removed, leaving behind a large, robust cavity that is perfect for stuffing and baking.

Above *Glossy purple aubergines (eggplants) are ideal carriers for a range of spices.*

AUBERGINES (EGGPLANTS)

Available in different varieties, the vibrant, deep purple aubergine is the most widely grown and commonly used type in Indian cooking. Aubergines have a strong flavour and some may have a slightly bitter taste.

PREPARING BUTTERNUT SQUASH

1 Cut off the top and bottom of the butternut squash. Cut the vegetable in half widthways, just above the bulbous bottom part. Stand each half upright on a board and carefully cut down to remove the skin.

2 Cut each piece in half lengthways. Scoop out the seeds using the knife or a spoon, then cube the flesh, or cut it into strips, as required.

To prepare, cut in half lengthways and then chop or slice as indicated in the recipe. The flesh may be sprinkled with salt to extract the bitter juices, if you like, then rinsed and patted dry with kitchen paper. The spongey flesh absorbs other flavours well, making them ideal for curries.

Left *Fresh vegetables are sold everywhere in India, including at this camel fair in Pushkar.*

BUTTERNUT SQUASHES

With soft, vibrant flesh and a sweet flavour, this vegetable is a brilliant partner for spices. Packed with carbohydrates and vitamins, including vitamin C, it can be used to add substance and colour to curries and other baked dishes. Encased in a tough skin, it does not require refrigeration (ideal in the heat of India) and also travels very well, which is perhaps why it is so popular.

YAMS

Packed with starch, this humble vegetable is an invaluable part of the local diet in India, providing a welcome alternative to rice as a staple carbohydrate. Although it does not have a strong flavour, the firm flesh can be cubed and cooked with a range of spices, whereupon it will soften and absorb all the wonderful flavours.

To prepare, peel the tough skin using a vegetable peeler and slice into rounds or cut into cubes, as required. If frying, it is best to first soak the prepared yam in cold water for 30 minutes to start softening it.

POTATOES

Like yams, potatoes are a very good source of carbohydrate, and are also infinitely versatile. They appear in many curries all over the country, especially vegetarian ones, providing flavour as well as substance. They can be peeled if you prefer, but for optimum nutrition and flavour, simply scrub the skins to remove all traces of soil and cut into cubes or slice into rounds.

SWEET POTATOES

Similar to yams in texture, sweet potatoes have, as their name suggests, a sweet flavour that marries perfectly with hot and fragrant spices. They require peeling before use, and the vibrant orange flesh can then be cubed or sliced and used in much the same way as potatoes, although they normally require a slightly longer cooking time. Due to their high starch content they add substance as well as colour and flavour to dishes, along with their many vitamins and minerals.

PLANTAINS

Related to bananas, these starchy fruits are usually cooked in savoury dishes, such as curries, or dusted with spices, fried and served as an accompaniment. Their earthy flavour is the perfect foil for a plethora of spices, and they are most popular in eastern India. They are very easy to prepare: simply peel and slice or cube.

CARROTS

Crunchy, sweet and packed with nutrients, carrots appear in all manner of curries and stewed vegetable dishes. Like other root vegetables, they keep well in heat and are easy to transport as they do not bruise and spoil easily, unlike many other vegetables. If they are tender young carrots, they may not need peeling and, if small enough, can be left whole, with the green top removed. Older specimens will usually require peeling before being chopped or sliced.

BLANCHING VEGETABLES

1 Prepare the vegetables by breaking into florets, trimming or chopping, according to the type of vegetable and the recipe instructions.

2 Bring a large pan of lightly salted water to the boil. Add the prepared vegetables and cook over a high heat, boiling rapidly, for 1–2 minutes.

3 Drain the vegetables in a colander and immediately plunge them into iced water or run under the cold tap to halt the cooking process. Drain.

Above *Courgettes (zucchini) come in all shapes and colours and can be eaten raw or cooked.*

Above *The tough outer skin of yams needs to be removed before the flesh can be diced or sliced.*

Above *Crunchy, vibrant carrots are packed with flavour and nutrition.*

PARSNIPS

Although not grown in India, parsnips make a wonderful addition to vegetable curries, where they impart their sweet flavour and add substance. They can also be fried and then blended with other flavourings to make sweet and spicy patties, which are shallow-fried in hot oil and served with chutney as an appetizer. Prepare in the same way as carrots.

TURNIPS

With their pretty purple and white skins and crunchy white flesh, turnips are attractive as well as tasty, and have many uses, appearing as dishes in their own right with spicy yogurt sauces and in mixed vegetable curries. High in carbohydrate, turnips have a sweet, mild flavour and, being easy to grow in even the poorest of soils and keeping well, they are an important crop during the winter months in India when other fresh, more perishable vegetables may be hard to come by.

CAULIFLOWERS

Usually braised with a range of spices and other vegetables, tender, creamy cauliflower is a popular ingredient in most regions of India. It can also be dipped in spicy batter and deep-fried to make a tasty appetizer, or separated into tiny florets and used in chutneys and preserves, including the famous British condiment piccalilli, which arguably originated in east India. Cauliflower florets are often blanched before being added towards the end of the cooking time.

BEANS

Among the most popular vegetables in India, beans are sold almost everywhere at colourful street markets. Both French (green) beans and runner (green) beans are used in spicy stir-fries, cooked with lentils, or lightly steamed and seasoned with whole spices to make salads. They can also be chopped into small pieces and used in chutneys and relishes, adding substance as well as flavour.

To prepare them, remove the tops and tails and, if they have them, the strings that run along either side of the bean. If they are tough and woody French beans, cut them into thin strips using a knife or a special implement that can be found in most cookshops. Beans are often blanched before being added at the end of the cooking time.

PEAS

Vibrant and sweet, fresh green peas are added to a number of Indian dishes, such as potato cakes, curries and side dishes, to add colour, texture and taste. Frozen ones are just as good as the fresh type, if not better, and require only a quick rinse in a sieve (strainer) before being used in the same way as fresh ones, making them the perfect stand-by ingredient.

SPINACH

Available all year round, this leafy green vegetable has a mild, delicate flavour. The leaves vary in size and only the large thick ones need to be trimmed of their stalks. Spinach is a favourite vegetable in Indian

cuisine, and it is cooked in many ways, with spicy sauces, other vegetables, and along with beans, peas and lentils.

GREENS (COLLARDS)

Both mustard and spring greens are grown and used in most parts of India where conditions permit the growing of vegetables. They are used in much the same way as spinach, and require only minimal preparation and cooking.

PREPARING GREENS (COLLARDS)

1 Separate the greens into separate leaves and thoroughly wash these in a colander under cold running water to remove all traces of dirt.

2 If the leaves have a tough, woody core, remove this with a knife. Tender leaves will not require this.

3 Roll up the leaves into a sausage shape and slice across this to finely shred the greens.

Above *Turnips are crunchy and sweet, and are especially popular served with creamy sauces.*

Above *Cauliflower appears in many guises in Indian food, from appetizers to chutneys.*

Above *Spring (collard) greens are quick to cook, nutritious and colourful.*

Above *Okra, or ladies' fingers, are one of the most commonly used vegetables in India.*

Above *Colourful (bell) peppers make a crunchy and tasty addition to many dishes.*

REMOVING THE SKINS FROM TOMATOES

1 Score the skins of the tomatoes with a sharp knife.

2 Place the tomatoes in a heatproof bowl and carefully pour over enough boiling water to cover. Leave for about 30 seconds, until the skins look loose around the tomatoes.

3 Lift out the tomatoes with a slotted spoon, leave until cool enough to handle, then peel off the skins.

DICING ONIONS

1 Using a sharp knife, make a shallow slit down the side of the onion. Peel off the skin, using your fingers.

2 Cut the onion in half, from top to bottom. Slice through the onion at regular intervals at right angles to the root end. Leaving the root intact will hold the onion together and make it easier to dice.

3 Cut across the slices you have made to dice the onion.

OKRA
Also known as ladies' fingers, okra are one of the most popular and ubiquitous vegetables. These small, green, five-sided pods are indigenous to India. They have a distinctive flavour and a sticky, pulpy texture when they are cooked. To prepare, simply trim off the ends, rinse in a colander and use as directed in the method.

ONIONS
A versatile vegetable belonging to the allium family, onions have a pungent flavour and aroma and are one of the key ingredients, along with garlic and ginger, used in almost every Indian dish. They are grown in most regions of the country, except in arid areas, where they are bought in.

Globe onions are the most commonly used variety for Indian cooking, although smaller, sweeter shallots are favoured in some dishes that call for onions to be left whole, such as do-piaza. Spring onions (scallions) are often added to some dishes towards the end of the cooking time, or to raitas, to add colour and for their mild taste.

CORN
Although it originated in South America, corn is now grown worldwide, and is produced extensively in north India. It has a sweet, juicy flavour, which is at its best just after picking. Baby corn can be eaten whole, in curries, or dipped in a spicy batter and deep-fried to make fritters.

TOMATOES
An essential ingredient in a huge range of Indian dishes, tomatoes grow well in the heat of India and are a common sight at most markets. Adding acidity as well as colour and flavour, they are used to make sauces for curries, chutneys and relishes. Peeled and deseeded salad tomatoes are often adequate for most recipes, but they do need to be really ripe and flavoursome. Use canned tomatoes in sauces and curries for their rich colour and intense flavour, and as an alternative to salad varieties when these are not at their best.

(BELL) PEPPERS
Large, crunchy, hollow pods belonging to the capsicum family, peppers are available in a variety of colours. Red peppers are the sweetest, orange and yellow ones are mild and quite sweet, while green ones have a stronger, more peppery flavour. They are used in a wide variety of dishes, adding both colour and flavour.

To prepare, cut the peppers in half lengthways, then remove the stem, core and all the bitter white membrane using your fingers or a knife. Slice or dice the remaining flesh as required.

Fruit, nuts and seeds

Indians love fruit and, as well as eating fresh varieties raw as a snack or for dessert at the end of a meal, they will also cook them in savoury dishes. Fruit is often preserved by being sun-dried or converted into spicy chutneys, and these invaluable ingredients are cherished in the months when the fresh type is not available. Nuts and seeds – especially cashew nuts, almonds and sesame seeds – are often used as a thickening agent in curries, or are sprinkled on top of dishes to add an extra layer of flavour and texture.

Most of the fruit that is indigenous to India is now widely available in supermarkets and Asian stores. Choose ripe, unblemished specimens, as these will taste best. Nuts and seeds should be bought fresh and used quickly, as they can become rancid.

MANGOES
These fruits grow in India throughout the summer months, and ripe ones are used in sweet dishes. Unripe green mangoes, sold in the springtime, are used to make pickles and chutneys, and are added to curries as a souring agent. The unripe fruit is also sun-dried and ground into a powder called amchur, which has a sour taste and is sprinkled over dishes as a garnish.

PAPAYAS
Also known as pawpaw, these pear-shaped fruits are native to tropical America, and were not introduced to Asia until the 17th century. When ripe, the skin turns yellow and the pulp is a vibrant orange-pink. The edible black seeds taste peppery when dried. Peel off the skin and eat the creamy flesh raw. The unripe green fruit is used to tenderize meat.

Above *Mangoes are one of the favourite fruits in India, and are enjoyed in many different dishes.*

PINEAPPLES
These distinctive-looking fruits have sweet, golden and exceedingly juicy flesh. Unlike most other fruits, pineapples do not ripen after picking, although leaving a slightly unripe fruit at room temperature will help to reduce its acidity. Pineapples are cultivated in India, mainly in the south, and are generally cooked with spices to make palate-cleansing side dishes.

Above *Soft, fragrant and juicy, pears are ideal for making refreshing salads.*

BANANAS
The soft and creamy flesh of bananas is high in starch, and is an excellent source of energy. Indians use several varieties of banana in vegetarian curries, including plantains, green bananas, and the sweet red-skinned variety.

POMEGRANATES
The seeds of these beautiful fruits can be extracted by cutting fresh pomegranates into quarters and then picking out the seeds. Discard the bitter white membrane. As doing this is quite time-consuming, for convenience they can be bought in jars from Asian food stores. Pomegranate seeds impart a delicious tangy flavour.

PEARS
With cool, sweet and soft flesh, pears are the perfect foil to spices and can be combined with cucumber and creamy yogurt to make a delicious raita, or used to top the many milk-based treats that feature on the Indian dessert menu.

Left *Bananas are sold at roadside stalls and are eaten as healthy snacks as well as in dishes.*

LEMONS AND LIMES

These citrus fruits are indigenous to India, although limes, which in India are confusingly called lemons, are the most commonly available of the two. Both fruits are used as souring agents and are added to curries at the end of the cooking process.

DRIED FRUITS

Raisins, figs, apricots, dates and prunes are among the many dried fruits that provide succour and sweetness during the cold winter months when the fresh fruits are not available. They appear in comforting desserts and spicy, flavoursome chutneys, as well as being enjoyed on their own as a healthy snack.

COCONUT

Used in both sweet and savoury Indian dishes, fresh coconut is available from Indian food stores and supermarkets. Desiccated (dry unsweetened shredded) coconut, as well as coconut cream and creamed coconut, which are made from the grated flesh, will all make acceptable substitutes in most recipes if the fresh type is out of season. Coconut milk is used in Indian curries to thicken and enrich sauces. In Western supermarkets, it is sold in cans and in powdered form, as a convenient alternative to the fresh fruit; the powdered milk has to be blended with hot water before use. Coconut milk can be made at home from desiccated coconut. Coconut cream is used to add fragrance and aroma to dishes, while creamed coconut adds richness.

ALMONDS

These nuts are often soaked and pulped, then used for making rich sauces, especially kormas and pasandas. They grow in abundance in Kashmir in the north, where a superb chutney is made from ground blanched almonds and spices. Flaked (sliced) almonds are often toasted and used as an attractive garnish.

CASHEW NUTS AND PEANUTS

These full-flavoured nuts are an important ingredient in Indian cooking. In the north they are soaked and ground to a purée to make thick, rich sauces, and they can also be used as a crunchy garnish.

PISTACHIO NUTS

These vibrant green nuts are used mainly in desserts and sweets or as a garnish for pilaus and biryanis.

WALNUTS

Creamy and flavoursome, walnuts are commonly used whole or chopped in sweetmeats, salads and raitas.

SESAME SEEDS

These small, flat pear-shaped seeds are usually white, but can be cream, brown, red or black. When ground and made into a paste they act as a thickening agent.

POPPY SEEDS

Both white and black poppy seeds are used in Indian cooking to make savoury sauces. and in spicy fried dishes.

PREPARING COCONUT

Both the flesh and milk of fresh coconuts are used in Indian cooking.

1 To crack the coconut, tap it firmly with a rolling pin until a crack appears.

2 Holding it over a bowl, prise apart the shell and pour the liquid into the bowl.

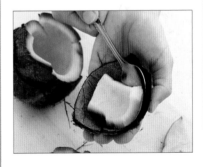

3 Scrape and prise out the white flesh using a spoon.

4 Slice the flesh intro strips or grate it with a grater, according to the recipe.

Above *Drying fruit is an excellent way to preserve it for use in the cold winter months.*

Above *Sesame seeds add flavour and texture, and can be ground and used as a thickener.*

Beans, peas and lentils

Playing an important role in regional cooking, pulses are an excellent source of protein and fibre, which is especially crucial for the many vegetarians in India. Some types are eaten whole, some are puréed and made into soups or dhals, and others are combined with vegetables or meat to make all manner of delectable and healthy dishes. It is important to follow the instructions regarding their preparation carefully, as some can be toxic if they are not treated properly.

Beans and chickpeas should be soaked before cooking, but if you are in a rush then you can use canned varieties. Lentils do not need to be soaked before use. Red and green split lentils have a soft consistency when cooked, while whole ones hold their shape. Do not add salt until the end of the cooking time when using lentils, apart from red split ones, as it will make them tough.

CHICKPEAS
These round, beige-coloured pulses have a strong, nutty flavour when cooked. As well as being used for curries, they are added to Indian snacks, and are also ground into gram flour (besan), which is used in many dishes, such as pakoras and bhajiyas.

PREPARING AND COOKING PULSES

It is very important to carefully follow preparation instructions when using beans and pulses.

1 Wash the beans or peas under cold running water, then place in a bowl of fresh cold water and leave to soak overnight. Drain and rinse again.

2 Put in a large pan and cover with cold water. Bring to the boil and cook on high for 10–15 minutes. Reduce the heat and simmer until tender. Lift out and drain, then use as required.

Above *Mung beans can be used in whole or split forms, and can also be sprouted.*

HARICOT (NAVY) BEANS
Ideal for Indian cooking because they retain their shape well and absorb flavours easily, these small, white oval beans contain more soluble fibre than any other type of pulse.

KIDNEY BEANS
These red-brown kidney-shaped beans hold their shape when cooked. It is important to soak and cook all beans before use, but especially kidney beans, as they are highly toxic if not prepared properly.

MUNG BEANS
Whole mung beans (sabut mung dhal) are small, round green beans with a sweet flavour and creamy texture, which are used in curries and to make dhal. When sprouted, mung beans produce nutritious beansprouts that can be used to make a wholesome and delicious bread as well as in salads. Skinless split mung beans (mung dhal) have a milder flavour than whole ones, and are often cooked with rice.

URID DHAL
This lentil-like bean is available split, with the blackish hull either retained or removed.

Above *Red split lentils (masoor dhal) are commonly used to make nutritious dhals.*

SPLIT BENGAL GRAM (CHANNA DHAL)
This round, skinless yellow split lentil is robust and versatile, which is perhaps why it is the most popular type of lentil used in Indian cooking. It is similar in taste to the yellow split lentil (moong or mung dhal), which will make a good substitute if you can not find split Bengal gram. It can cause wind, but cooking it with a small amount of Asafoetida helps combat this side effect.

GREEN LENTILS
Also known as continental lentils, these have a strong flavour and retain their shape well. They can be used in place of red split lentils.

RED SPLIT LENTILS (MASOOR DHAL)
These delicately flavoured lentils cook to a soft paste and are commonly used to make dhal in India, and soups elsewhere.

PIGEON PEAS (TOOR OR TUVAR DHAL)
A dull orange-coloured split pea with a distinctive earthy flavour, tuvar dhal is available plain and in an oily variety.

Dairy products, butter and oils

Used on a daily basis, these ingredients are the cornerstone of the Indian diet, except in regions where veganism is practised. Milk, yogurt and cheese appear in a huge range of dishes, adding much-needed protein and flavour, as well as being consumed on their own as drinks or snacks. Yogurt is especially popular with vegetarians and is used in cooking as well as for raitas and sauces. Butter (often in the form of ghee) or oil appear in almost every recipe, adding calories as well as flavour.

Used in drinks or cooked in both savoury and sweet dishes, milk is important in the Indian diet. Natural (plain) yogurt accompanies most Indian meals, and drinks based on yogurt, such as lassis, are also very popular. Paneer, the only Indian cheese, is a key ingredient in many specialities, such as Indian Cheese Curry in Milk.

Sunflower oil is the most popular cooking medium because of its neutral flavour, but in some regions cooks favour groundnut or mustard oil. Rich, nutty-tasting ghee was the traditional cooking medium until recent years.

MILK AND BUTTERMILK
The volume of milk produced in India is one of the highest in the world and the dairy industry is big business. In addition to milk from cows, more than half of the milk comes from buffalo, and is sold in liquid form, as a stable, creamy yogurt and as cheese. Buttermilk, the by-product of the butter-making process, is also drunk and used in cooking.

YOGURT
In India, yogurt is known as curd, and is very thick and rich as it is made with buffalo's rather than cow's milk. It can be added to sauces to give a creamy texture, although it is most often used as a souring agent, particularly in the dairy-dominated north.

Yogurt will curdle quickly when heated, especially if it does not have a high enough fat content, so it is best to use a full-fat (whole) version, such as Greek (US strained plain) yogurt. Other types of full-fat yogurt can be strained through muslin (cheesecloth) to remove water and make them more stable.

CREAM
Double (heavy) cream is added to some curries, such as kormas, where it adds depth of flavour and a silky texture to the dish.

PANEER
This traditional north Indian cheese is made from rich dairy milk. Paneer is white in colour and smooth-textured. It is usually available from large supermarkets, but halloumi, tofu and beancurd are adequate substitutes.

GHEE
The main fat used in Indian cooking until recent years, ghee is still widely used, although people are increasingly using vegetable oil, as it is healthier. There are two types: the traditional one, made from pure butterfat; and a more recent kind, which is made from vegetable fat. Butterfat ghee is rich with a golden colour and nutty taste. It is made by separating the milk solids and eliminating the moisture from unsalted butter. The result is a pure golden liquid, which is strained and stored in an airtight jar at room temperature. The kind made from vegetable fat has less flavour but is healthier. Unsalted butter, mixed with 15ml/1 tbsp oil, can be used as a substitute.

Above *Ghee is a cooking fat traditionally used in Indian kitchens.*

COOKING OILS
Corn oil and sunflower oil are most popular types of oil in India. Sesame oil and groundnut oil are also used, and in the south, where coconuts are abundant, coconut oil is most popular. Pungent mustard oil is used in everyday cooking in Kashmir, Bengal and in the north-eastern states. When it reaches a high temperature it loses its astringent taste and aroma.

Below *Buffalo are a common sight in India, and their milk is used to make a range of products.*

Rice

A staple grain that is grown nearly everywhere, rice is served with almost every meal in most parts of India, so it is no surprise that the Indians have created a variety of distinctive ways of cooking it. Plain boiled rice, cooked by the absorption method, is an everyday accompaniment to curries and other wet dishes. For special occasions and entertaining, it is often combined with other ingredients to make delectable pilaus and biryanis. Basmati rice is the grain of choice in most regions.

There is no definitive way to cook plain rice, but whatever the recipe, the aim is to produce dry, separate-grained rice that is cooked through yet still retains some bite. The secret is the amount of water added: the rice must be able to absorb it all, so it must be added in the correct ratio.

BASMATI RICE

Known as the 'prince of rices', basmati is the recommended rice for Indian curries – not only because it is easy to cook and produces an excellent finished result, but because it has a cooling effect.

Basmati is a slender, long grain, milled rice grown in northern India, the Punjab, parts of Pakistan and in the foothills of the Himalayas. Its name means 'fragrant', and it has a distinctive and appealing aroma. After harvesting it is aged for a year, which gives it its characteristic flavour and a light, fluffy texture. Basmati can be used in almost any savoury dish, particularly curries or pilaus, and is the essential ingredient in biryanis. White and brown basmati rices are widely available from supermarkets and Indian food stores.

Above *White basmati rice is grown in the north, and is the most common type of rice in India.*

PATNA RICE

This rice takes its name from Patna in Bihar, eastern India. At one time, most of the long grain rice sold in Europe came from here, and the term was used to mean any long grain rice, whatever its origin. The custom still persists in parts of the United States, but elsewhere patna describes this specific variety of rice. It is used in the same way as other long grain rices.

Above *Ground rice is the thickening agent used to make Indian milk-based desserts.*

OTHER RICE PRODUCTS

Rice can be used to make other ingredients, such as ground rice, which is used for making desserts, and rice flour, which is used in sweetmeats, dumplings and pancakes. The grains may also be flattened to make flaked rice, which is used for creating delicious snacks; or placed in very hot sand to make puffed rice, which is used for various snacks and sweets.

PLAIN BOILED RICE

Always wash rice in several changes of water until the water runs clear, and soak it for 15–20 minutes before cooking, then drain.

Serves 4
275g/10oz/1⅓ cups basmati rice
15ml/1 tsp butter
2.5ml/½ tsp salt

1 Wash the rice in several changes of water until the water runs clear. Soak it in fresh water for 20 minutes. Drain well.

2 In a medium-sized pan, bring 550ml/ 18fl oz/2½ cups water to the boil and add the butter, salt and the drained rice. Bring it to the boil and let it boil steadily for 1 minute.

3 Reduce the heat to low and cover the pan tightly. Cook for 8–9 minutes, then switch off the heat source. Leave the pan to stand undisturbed for 10–12 minutes.

4 Fluff up the rice with a fork and serve with a main course or vegetable side dishes.

Per Portion Energy 256kcal/1071kJ; Protein 5.1g; Carbohydrate 54.9g, of which sugars 0g; Fat 1.4g, of which saturates 0.7g; Cholesterol 3mg; Calcium 13mg; Fibre 0g; Sodium 255mg.

Bread

An integral part of many meals, Indian breads are served alongside or instead of rice as a staple carbohydrate to balance out the other dishes. Most traditional Indian breads are unleavened – that is, made without any raising agent – and recipes tend to use wholemeal (whole-wheat) flour, known as chapati flour or atta. They are all delicious hot from the oven, but generally do not keep very well so should be made and eaten on the same day. They are also cheap and readily available to buy.

Throughout India, breads vary from region to region, depending on local ingredients and customs. Some breads are cooked dry on a hot griddle, while some are fried with a little oil, and others are deep-fried to make small savoury puffs.

NAAN

Probably the most well-known Indian bread outside India is naan, from the north of the country. Naan is made with plain (all-purpose) flour, yogurt and yeast; some contemporary recipes favour the use of a raising agent such as bicarbonate of soda (baking soda) or self-raising (self-rising) flour as a leaven in place of yeast. The yogurt is important for the fermentation of the dough, and some naan are made entirely using a yogurt fermentation. This gives the bread its soft, puffy texture and soft crust.

The flavour comes partly from the soured yogurt and partly from the *tandoor*, in which the bread is traditionally cooked. The dough is flattened against the hot walls of the oven and the pull of gravity produces the teardrop shape. As the dough scorches and puffs up, it produces a bread that is soft and crisp.

CHAPATIS

The favourite bread of central and southern India, the chapati is a thin, flat, unleavened bread usually made from ground wholemeal (whole-wheat) flour. Chapatis are cooked on a hot *tava*, a concave-shaped Indian griddle. They have a light texture and fairly bland flavour, which makes them an ideal accompaniment to curry dishes. Spices can be added to the flour to give more flavour.

ROTIS

There are many variations of chapatis, including rotis and dana rotis. These are unleavened breads, made using chapati flour to which ghee, oil, celery seeds and/or fresh coriander (cilantro) are added. They are rolled out thinly and cooked like chapatis.

POORIS

Another popular variation on the chapati is the poori, which is a small, deep-fried puffy bread made from chapati flour. Pooris are best eaten sizzling hot and are traditionally served for breakfast. They can be plain or flavoured with spices, such as cumin, turmeric and chilli powder.

Above *Chapatis are traditionally cooked on a tawa over a wood fire, giving them a smoky flavour.*

PARATHAS

A paratha is a flat bread that contains a substantial amount of ghee, which gives the bread a rich flavour and flaky texture. Parathas are much thicker than chapatis and are shallow-fried. Plain ones are often eaten for lunch, and they go well with most vegetable dishes. They can be stuffed with various fillings, the most popular being spiced potato, and served as a snack.

POPPADUMS

Now widely available outside of India, poppadums are large, thin, crisp discs, which can be bought ready-cooked or ready-to-cook. In India they are served with vegetarian meals. They are sold in markets and by street vendors, and are available plain or flavoured with spices or seasoned with ground red or black pepper. The dough is generally made from gram flour (besan), but can also be made from potatoes or sago.

Above *North-Indian naan is the best-known bread outside India, and has a lovely fluffy texture.*

Above *Crunchy poppadums are the ideal accompaniment to chutneys and relishes.*

Herbs, spices and other flavourings

The key to Indian cooking lies in the various combinations and treatments of the panoply of spices and flavourings that are indigenous to the region. Some types are used principally for the taste they impart, while other ones, known as aromatics, are used mainly for their aroma. One individual spice can completely alter the taste of a dish and a combination of several will also affect its colour and texture, so it is little wonder that there is such a huge number of possible variations in Indian cuisine.

In order to get the most from herbs, spices and flavourings you need to buy the freshest ones you can, which means it is often better to buy smaller quantities more often. This is especially true of spices, which go stale and lose their piquancy fairly quickly.

HERBS

Fresh and dried herbs add colour, flavour, aroma and texture to a curry. Because herbs require only a minimal amount of cooking, they retain a marvellous intensity of flavour and fragrance.

Chillies

It is surprising that chillies, without which Indian food is difficult to imagine, were not known in India until the 16th century when the Portuguese introduced them to the southern region. South Indians consume the most fresh chillies, while the state of Andhra Pradesh in central India produces the largest quantity. Removing the seeds will reduce the potency of fresh chillies (*see* box), or you can reduce the quantity used. Dried red chillies, dried chilli flakes and chilli powder are popular all over India. A little goes a long way with these products, so be sure to measure quantities carefully.

Below Dried chilli flakes add a fiery punch to dishes and can be used instead of fresh chilli.

Fenugreek

This fresh herb has very small leaves and is sold in fragrant bunches as well as in its dried form (kasuri methi) at street markets. The stalks of fresh fenugreek should be discarded as they will impart a bitterness to a dish if used. Fenugreek seeds are flat, extremely pungent and slightly bitter.

Fresh coriander (cilantro)

The leaves of this fragrant and attractive plant are used to garnish almost every savoury dish throughout the country, and the stems and leaves are also chopped and added during cooking to impart a freshness and their unique flavour.

Bay leaves

Glossy green bay leaves can be used fresh or dried to add flavour to stocks and slow-cooked curries.

Curry leaves

These pungent leaves (kariveppilai) are ubiquitous in the dishes from the south of country, especially in Tamil Nadu. They are available fresh or dried, although the fresh version has a much stronger flavour and is generally the preferred form.

Below Dried fenugreek has a strong taste.
Right Coriander (cilantro) makes a pretty garnish.

PREPARING CHILLIES

You should always wash your hands after touching chillies. Wear gloves if you have sensitive skin.

1 Cut the chillies in half lengthways. Remove the membranes and seeds.

2 Cut the flesh lengthways into long, thin strips, and then into tiny dice.

Above *Cardamom seeds can be used whole or crushed to add aroma to dishes.*

Above *Cloves have a very powerful flavour so make sure you use the amount stated.*

GARAM MASALA

This spice mix is added at the end of the cooking time in many curries.

Makes about 90g/3oz
15g/½oz brown cardamom seeds
15g/½oz whole green cardamom pods
15g/½oz cinnamon sticks
10 cloves
7g/¼oz black peppercorns
1 whole nutmeg, lightly crushed
1 mace blade

1 Preheat a small, heavy frying pan over a low-medium heat and add all the spices. Dry-roast for 30–40 seconds, when they will release their aroma. Immediately remove from the heat.

2 Transfer the spices to a plate to stop them roasting further. Let them cool completely, then grind in a coffee grinder or with a mortar and pestle until fine.

3 Store in an airtight container away from direct light. The spice mix will keep well for 3–4 months.

SPICES

The quantities of spices specified in recipes are measured to achieve a balance of flavours, so it is important that you follow them. Having tried a dish, however, you may prefer to change the amounts according to taste.

Asafoetida

This spice has a powerful aroma and is often used when cooking pulses, as it is a digestive aid. It is usually fried in hot oil, which mellows its strong smell and changes its flavour from bitter to onion-like.

Cardamom, cinnamon and cloves

These three sweetish spices have been an integral part of Indian cooking since ancient times, and they appear as a flavour trio found together in any number of dishes. They are also used in the north to make an infusion that raises the body temperature – ideal in the bitterly cold winter climate of the Himalayas.

Cardamom is native to India, where it is considered to be the most prized spice after saffron. The pods can be used whole or the husks can be removed to release the seeds, which have a slightly pungent, aromatic taste. Southern Indians use ground cardamom in sweetmeats and desserts, while northerners are passionate about its heady aroma in many chicken dishes, pilaus and biryanis.

Cinnamon is usually used in its bark form, rather than ground, and cloves are also normally left whole, so you may choose to remove them prior to serving.

Below *A dazzling array of dried spices are available at colourful markets in India.*

Above *Yellow and black mustard seeds, along with mustard oil, are widely used in Indian food.*

Above *Nutmeg and mace are from the same plant and feature in north-Indian cuisine.*

PREPARING GINGER

It is best to grate fresh root ginger rather than puréeing it in a food processor, as it removes the fibres.

1 Peel the ginger either with a peeler, a knife, or by scraping with a teaspoon.

2 Chop or grate the flesh as required, cutting or grating in the same direction as the hairy fibres of the ginger.

Aniseed

These liquorice-flavoured seeds are used in many fried and deep-fried Indian dishes as an aid to digestion, and is also sometimes chewed after meals as a mouth freshener. It has a potent flavour that can overwhelm dishes, so it should be used sparingly, according to the recipe.

Coriander and cumin

These two spices appear in almost every savoury dish in India. Dried coriander seeds are pale and round, and have a sweet, mellow flavour, while white cumin seeds are oval, ridged and greenish-brown in colour. They have a strong aroma and flavour and can be used whole or ground. Ready-ground cumin powder is available, but it should be bought in small quantities as it loses its flavour rapidly. Black cumin seeds are dark and aromatic and are sometimes used to make the spice blend garam masala. Whole seeds should be dry-roasted to bring out their full flavour and aroma before being ground in a coffee grinder or mortar and pestle, or added to dishes.

DRY-ROASTING SPICES

Dry spices, ground or whole, should be gently sizzled over a very low heat so that they do not burn, as this would make the dish bitter. It is crucial not to rush this process as the raw smell of the spices must be eliminated in order to achieve a fragrant, well-rounded flavour.

Fennel seeds

These are similar in appearance to cumin seeds, have a sweet taste and are used to flavour curries. Fennel seeds can also be chewed as a mouth-freshener after a meal.

Mustard seeds

These are another essential ingredient in Indian cooking, especially in vegetarian dishes. In the south, jet-black mustard seeds adorn yogurt as a dressing for all kinds of salads. On the other hand, the creamy-yellow variety is used to make curries as well as the majority of pickles.

Onion seeds

Black, triangular shaped and aromatic, onion seeds are used in pickles and to flavour vegetable curries and lentil dishes as well as on top of Peshwari naan.

Nigella

This spice has a sharp, tingling taste and is mainly used to add flavour to vegetable dishes. They are often referred to as onion seeds as they are similar in appearance.

Nutmeg and mace

The nutmeg plant is unique as it produces two spices in one: nutmeg and mace. These are both highly aromatic and are used extensively in northern Indian cuisine. It is best to grate whole nutmeg as needed. Mace is often available in its ground form.

Saffron

Used in both sweet and savoury dishes, saffron is known to have medicinal values such as curing skin and stomach disorders.

The stigmas of the saffron crocus flower are hand picked and sun-dried, and they are so light that it takes about 500,000 dried stigmas to make 450g (1lb) of saffron. A few strands soaked in milk or water add an exotic taste and appearance to any dish.

Star anise

The fruit of the Chinese evergreen magnolia tree, star anise is an eight-pointed liquorice-flavoured pod that adds a warm and pungent note to curries all over India.

Turmeric

With a rich golden hue, turmeric has a bitter taste that disappears when it is blended with other ingredients. It is highly antiseptic, with exceptional preserving qualities. Fish is often sprinkled with turmeric and salt if it cannot be cooked on the same day as it is bought. It stains, so be careful when using it!

OTHER FLAVOURINGS

Often termed 'wet spices', the main trio of flavourings in Indian cooking undoubtedly consists of ginger, onion and garlic, which appear in almost every dish. Salt is also key and plays a vital role in developing and blending flavours. The addition of sweet and sour notes lends an extra dimension to many curries, and these are usually imparted by the judicious use of flavoursome palm sugar (jaggery), dry mango powder (*amchur*) and tamarind.

Garlic, ginger and onion

These three aromatics are often the key elements in Indian food. Garlic and ginger are standard ingredients in most curries, and they are generally pulped, crushed or chopped. In the north, the trio are often used as an all-in-one paste, or onions are boiled and puréed before being cooked with ginger, garlic and dry spices. Browned onion purée, used in conjunction with the other two ingredients, creates a distinctive rich flavour.

Salt

This essential ingredient is always added at the beginning of or during the cooking process rather than at the end, except in lentil dishes, where the addition of salt too early would cause the lentils (except red split ones) to become tough. Although the quantity of salt used in Indian cooking may seem excessive at times, it is treated almost as a spice and is vital for balancing the other flavours in a dish.

PREPARING COMPRESSED TAMARIND

Asian food stores sell compressed tamarind in a solid block, which resembles a packet of dried dates.

1 Tear off a piece of tamarind that is equivalent to 15ml/1 tbsp. Put it in a jug (pitcher). Add 150ml/ ¼ pint/⅔ cup warm water. Leave it to soak for 10 minutes.

2 Swirl the tamarind around with your fingers so that the pulp is released.

3 Strain the juice into a bowl. Discard the pulp. Use the liquid as required.

4 Store any leftover juice in the refrigerator for up to 2 weeks, for use in another recipe.

Palm sugar (jaggery)

Available as blocks of solidified sugar or in paste form, this distinctive sugar is used as a sweetener in savoury dishes and desserts. It is made from the concentrated juice that is extracted from sugarcane or palm trees, with that made from the date palm being the most highly prized as it has a better flavour. Soft dark brown sugar can be used as an adequate substitute.

Dry mango powder

Mangoes are indigenous to India, and they have many uses in Indian cooking. The fruit is used in curries at different stages of ripeness as well as in desserts and as a snack, but the unripe fruit is also sun-dried and ground into a dry powder called amchur. The powder has a sour taste, and is sprinkled over dishes as a garnish; it is not used in cooking.

Tamarind

Dried black tamarind pods are sour in taste and very sticky. Tamarind can be bought in paste form or compressed form (*see* box), but lemon juice can be used as a substitute if you prefer.

PULPING GARLIC

Garlic is one of the most common ingredients, and is easy to prepare.

1 Separate the cloves from the bulb and remove the papery skin.

2 Sprinkle each garlic bulb with a little sea salt and finely chop, then press with the flat of a knife and scrape on a board to make a purée.

Above *Garlic is one of the three key wet spices used in Indian cooking.*

Above *Palm sugar (jaggery) has a molasses-like flavour and is available in block or paste form.*

Accompaniments

There is a vast range of salads, chutneys and raitas on offer in India, and they vary tremendously from one region to another, depending on what ingredients are available locally. Chutneys are used as a way of preserving ingredients for the months when fresh produce is not available, but they have the added benefit of being extremely tasty. Usually served alongside main dishes, all these tempting accompaniments are eaten in small quantities to add zest, as well as being used for flavoursome garnishes and dips.

An Indian meal would not be complete without several small bowls of assorted accompaniments, which enable diners to mix and match and create different flavour sensations with every mouthful. Often served at the start of the meal with poppadums in Indian restaurants in the West, they should also accompany the main dishes and be almost like additional seasonings.

RAITAS

Originating in northern India, raita always consists of a yogurt base to which grated or finely chopped vegetables are added. In southern India, *pachadi* is flavoured with whole spices such as mustard and cumin seeds, curry leaves and chillies, which are added to a small quantity of hot oil and incorporated into the yogurt mixture. In northern India the spicing is different, comprising a fiery combination of crushed black pepper, roasted cumin seeds and chilli powder. In the state of Maharashtra in western India the flavourings are different again, and *koshimbir* generally contains lemon juice, fresh green chillies, finely chopped onion and coriander (cilantro). Raita is also occasionally made with fruit, such as banana, in place of the cucumber.

Above *Pickles, often made with sour vegetables or fruits such as limes, add an acidic, zesty note to Indian meals.*
Below *Salads and raitas can be made from many different ingredients, depending on what is available locally and what is in season.*

CUCUMBER RAITA

Makes about 600ml/1 pint/2½ cups
½ cucumber
1 fresh green chilli, deseeded and finely chopped
300ml/½ pint/1¼ cups natural (plain) yogurt
1.5ml/¼ tsp salt
1.5ml/¼ tsp ground cumin

1 Dice the cucumber finely and place it in a large mixing bowl. Add the chilli.

2 Gently beat the yogurt with a fork until it becomes smooth, then stir it into the cucumber and chilli mixture.

3 Next, stir in the salt and cumin. Cover the bowl with clear film (plastic wrap) and leave in the refrigerator to chill before serving.

SALADS

Served hot or cold, as an accompaniment or as the star of the show, Indian salads are an important element of many meals. Often consisting of simple mixtures of vegetables such as carrots, they add a lightness and crunch to contrast with the softer textures of rice and curries. More robust versions made with beans, peas and lentils are also popular, and these are usually liberally doused with a spicy dressing and served as a main course.

GARNISHES

Fresh coriander (cilantro) is the most common garnish in Indian cooking, and its bright green leaves and fresh flavour provide a visual and taste sensation. Parsley and mint are also sometimes used. Finely chopped fried onions give a crispy topping to rice dishes, while wedges of lemon or lime are served with other dishes, to be squeezed over by the diner. Slivers of raw chilli add a vibrant, fiery note to spicy foods, and this can be offset by a spoonful of raita or plain yogurt. Toasted slivers of coconut or nuts such as flaked (sliced) almonds can be sprinkled over sweet and savoury dishes, including the much-loved rice puddings.

TOASTING ALMONDS

Flaked (sliced) almonds make a lovely garnish, and have the best flavour and texture if toasted.

1 There are two ways of toasting almonds: in the oven or in a frying pan. If toasting in the oven, preheat it to 180ºC/350ºF/Gas 4. Spread out the almonds on a baking sheet and bake for 5–8 minutes, checking them often.

2 To toast in a frying pan, cook over a medium heat for 3–5 minutes.

Above *Chutneys were originally devised as a tasty means of preserving fresh produce prior to refrigeration, and are still enjoyed today.*

PRESERVES

A ubiquitous element of an Indian meal, chutneys, or *chatnis*, originally evolved during the British Raj in the days before refrigeration, as a means of preserving fresh foods that were slightly past their best. Cooked with vinegar and sugar, the fruit and vegetable mixtures are then flavoured with a huge range of spices to create myriad different variations. Pickles were created for similar reasons, although in this instance only seasonal produce in peak condition is used. In the summer, seasonal fruits and vegetables are also dried in the sun and made into leathers for use during the colder months.

Chutney

There are two categories of chutney: fresh and cooked. In India, fresh chutneys are made in small quantities and consumed there and then, as they do not keep well. Made daily, the ingredients, such as peanuts, cashew nuts, dried peas, fresh herbs, chillies, ginger and garlic, are ground in a traditional grinding stone, which produces a fine texture and blends the flavours. A mortar and pestle can also be used.

Cooked chutneys are made from seasonal fruits and vegetables such as raw and ripe mangoes, pineapples, plums and tomatoes. In addition to the traditional method of cooking the ingredients with vinegar and sugar, there is another type of

POTTING PRESERVES

Before potting chutneys or pickles it is essential to sterilize containers to destroy any micro-organisms.

1 Check jars or bottles for damage or cracks. If you have a dishwasher, place the containers and their lids in it and run it on its hottest setting. This will both wash and sterilize in one go.

2 If you don't have a dishwasher, wash the containers in hot, soapy water, rinse well and turn up-side down to drain.

3 Stand the containers on a baking sheet. Rest any lids on top. Place in a cold oven, then heat to 110ºC/225ºF/Gas ¼ and bake for 30 minutes.

4 Leave to cool slightly befor filling. Screw on the lids and label the containers with the contents and date.

cooked chutney which is made by dry-roasting certain types of lentils and dried peas and mixing these with selected spices.

Pickles

Comprising small chunks of fruits and vegetables cooked in oil with spices such as Asafoetida, chilli powder, turmeric and an ample amount of salt, pickles are usually prepared in the summer, when the ingredients are at their best. Ones made with mangoes and limes are very common, although they can be made with a huge range of produce – from carrots, onions and tomatoes to rose petals, jackfruit and Indian gooseberries. The flavour of the condiments is affected by the choice of spices as well as the type of oil used, with mustard oil being the preference in the north and sesame oil more often used in the south. Meat and fish are also pickled in brine in some regions.

Soups, Appetizers and Snacks

Whether served at home or on street corners, soups and light bites are very much an integral part of everyday life in India, whetting the appetite and satisfying the desire for a delicious morsel at any time of the day. From warming, nutritious soups made with seasonal vegetables to crisp, deep-fried treats and all manner of kebabs, every dish is sure to stimulate the senses.

Tempting, tasty and aromatic

Traditionally, Indian meals are not divided into categories such as appetizers and main courses; instead, all the dishes are served at the same time, and diners simply help themselves to them in any order. In recent times, however, dishes have been categorized, particularly outside India, in order to conform with other countries' eating habits. For this reason, almost all Indian restaurants now divide their menus into distinct courses and the same practice is also being followed in some homes when entertaining.

Generally, people do not associate soups with Indian cuisine, but there is, in fact, a very special – albeit limited – repertoire that is enjoyed before or during a meal. History has it that soups were first served in India in the fourteenth century, having been brought from ancient Persia to north India by the Mughals. The Hindi name for soups, *shorba*, literally means 'broth', and indeed many do consist of a range of vegetables in a highly flavoured stock. Rich *shorbas*, which may have been thickened by puréeing the ingredients, were an integral part of most Mughal banquets and remain popular today, especially during the bitterly cold winter months in the northern and eastern regions. Traditionally, they were served during a meal rather than before it, and this practice continues in some private homes. North Indian soups tend to be rich and the spicing is subtle, whereas in southern India they are often lighter and spicier, and may include the ubiquitous coconut milk.

Within the huge diversity of Indian cuisine there exists a large range of dishes that can be enjoyed both as appetizers and snacks, from world-famous favourites such as Onion Bhajiyas to less well-known delicacies such as Lotus Root Kebabs. While these are generally eaten in the afternoon with tea in India, they are equally delicious served with drinks before a meal or as a first course. Outside the home, snacks are a big part of the Indian way of life. There are street vendors in every city, town and village, selling enticing treats that are enjoyed in cinemas, at sports events and even walking down the road. Indians simply love to nibble on choice morsels at any time, and the range on offer reflects this national obsession.

Most of the snacks can be served with a garnish of salad, which provides freshness and cleanses the palate before the next course is served, and they are almost always accompanied by several types of chutney. The importance of these irresistible condiments cannot be overstated, as their diverse flavours, colours and textures both contrast with and complement the foods they accompany.

Mushroom soup with green chilli and garlic

This recipe, *Khumb Ka Shorba*, is from the strikingly beautiful district of Arunachal Pradesh in the foothills of the Himalayas. It is ideal on a cold winter's night and, when made to perfection, you can taste and savour each ingredient. A good stock is essential, so it is worth paying a little extra or making your own.

SERVES 4

900ml/1½ pints/3¾ cups fresh vegetable stock or 2 vegetable stock (bouillon) cubes

250g/9oz potatoes, cubed

2.5cm/1in piece of fresh root ginger, finely grated

4 large garlic cloves, crushed to a pulp or grated

1 fresh green chilli, finely chopped (deseeded if preferred)

250g/9oz button (white) mushrooms, sliced

15ml/1 tbsp fresh coriander (cilantro) leaves, chopped

hot crusty rolls, to serve

1 Put the stock in a pan. If using stock cubes, put them in a heatproof jug and dissolve them in 900ml/1½ pints/3¾ cups hot water. Add the potatoes, ginger, garlic and chilli.

2 Bring to the boil and cook over a medium heat for 10 minutes.

3 Add the mushrooms and cook for a further 10 minutes, until the mushrooms are cooked.

4 Stir in the chopped coriander and serve immediately with hot crusty rolls.

Per portion Energy 69kcal/290kJ; Protein 3g; Carbohydrate 12g, of which sugars 1g; Fat 1g, of which saturates 0g; Cholesterol 0mg; Calcium 11mg; Fibre 2.4g; Sodium 596mg.

Fresh vegetables in chilli and ginger broth

This dish, *Oying*, originates in the scenic mountain state of Arunachal Pradesh. The cuisine of this region is simple, delicious and extremely nutritious. Most of the cooking is done without using any fat, as in this recipe, relying instead on the addition of herbs and spices to give it superb, distinctive flavours.

SERVES 4

250g/9oz/1 cup potatoes, cut into
  2.5cm/1in cubes
1–2 fresh green chillies, sliced diagonally
150g/5oz/1 cup green beans, cut into
  2.5cm/1in lengths
150g/5oz/1 cup cabbage, shredded
5ml/1 tsp salt, or to taste
10ml/2 tsp grated fresh root ginger
1 large garlic clove, crushed
150g/5oz/1 cup fresh spinach, washed
  and roughly chopped
15–30ml/1–2 tbsp fresh coriander (cilantro)
  leaves, chopped
hot crusty rolls, to serve

1 Put the potatoes in a medium pan, pour in 700ml/1¼ pints/3 cups water and bring to the boil. Add the chillies, reduce the heat to low, cover and cook for 7–8 minutes.

2 Add the green beans and cabbage, bring back to the boil, then cover and cook over a medium heat for 5 minutes.

3 Add the salt, ginger and garlic, replace the lid and continue to cook for 5 minutes.

4 Stir in the spinach and cook for a further 1–2 minutes, until it has wilted.

5 Add the coriander leaves, cook for about 1 minute, then remove from the heat and serve with hot crusty rolls.

Per portion Energy 77kcal/322kJ; Protein 3.7g; Carbohydrate 14.1g, of which sugars 4.4g; Fat 0.9g, of which saturates 0.2g; Cholesterol 0mg; Calcium 125mg; Fibre 3.7g; Sodium 66mg.

Tomato and coriander soup

Based on a recipe from southern India, this soup, *Rasam*, is traditionally served in a cup to accompany a meal. However, it is rather a novel idea to serve this in shot glasses or coffee cups as an appetizer. Fresh curry leaves provide the main flavour here, but if you cannot obtain them, use the dried ones instead.

2 Add the tomatoes and pour in 300ml/ ½ pint/1¼ cups hot water. Bring it to the boil, add the salt and sugar, cover and reduce the heat to low.

3 Simmer for 15–20 minutes, cool slightly, then process in a blender or food processor. Push through a sieve (strainer) into the pan.

4 Reheat the soup gently until it is just simmering. Garnish with the coriander leaves and serve immediately.

SERVES 4

30ml/2 tbsp sunflower oil or light
  olive oil
2 cloves garlic, crushed
1cm/½in piece of fresh root ginger,
  peeled and grated
2 dried red chillies, finely snipped
2.5ml/½ tsp black peppercorns,
  crushed
8 fresh or 10 dried curry leaves
600g/1lb 6oz chopped fresh tomatoes
  or canned chopped tomatoes
5ml/1 tsp salt
5ml/1 tsp sugar
30ml/2 tbsp fresh coriander (cilantro)
  leaves, to garnish

1 Heat the oil in a pan over a low heat, then add the garlic, ginger, chillies, peppercorns and curry leaves and fry for 2–3 minutes, until the garlic and ginger have browned and the chillies have blackened a little.

COOK'S TIP

Fresh curry leaves are often available from Asian stores. The best way to preserve them is to wash them, then pat them dry with kitchen paper and freeze them in a single layer. Once frozen, transfer them to an airtight freezer bag and use them direct from the freezer, as required.

Per portion Energy 101kcal/421kJ; Protein 2g; Carbohydrate 7g, of which sugars 6g; Fat 8g, of which saturates 1g; Cholesterol 0mg; Calcium 24mg; Fibre 1.2g; Sodium 1043mg.

Coconut kebabs

In India, these little morsels, *Nariyal Ke Kabab*, are made from grated fresh coconut. To make life easier, this recipe uses desiccated (dry unsweetened shredded) coconut moistened with milk to replenish some of its richness. They make an ideal appetizer served with chutney and a glass of cold beer or white wine.

MAKES 16

150g/5oz desiccated (dry unsweetened shredded) coconut

150ml/¼ pint/⅔ cup full-fat (whole) milk, heated until warm

2 large slices of white bread, crusts removed

75g/3oz/⅔ cup gram flour (besan)

1–3 fresh green chillies, roughly chopped (deseeded if preferred)

2.5cm/1in piece of fresh root ginger, peeled and roughly chopped

1 large garlic clove, peeled and roughly chopped

15ml/1 tbsp fresh coriander (cilantro) leaves and stalks, roughly chopped

2.5ml/½ tsp chilli powder, or to taste

3.75ml/¾ tsp salt, or to taste

1 medium onion, finely chopped

sunflower oil, for shallow-frying

chutney, to serve

1 Put the desiccated coconut in a large mixing bowl and pour over the warm milk. Set aside for 10 minutes for the coconut to absorb the milk and rehydrate slightly. Cut the bread into small pieces.

2 Place all the ingredients, except the onion and the oil, in a food processor and blitz for a few seconds, until you have a smooth paste.

3 Transfer the mixture to a bowl and add the onion. Mix thoroughly and divide the mixture into 16 balls, each the size of a lime.

4 Flatten the coconut balls to form 16 smooth, round cakes. If the mixture sticks to your fingers, moisten your palms with cold water between cakes.

5 Pour enough oil in a frying pan to measure about 1cm/½in in depth, and heat over a high heat.

6 Fry the kebabs in batches, without overcrowding the pan, for 3–4 minutes on each side, until browned all over.

7 Lift out the kebabs with a slotted spoon, drain on kitchen paper and keep warm while you fry the remaining kebabs. Serve with a chutney of your choice.

Per portion Energy 121kcal/502kJ; Protein 3g; Carbohydrate 8g, of which sugars 2g; Fat 9g, of which saturates 6g; Cholesterol 1mg; Calcium 34mg; Fibre 3.1g; Sodium 125mg.

Lotus root kebabs

In the Hindu religion, the strikingly beautiful lotus flower is synonymous with spiritual awakening. In this Kashmiri recipe, *Nadhru Kababs*, exotic lotus flower roots are lightly mashed and blended with potatoes and spices, then shaped into cakes and fried to create kebabs that are as enticing as they are delectable.

MAKES 12

400g/14oz canned lotus roots, drained and rinsed well
350g/12oz boiled potatoes
30ml/2 tbsp sunflower oil or light olive oil
1 small onion, finely chopped
1cm/½in piece of fresh root ginger, grated
1 fresh green chilli, finely chopped (deseeded if preferred)
1 fresh red chilli, finely chopped (deseeded if preferred)
2.5ml/½ tsp fennel seeds
5ml/1 tsp garam masala
7.5ml/¾ tsp salt, or to taste
30ml/2 tbsp fresh coriander (cilantro) leaves, chopped, plus sprigs, to garnish
1 egg, beaten
75g/3oz white poppy seeds
vegetable oil, for shallow-frying
Almond Chutney (*see* page 196), to serve

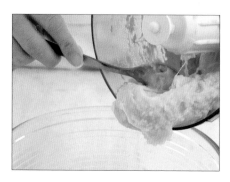

1 Blend the lotus roots and potatoes in a food processor; the potatoes should be smooth, but the lotus roots should still have a rough texture. Transfer the mixture to a bowl.

2 Heat the oil over a medium heat and fry the onion, ginger, and green and red chillies for 3–4 minutes, until the onion is soft.

3 Add the fried mixture to the lotus root and potato mixture and stir in the fennel seeds, garam masala, salt and chopped coriander. Mix well, then chill for 35–40 minutes.

4 Divide the mixture into 12 equal parts and make flat cakes 1cm/½in thick. Dip each cake in the beaten egg, then roll in the poppy seeds.

5 Heat the oil in a frying pan over a medium heat and fry the kebabs for 2 minutes on each side. Drain on kitchen paper, garnish with coriander and serve with Almond Chutney.

Per portion Energy 118kcal/491kJ; Protein 2.4g; Carbohydrate 5.5g, of which sugars 1g; Fat 9.8g, of which saturates 1.3g; Cholesterol 16mg; Calcium 63mg; Fibre 1.3g; Sodium 32mg.

Wild fig kebabs

In India, wild figs are used for this recipe, *Goolar Kabab*, but when these are not available dried ones can be used instead. Split Bengal gram (channa dhal) and figs are ground together and combined with fresh root ginger, garlic, chillies and garam masala to produce these wonderfully fragrant kebabs.

MAKES 15

250g/9oz/1½ cups dried figs, chopped
250g/9oz/1½ cups split Bengal gram
  (channa dhal or skinless split chickpeas)
5ml/1 tsp salt, or to taste
2.5cm/1in piece of fresh root ginger, chopped
2 large garlic cloves, chopped
1 small onion, chopped
2.5ml/½ tsp ground turmeric
1 fresh green chilli, chopped
  (deseeded if preferred)
2.5ml/½ tsp chilli powder
2.5ml/½ tsp ground cumin
2.5ml/½ tsp garam masala
juice of 1 lemon
sunflower oil, for shallow-frying
fresh coriander (cilantro) sprigs, to garnish
chutney, to serve

1 Put the figs, split Bengal gram, salt, ginger, garlic and onion into a pan and add 425ml/14fl oz/1¾ cups water. Bring it to the boil, reduce the heat to low and simmer, uncovered, for 25–30 minutes until the water has been absorbed.

2 Cool slightly, then add the turmeric, green chilli, chilli powder, cumin, garam masala and lemon juice.

COOK'S TIP
Figs are native to Asia, Africa and southern Europe, and are a good source of iron and calcium.

3 Blend the ingredients in a food processor until they are finely chopped and well combined. Transfer to a mixing bowl, cover with clear film (plastic wrap) and chill in the refrigerator for 1 hour.

4 Shape the mixture into 15 equal balls and flatten each one into a neat, round cake.

5 Heat the oil in a large frying pan over medium heat and fry the kebabs in batches on low/medium heat for about 2 minutes on each side, until they are a rich brown colour on both sides.

6 Drain on kitchen paper, garnish with coriander and serve with chutney.

Per portion Energy 139kcal/585kJ; Protein 5.2g; Carbohydrate 21.1g, of which sugars 10.7g; Fat 4.4g, of which saturates 0.5g; Cholesterol 0mg; Calcium 59mg; Fibre 2.5g; Sodium 17mg.

Green pea kebabs

Only fresh peas are used in India for making these delectable kebabs, *Hare Mattar Ke Kabab*, but this recipe uses frozen ones for convenience. These are cooked and lightly crushed, and boiled and mashed potatoes are added for binding. The spicing is simple, delicious and quite fragrant.

3 Dry-roast the coriander and cumin seeds in a small pan over a medium heat for about 1 minute, until they release their aroma. Allow to cool, then crush them in a mortar and pestle or place them in a plastic bag and crush them with a rolling pin. Add to the potato mixture and stir to combine.

4 Melt the ghee or butter in a pan and add the onion and chillies. Cook for 6 minutes, until softened, then add the garlic.

5 Cook for about 1 minute, then add the garam masala. Remove from the heat and add to the potato/pea mixture along with the salt, breadcrumbs, flour and egg. Stir to combine. Cover and chill for 30 minutes.

6 Divide the mixture into 12 equal portions and flatten them to form round cakes.

7 Heat the oil in a frying pan and fry the kebabs in batches for about 3–4 minutes on each side, until browned all over. Serve with Roasted Tomato Chutney.

MAKES 12

350g/12oz frozen garden peas
175g/6oz boiled potatoes, mashed
5ml/1 tsp coriander seeds
5ml/1 tsp cumin seeds
30ml/2 tbsp ghee or unsalted butter
1 large onion, finely chopped
2–3 fresh red chillies, finely chopped
10ml/2 tsp garlic purée
2.5ml/½ tsp garam masala
5ml/1 tsp salt, or to taste
65g/2½oz/1 cup soft fresh breadcrumbs
45ml/3 tbsp plain (all-purpose) flour
1 egg, beaten
sunflower oil, for shallow-frying
Roasted Tomato Chutney (*see* page 195),
  to serve

1 Cook the peas in a pan of boiling water for about 5 minutes, until tender, then drain, transfer to a bowl and mash with a fork.

2 Add the mashed potatoes, stir well to combine and set aside.

Per portion Energy 128kcal/535kJ; Protein 4g; Carbohydrate 12g, of which sugars 2g; Fat 8g, of which saturates 2g; Cholesterol 25mg; Calcium 31mg; Fibre 2.7g; Sodium 225mg.

Yogurt and gram flour kebabs

Yogurt and gram flour (besan) are two extremely healthy ingredients, offering protein, vitamins and minerals in abundance. These kebabs, *Dahi Ke Kabab*, are easy to make and, served with flavoursome chutney, they are deliciously moreish. They are also great topped with tomato salsa.

MAKES 14

400g/14oz/3½ cups gram flour (besan)

5ml/1 tsp salt, or to taste

1.25ml/¼ tsp Asafoetida

5ml/1 tsp ground turmeric

2.5cm/1in piece of fresh root ginger, finely grated

4 cloves garlic, finely choped

2 fresh green chillies, finely chopped (deseeded if preferred)

2.5–5ml/½–1 tsp dried chilli flakes

5ml/1 tsp garam masala

1 red onion, finely chopped

10ml/2 tsp dried fenugreek leaves

30ml/2 tbsp fresh coriander (cilantro) leaves, chopped

250g/9oz/generous 1 cup Greek (US strained plain) yogurt

sunflower oil, for deep-frying

Sweet Tamarind Chutney (*see* page 194), to serve

1 Put the gram flour in a non-stick frying pan and add the salt, Asafoetida, turmeric, ginger, garlic, both types of chilli and the garam masala.

4 Grease your palms and divide the mixture into 14 equal portions. Rotate them between your palms and flatten them to a smooth round cake about 5mm/¼in thick.

5 Heat the oil over a low-medium heat in a wok or other suitable pan for deep-frying.

6 Reduce the heat to low and fry the kebabs for about 3 minutes on each side, until well browned all over.

7 Lift out with a slotted spoon and drain on kitchen paper. Serve immediately with Sweet Tamarind Chutney.

2 Mix well, then add the onion, fenugreek leaves, coriander and yogurt, and stir to combine well.

3 Place the frying pan over a low heat and stir until a sticky paste is formed. Continue to cook for 2–3 minutes, then remove from the heat and set aside until cool enough to handle.

Per portion Energy 158kcal/661kJ; Protein 7g; Carbohydrate 16g, of which sugars 2g; Fat 8g, of which saturates 2g; Cholesterol 3mg; Calcium 80mg; Fibre 4.0g; Sodium 165mg.

Crispy gram flour rounds

Papris are a very popular snack in central India, especially during the festival of colours (Holi), which is celebrated throughout the country in the spring. The predominant flavour and aroma comes from the small amount of pungent dried fenugreek (kasuri methi) used. These tasty little cakes can be served on their own with drinks or used as a base for canapés with a chutney or a dip.

SERVES 4

225g/8oz/2 cups gram flour (besan), sifted, plus extra for dusting
a pinch of bicarbonate of soda (baking soda)
5ml/1 tsp salt, or to taste
5ml/1 tsp chilli powder
5ml/1 tsp cumin seeds
15ml/1 tbsp dried fenugreek leaves (kasuri methi)
15ml/1 tbsp sunflower oil or light olive oil
vegetable oil, for deep-frying

COOK'S TIP
Fenugreek is thought to both inhibit and alleviate arthritis.

1 In a large mixing bowl, mix the gram flour, bicarbonate of soda, salt, chilli powder, cumin seeds and fenugreek leaves.

2 Make a well in the centre, add the oil and mix well.

3 Add 125ml/4fl oz/½ cup water and mix until a dough is formed.

4 Transfer to a lightly floured surface and knead it briefly, then form the dough into a large flat cake.

5 Dust with a little flour and roll out thinly to a 30cm/12in circle about 2.5mm/⅛in thick.

6 Using a round cookie cutter, cut out as many small circles as possible, then gather up the remaining dough and roll again. Cut out into circles as before. You should end up with about 24 small circles.

7 Heat the oil in a wok or other suitable pan for deep-frying over a medium heat. Fry the rounds in hot oil in two or three batches, until they are crisp and golden brown.

8 Drain on kitchen paper and serve. Once fried, they will keep well in an airtight container for up to a week.

Per portion Energy 358kcal/1498kJ; Protein 7.7g; Carbohydrate 37.3g, of which sugars 1.2g; Fat 21g, of which saturates 2.6g; Cholesterol 0mg; Calcium 28mg; Fibre 5.1g; Sodium 3mg.

Golden mung bean patties

These delicious morsels, *Mung Ke Tikkia*, are made of skinless split mung beans (mung dhal) that are ground to a paste and cooked with spices, until the mixture reaches a mashed potato-like consistency. This is then formed into small, round cakes and deep-fried until crisp and golden brown. These patties have a wholesome, earthy taste and make a substantial snack or appetizer.

MAKES 12

250g/9oz/1½ cups skinless split mung beans (mung dhal)
2.5cm/1in piece of fresh root ginger, chopped
1–2 dried red chillies, chopped
5ml/1 tsp ground turmeric
15ml/1 tbsp fresh coriander (cilantro) leaves, chopped
1 fresh green chilli, finely chopped
50g/2oz natural (plain) yogurt
3.75ml/¾ tsp salt, or to taste
vegetable oil, for deep-frying
chutney, to serve

1 Wash the beans and soak for 3–4 hours. Drain and transfer to a food processor with the ginger and red chillies. Grind to a coarse consistency, then transfer to a non-stick pan over a low heat.

2 Add the turmeric and cook, stirring, until the mixture is dry and slightly crumbly.

3 Remove from the heat and add all the remaining ingredients except the oil.

4 Mix thoroughly and make 12 equal balls, then flatten them into neat, round cakes.

5 Heat the vegetable oil in a wok or other pan suitable for deep-frying over a low/medium heat.

6 Fry the patties in several batches for 2–3 minutes, until they are golden brown.

7 Remove with a slotted spoon and drain on kitchen paper while you cook the rest of the patties. Serve with any chutney.

Per portion Energy 148kcal/620kJ; Protein 5.4g; Carbohydrate 12.6g, of which sugars 0.8g; Fat 8.9g, of which saturates 1g; Cholesterol 0mg; Calcium 22mg; Fibre 1g; Sodium 12mg.

Vegetable samosas

The original recipe for *Samosas* is a vegetarian one. Potatoes and garden peas are the most common fillings, but other vegetables such as carrots and cauliflower are also used in some regions. Filo pastry is a quick and easy alternative to traditional Indian pastry, and makes a delicious samosa that is also lower in fat. These samosas have been baked in the oven, but they can also be deep-fried in a light cooking oil.

MAKES 12

60ml/4 tbsp sunflower oil or light olive oil
1.25ml/¼ tsp Asafoetida
2.5ml/½ tsp black mustard seeds
5ml/1 tsp cumin seeds
2.5ml/½ tsp nigella seeds
1 medium onion, finely chopped
2 fresh green chillies, finely chopped
    (deseeded if preferred)
2.5ml/½ tsp ground turmeric
5ml/1 tsp ground cumin
350g/12oz boiled potatoes, cut into
    bitesize pieces
110g/4oz/1 cup fresh peas, cooked or
    frozen peas, thawed
50g/2oz/½ cup carrots, coarsely grated
5ml/1 tsp salt, or to taste
2.5ml/½ tsp garam masala
30ml/2 tbsp fresh coriander (cilantro)
    leaves, chopped
12 sheets filo pastry, each about
    18 x 29cm/7 x 11in
75g/3oz/6 tbsp butter, melted

1 Heat the oil over a medium heat. When it is hot but not smoking, add the Asafoetida, mustard, cumin and nigella. Add the onion and chillies and fry until the onion is brown.

2 Add the turmeric and cumin, cook for about 1 minute, then add the potatoes, peas, carrots and salt. Stir them around until the vegetables are coated with the spices. Stir in the coriander and remove from the heat. Allow to cool completely.

3 Preheat the oven to 180°C/350°F/Gas 4. Line a baking sheet with baking parchment.

4 Remove the filo pastry from its packaging and cover with a moist cloth or clear film (plastic wrap). Place one sheet of filo pastry on a board and brush generously with melted butter.

5 Fold the pastry sheet in half lengthways, brush with some more butter and fold lengthways again to form a long strip.

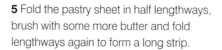

6 Place about 15ml/1 tbsp of the vegetable filling on the bottom right-hand corner of the pastry sheet.

> ## COOK'S TIP
> It is important to work quickly when using filo pastry, and keep sheets that you are not using covered, as it dries out quickly.

7 Fold over the pastry and filling to form a triangle. Continue to fold to the top of the strip, maintaining the triangular shape. Moisten the ends and seal the edges.

8 Place on the prepared baking sheet and brush the outside with melted butter. Make the rest of the samosas in the same way. Bake just below the top of the oven for 20 minutes or until browned.

Per portion Energy 180kcal/752kJ; Protein 3.6g; Carbohydrate 19.6g, of which sugars 2.5g; Fat 10.4g, of which saturates 4.1g; Cholesterol 26mg; Calcium 38mg; Fibre 1.6g; Sodium 58mg.

Bread fritters

Sold by street vendors everywhere in north India, *Double Roti Ke Pakore* are an ideal way to liven up stale bread and are absolutely irresistible eaten hot, straight from the pan. Store-bought sauces are used in this recipe to make a quick and easy snack or appetizer, but you can vary the fillings.

2 Mix the remaining ingredients, except the oil, in a bowl and gradually add 175ml/6fl oz/ ¾ cup cold water. Stir until you have a thick batter of coating consistency.

3 Heat the oil in a wok or other suitable pan for deep-frying over a medium heat. Test that the temperature is right by dropping a tiny (size of a lemon pip) amount of the batter into the oil. If it floats quickly to the surface without browning, then the temperature is just right.

MAKES 12

45ml/3 tbsp chilli sauce

5ml/1 tsp mint sauce

15ml/1 tbsp mango chutney, mashed to a pulp

6 large slices of slightly stale white bread, crusts removed

115g/4oz/1 cup gram flour (besan)

2 fresh green chillies, finely chopped (deseeded if preferred)

30ml/2 tbsp fresh coriander (cilantro) leaves, chopped

5ml/1 tsp fennel seeds

7.5ml/1½ tsp garam masala

2.5ml/½ tsp ground turmeric

3.75ml/¾ tsp salt, or to taste

sunflower oil, for deep-frying

1 Mix together the chilli sauce, mint sauce and mango chutney in a small bowl. Divide the mixture between three slices of bread. Top each slice with the remaining bread to make three sandwiches. Cut each sandwich into four triangles or squares.

4 Dip one triangle into the batter, using your fingers or two forks. Make sure it is well coated with batter all over, including the edges.

5 Carefully lower the triangle into the hot oil and fry for 3–4 minutes, until crisp and well browned. Lift out using a slotted spoon and drain on kitchen paper.

6 Repeat the dipping and frying with the remaining triangles. Serve immediately.

Per portion Energy 341kcal/1441kJ; Protein 12g; Carbohydrate 53g, of which sugars 9g; Fat 11g, of which saturates 1g; Cholesterol 0mg; Calcium 141mg; Fibre 6.4g; Sodium 1061mg.

Onion bhajiyas

One of the most popular snacks in India, and indeed the rest of the world, there are numerous versions of *Kanda Bhaje*. This southern Indian recipe comes from the mainly vegetarian state of Karnataka. Bhajiyas are delicious served on their own or accompanied by a chutney of your choice.

SERVES 4–6

150g/5oz/1¼ cups gram flour (besan)
25g/1oz ground rice
5ml/1 tsp salt, or to taste
a pinch of bicarbonate of soda (baking soda)
2.5ml/½ tsp ground turmeric
5ml/1 tsp ground cumin
5ml/1 tsp cumin seeds
2.5ml/½ tsp Asafoetida
2 fresh green chillies, finely chopped
 (deseeded if preferred)
450g/1lb onions, sliced into half rings
 and separated
15ml/1 tbsp fresh coriander (cilantro) leaves
 and stalks, finely chopped
sunflower oil or light olive oil, for deep-frying
chutney, to serve (optional)

1 Sift the flour into a large mixing bowl and add the ground rice, salt, bicarbonate of soda, turmeric, ground cumin, cumin seeds and Asafoetida.

2 Mix these dry ingredients together thoroughly, then add the chillies, onion rings and coriander.

3 Gradually pour in 200ml/7fl oz/¾ cup water and mix until a thick batter is formed and all the ingredients are well coated.

4 Heat the oil in a pan suitable for deep-frying over a medium heat until it reaches 180ºC/350°F on a thermometer. To measure the temperature without a thermometer, drop about 1.25ml/¼ tsp of the batter into the hot oil. If it floats up to the surface immediately without turning brown, then the oil is at the right temperature.

5 Lower about 15ml/1 tbsp of the onion batter mixture at a time into the hot oil, in a single layer. Avoid overcrowding the pan as this will lower the temperature of the oil and the bhajiyas will not crisp up.

6 Reduce the heat slightly and continue to cook until the bhajiyas are golden brown and crisp. This should take 8–10 minutes.

7 Drain on kitchen paper and serve on their own or with a chutney of your choice.

COOK'S TIPS
• If the oil is not hot enough the bhajiyas will be soggy.
• Maintaining a steady temperature is important to ensure that the centre of each bhajiya is cooked and the outside turns brown.

Per portion Energy 284kcal/1181kJ; Protein 5.1g; Carbohydrate 27g, of which sugars 4.7g; Fat 18g, of which saturates 1.9g; Cholesterol 0mg; Calcium 38mg; Fibre 3.3g; Sodium 5mg.

Batter-fried peppers

If your taste buds ever crave a change from Onion Bhajiyas (*see* page 61), try these sweet (bell) peppers, *Mirchi Bhaje,* which are cut into rings, dipped in a spiced batter and deep-fried until crisp and brown. They make a wonderful snack, a delicious appetizer or a tasty canapé piled high to serve with drinks.

MAKES 15

1 green (bell) pepper
1 red (bell) pepper
1 yellow (bell) pepper
200g/7oz/1¾ cups gram flour (besan)
a pinch of bicarbonate of soda
  (baking soda)
5ml/1 tsp fennel seeds
5ml/1 tsp cumin seeds
5ml/1 tsp coriander seeds, lightly crushed
2.5ml/½ tsp ground turmeric
3.75ml/¾ tsp salt, or to taste
1–3 fresh green chillies, finely chopped
  (deseeded if preferred)
sunflower oil or light olive oil, for
  deep-frying

1 Wash the peppers, pat dry with kitchen paper and then cut them widthways into 5mm/¼in-wide rings. Remove and discard the seeds and the bitter white membrane. Set aside.

2 Sift the gram flour into a large mixing bowl, lifting the sieve (strainer) up high.

3 Add all the remaining ingredients except the oil. Mix well and gradually add 200ml/7fl oz/¾ cup water. Stir thoroughly to make a thick batter.

4 Heat the oil in a pan suitable for deep-frying over a medium heat until it reaches 180°C/350°F on a thermometer. To measure the temperature without a thermometer, drop about 1.25ml/¼ tsp of the batter into the hot oil. If it floats up to the surface immediately without turning brown, then the oil is at the right temperature.

5 Ensure the pepper rings are well coated with the spiced batter, then add them one by one to the hot oil without overcrowding the pan, as this will result in soggy rings.

6 Fry until they are crisp and golden brown. Drain on kitchen paper and repeat with the remaining pepper rings.

Per portion Energy 104kcal/433kJ; Protein 2.3g; Carbohydrate 11.4g, of which sugars 2.6g; Fat 5.7g, of which saturates 0.6g; Cholesterol 0mg; Calcium 11mg; Fibre 1.8g; Sodium 2mg.

Spiced yam fingers

These crispy yam bites, *Kath Alu Bhoja*, are rather like French fries with a spicy coating, and are often served at informal parties as an appetizer with drinks. They are easy to make and very tasty. Yams are usually readily available in larger supermarkets, as well as in Asian and African stores.

SERVES 4

450g/1lb yam
45ml/3 tbsp sunflower oil or light olive oil
10ml/2 tsp garlic purée
2.5–5ml/½–1 tsp chilli powder
2.5ml/½ tsp ground turmeric
5ml/1 tsp salt, or to taste

1 Peel the yam and slice the flesh into thin fingers to resemble French fries. Wash and dry thoroughly with a dish cloth.

2 In a large frying pan, heat the oil over a low heat. Add the garlic and fry gently until it is light brown.

3 Add the chilli powder, turmeric and salt and stir to combine.

VARIATION

Parsnips make a good alternative to yams, if you prefer. Reduce the cooking time to 5 minutes.

4 Add the yam fingers to the pan and stir over a medium heat for 2–3 minutes. Reduce the heat slightly, cover the pan and cook for 8–9 minutes, until the yam is tender.

5 Remove the lid and increase the heat slightly. Cook, stirring frequently, until the yam has browned. Remove from the heat and serve immediately.

Per portion Energy 209kcal/880kJ; Protein 2.2g; Carbohydrate 32.8g, of which sugars 0.9g; Fat 8.6g, of which saturates 1.1g; Cholesterol 0mg; Calcium 18mg; Fibre 1.7g; Sodium 3mg.

Tangy potato canapés with mint and yogurt

Papri Chaat are a street-side snack full of amazing aromas and sensational tastes. They are easy to cook and are ideal as a light bite or appetizer. If you do not have time to make the small crisp-fried bread (papri), you can serve the potato topping on small crackers instead. In India, these are served with a yogurt sauce, a chilli-coriander chutney and tamarind chutney, but you can use any chutney you like.

SERVES 4

For the crisp-fried bread:
250g/9oz/2¼ cups gram flour (besan),
   sifted, plus extra for dusting
a pinch of bicarbonate of soda
   (baking soda)
5ml/1 tsp salt, or to taste
5ml/1 tsp chilli powder
5ml/1 tsp cumin seeds
15ml/1 tbsp dried fenugreek leaves
   (kasuri methi)
15ml/1 tbsp sunflower oil or light
   olive oil
sunflower oil, for deep-frying

For the potato topping:
450g/1lb potatoes, peeled and cut into
   bitesize pieces
2.5ml/½ tsp ground cumin
2.5ml/½ tsp chilli powder
1.25ml/¼ tsp salt
30ml/2 tbsp lime juice

To serve:
115g/4oz natural (plain) yogurt
1.25ml/¼ tsp salt
5ml/1 tsp sugar
chutneys of your choice

1 To make the crisp-fried bread, mix the gram flour, bicarbonate of soda, salt, chilli powder, cumin seeds and fenugreek leaves in a bowl. Add the oil and stir to combine. Add 120ml/4fl oz/½ cup water and mix until a dough is formed.

2 Transfer the dough to a lightly floured surface and knead it briefly, then form it into a flat circle.

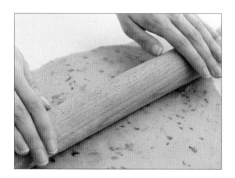

3 Dust the dough with flour and roll it out to form a disc 30cm/12in in diameter and with a thickness of 2.5mm/⅛in.

4 Using a small round cookie cutter, cut out as many circles as possible, then gather up the remaining dough and roll again. Cut out into circles as before. You should have about 24 in total.

5 Heat the oil in a pan suitable for deep-frying over a medium heat. Fry the breads in two or three batches for 4–5 minutes, until they are crisp and golden brown. Drain on kitchen paper. Repeat with the remaining circles of dough.

6 To make the potato topping, boil the potatoes in boiling water for 10 minutes, until tender. Drain and leave to cool.

7 Mix the cold potato with the cumin, chilli powder, salt and lime juice.

8 Beat the yogurt with a fork and add the salt, sugar and 30ml/2 tbsp water.

9 Top each crisp-fried bread with some of the potato mixture and drizzle the yogurt sauce over it. Spoon over the chutneys and serve immediately.

Per portion Energy 410kcal/1724kJ; Protein 17g; Carbohydrate 54g, of which sugars 6g; Fat 16g, of which saturates 2g; Cholesterol 3mg; Calcium 189mg; Fibre 10.2g; Sodium 775mg.

Spiced potato cakes

These delicious Bengali deep-fried spiced potato cakes, *Alur Bora*, are traditionally enjoyed at afternoon tea – a legacy left behind by the British tea plantation owners – which is still a big occasion in this part of the country. They are also lovely as an appetizer, and can easily be made in advance, frozen and then reheated in a hot oven for 10–12 minutes – perfect for those unexpected guests.

2 Put the mashed potato into a mixing bowl and add the onion mixture, stir well and add the cornflour and egg. Stir until all the ingredients are well blended.

3 Heat the oil for deep-frying in a wok or other suitable pan over a medium/high heat. Drop a tiny amount of the potato mixture into the oil to test the temperature. If the potato mixture starts sizzling and floats to the surface immediately, then the oil is at the right temperature.

4 Take 15ml/1 tbsp of the potato mixture and, with two spoons, make a rough croquette shape, then gently and carefully lower it into the hot oil.

SERVES 4–5

30ml/2 tbsp sunflower oil or vegetable oil
2.5ml/½ tsp fennel seeds
1 medium onion, finely chopped
1–2 fresh green chillies, chopped
  (deseeded if preferred)
10ml/2 tsp ginger purée
2.5ml/½ tsp ground turmeric
30ml/2 tbsp fresh coriander (cilantro)
  leaves, chopped
5ml/1 tsp salt, or to taste
450g/1lb potatoes, boiled and mashed
15ml/1 tbsp cornflour (cornstarch)
1 large (US extra large) egg, beaten
sunflower oil, for deep-frying
Roasted Tomato Chutney (*see* page 195),
  to serve

1 Heat the oil in a pan over a medium heat and add the fennel seeds. Allow them to sizzle for a few seconds, then add the onion, chillies and ginger. Fry for 3–4 minutes, until the onions soften. Stir in the turmeric, coriander and salt. Remove from the heat.

5 Fry as many cakes as the pan will hold in a single layer without overcrowding it. Fry for 5–6 minutes, until well browned. Remove with a slotted spoon and drain on kitchen paper. Repeat with the remaining mixture. Serve with Roasted Tomato Chutney.

Per portion Energy 256kcal/1064kJ; Protein 3.8g; Carbohydrate 23.6g, of which sugars 5.7g; Fat 16.9g, of which saturates 2.3g; Cholesterol 38mg; Calcium 32mg; Fibre 2g; Sodium 421mg.

Spiced gram flour dumplings

In this recipe for *Methi Na Muthia*, a golden gram flour (besan) mixture is combined with dried fenugreek leaves (kasuri methi) and a range of spices, then formed into small dumplings and steamed. The cooked dumplings are then sliced into bitesize pieces and doused with tempered oil redolent with whole spices, curry leaves and chillies. The dumplings can be made ahead and then steamed when required.

SERVES 4

For the dumplings:
300g/10½oz/2½ cups gram flour (besan)
30ml/2 tbsp dried fenugreek leaves
  (kasuri methi)
1.25ml/¼ tsp bicarbonate of soda
  (baking soda)
1.25ml/¼ tsp Asafoetida
2.5ml/½ tsp chilli powder
2.5ml/½ tsp ground turmeric
3.75ml/¾ tsp salt, or to taste
juice of 1 lime
30ml/2 tbsp sunflower oil or light
  olive oil, warmed

For the tempering:
30ml/2 tbsp sunflower oil or light
  olive oil
2.5ml/½ tsp black mustard seeds
2.5ml/½ tsp cumin seeds
1.25ml/¼ tsp Asafoetida
8–10 curry leaves
30ml/2 tbsp fresh coriander (cilantro)
  leaves, finely chopped

3 Divide the dough into four equal portions and roll each one into a cylinder shape 8cm/3¼in long.

4 Place the dumplings in an electric steamer or a metal steamer positioned over a pan of simmering water, and cook for 15–16 minutes.

5 Remove from the heat, transfer them to a cutting board and leave to cool a little.

6 Cut the cylinders into 1cm/½in-thick slices and put them on a serving dish.

7 Heat the oil for the tempering over a medium heat. When hot, add the mustard seeds. As soon as they pop, add the cumin seeds, Asafoetida and curry leaves.

8 Let them sizzle for 10–15 seconds, then pour the oil and spices over the dumplings. stir in the coriander and serve immediately.

1 Sift the gram flour into a large mixing bowl and add all the remaining dumpling ingredients except the lime juice and oil. Mix thoroughly to combine.

2 Make a well in the centre, then add the lime juice and warmed oil, and mix again. Make another well in the centre, add 100ml/3½fl oz/⅓ cup cold water and mix until a dough is formed.

Per portion Energy 285kcal/1201kJ; Protein 8.7g; Carbohydrate 40.8g, of which sugars 1.3g; Fat 11g, of which saturates 1.4g; Cholesterol 0mg; Calcium 35mg; Fibre 5.4g; Sodium 4mg.

Chickpea flour squares with coconut and mustard

This is a new version of a delicious savoury snack, *Khandvi*, from the state of Gujarat, which uses yogurt in place of curds and incorporates chilli and desiccated (dry unsweetened shredded) coconut for added flavour. They are low in fat and packed with essential nutrients. Served with chutney, they make a perfect appetizer.

SERVES 4

275g/10oz/2½ cups gram flour (besan)
115g/4oz/½ cup full-fat (whole) natural
  (plain) yogurt
5ml/1 tsp salt, or to taste
2.5ml/½ tsp ground turmeric
2 fresh red chillies, finely chopped
  (deseeded if preferred)
30ml/2 tbsp sunflower oil or light olive oil,
  plus extra for brushing over
15ml/1 tbsp desiccated (dry unsweetened
  shredded) coconut
30ml/2 tbsp fresh coriander (cilantro)
  leaves, chopped
tangy chutney, to serve

For the tempering:
10ml/2 tsp sunflower oil or light olive oil
2.5ml/½ tsp black mustard seeds
1 dried red chilli, torn into pieces
6 fresh or 8 dried curry leaves
1.25ml/¼ tsp Asafoetida

1 Sift the gram flour into a large mixing bowl and make a well in the centre.

2 Blend the yogurt with 90ml/6 tbsp water in a separate bowl or jug, and add the mixture to the flour.

3 Add the salt, turmeric, chillies and oil. Mix everything thoroughly with a wooden spoon, making sure that all the ingredients are well blended together, to make a thick paste. Cover the bowl with a damp dish towel and set aside for 30 minutes.

4 Brush a little oil on a 30cm/12in heatproof plate and spread over half the gram flour mixture, like a thick pancake, covering the entire surface of the plate. It is easier to spread the mixture if you use lightly greased palms or a greased metal spoon.

5 Divide the coconut and coriander equally into two portions and sprinkle one portion on the surface of the mixture.

6 Place the plate on a steamer positioned over a pan of simmering water and steam the pancake for 8 minutes, or until the surface is set.

7 Remove the plate from the steamer and set aside for 5 minutes to cool slightly, then gently ease away the steamed pancake with a thin metal spatula or a fish slice.

8 Place the pancake on a cutting board and cut it into 2.5cm/1in squares. Cook the remaining mixture in the same way, and cut into squares.

9 In a non-stick wok or other pan, heat the remaining oil over a medium heat until it reaches smoking point, then switch off the heat source.

10 Add the mustard seeds and as soon as they start popping add the chillies, curry leaves and Asafoetida and let them sizzle for 15–20 seconds.

11 Add the pancake squares and mix gently, being careful not to break them up. Transfer to a serving dish and serve hot or cold with a tangy chutney.

VARIATION
You could also leave the pancakes whole, spread them with chutney and then roll them up.

Per portion Energy 353kcal/1482kJ; Protein 16g; Carbohydrate 37g, of which sugars 5g; Fat 17g, of which saturates 4g; Cholesterol 3mg; Calcium 191mg; Fibre 10.1g; Sodium 544mg.

Split chickpea squares with coconut

This simple, delicious and highly nutritious dish, *Amiri Khaman*, comes from the mainly vegetarian state of Gujarat, which is well known for its aromatic spiced snacks, known as *farsan*. Every Gujarati housewife has a supply of home-made *farsan* in the store cupboard, which helps them to follow the age-old Indian custom of looking after their guests, whether invited or unexpected. These wonderfully flavoursome squares make a fabulous appetizer when served with chutney, and are ideal for afternoon tea.

SERVES 4–5

350g/12oz/2 cups split Bengal gram
  (channa dhal or skinless split chickpeas)
45ml/3 tbsp sunflower oil or light olive oil
2.5ml/½ tsp black mustard seeds
1.25ml/¼ tsp Asafoetida
10ml/2 tsp ginger purée
10ml/2 tsp garlic purée
2–4 fresh green chillies, finely chopped
  (deseeded if preferred)
2.5ml/½ tsp ground turmeric
5ml/1 tsp salt, or to taste
5ml/1 tsp sugar
425ml/¾ pint/1¾ cups full-fat (whole) milk
30ml/2 tbsp lemon juice
15ml/1 tbsp fresh coriander (cilantro)
  leaves, finely chopped
15ml/1 tbsp desiccated (dry unsweetened
  shredded) coconut
chutney, to serve

VARIATION
You can vary the topping, adding very finely chopped fresh chilli if you like a fiery kick, or use other soft herbs, such as chopped mint or flat leaf parsley.

1 Wash the split Bengal gram in a sieve (strainer), then transfer to a bowl and soak in cold water for 5–6 hours or overnight.

2 Drain the split Bengal gram well, then process in a food processor or blender until a fine paste is formed.

3 In a wok or non-stick pan, heat the oil over a medium heat. When hot, but not smoking, add the mustard seeds and reduce the heat to low.

4 Add the Asafoetida, followed by the ginger, garlic, chillies and turmeric. Stir to combine well and fry them gently for about 1 minute.

5 Add the gram paste, salt and sugar, and cook over a medium/low heat, stirring constantly so it doesn't stick, for about 6 minutes, until the mixture is completely dry and looks crumbly.

6 Add one-third of the milk and continue to cook, stirring, for 3–4 minutes. Repeat the process with the remaining milk. Add the lemon juice and stir until well blended.

7 Spread the mixture on a lightly greased plate to a 30cm/12in rectangle and sprinkle over the coriander and coconut.

8 Press down the coconut and coriander so that they stick. Cut into squares or diamonds and serve hot or cold with chutney.

Per portion Energy 357kcal/1499kJ; Protein 18.5g; Carbohydrate 40.9g, of which sugars 5.9g; Fat 14.5g, of which saturates 3.3g; Cholesterol 12mg; Calcium 221mg; Fibre 7.5g; Sodium 76mg.

Rice pancakes filled with spiced potatoes

Crispy rice pancakes filled with spiced potatoes and served with coconut chutney are a popular breakfast or brunch dish in south India. This version of *Masala Dosai* is simplified for cooks with limited time in the kitchen and is easy and quick to put together – perfect for a light snack or appetizer.

MAKES 8

For the pancakes:
75g/3oz/⅔ cup plain (all-purpose) flour
110g/4oz/⅔ cup semolina
110g/4oz/⅔ cup ground rice
2.5ml/½ tsp salt, or to taste
150g/5oz/⅔ cup natural (plain) yogurt
sunflower oil or light olive oil, for cooking
  the pancakes

For the filling:
600g/1¼lb potatoes
60ml/4 tbsp sunflower oil or light
  olive oil
2.5ml/½ tsp black mustard seeds
2.5ml/½ tsp cumin seeds
1.25ml/¼ tsp fenugreek seeds
1 large onion, finely sliced
1–3 fresh green chillies, finely chopped
  (deseeded if preferred)
2.5ml/½ tsp ground turmeric
5ml/1 tsp ground coriander
5ml/1 tsp ground cumin
5ml/1 tsp salt, or to taste
30ml/2 tbsp fresh coriander (cilantro)
  leaves, chopped

1 To make the pancakes: mix all the dry ingredients in a large mixing bowl. Make a well in the centre of the ingredients.

2 Beat the yogurt in a bowl until smooth, then blend with 450ml/16fl oz/scant 2 cups water. Gradually add the blended yogurt to the dry ingredients, beating well with a wire whisk.

3 Place a heavy non-stick griddle (23cm/9in wide) or frying pan over a medium heat and add 10ml/2 tsp oil. Brush the oil quickly all over the surface and allow to heat up for a few minutes.

4 Using a measuring jug (cup), pour about 125ml/4fl oz/½ cup of the batter on to the griddle, spread it quickly and evenly and let the mixture set for 2 minutes.

5 Sprinkle 15ml/1 tbsp water around the edges, wait for 15–20 seconds, then turn the pancake over with a metal spatula or a fish slice.

6 Cook for a further 2–3 minutes or until brown patches appear underneath. Cook the remaining pancakes the same way and place on a wire rack in a single layer.

7 For the filling: boil the potatoes in their skins to stop them going mushy. Cool, peel and cut them into 2.5cm/1in cubes. You can also cook them in advance and store them in the refrigerator.

8 Heat the oil over a medium heat. When hot, but not smoking, add the mustard seeds, followed by the cumin and fenugreek seeds.

9 Add the onion and green chillies and stir-fry for 8–9 minutes or until the onions are a light golden colour. Add the turmeric, coriander and cumin. Cook for 1 minute.

10 Add the cooked potatoes and salt to the spice mixture and stir until the potatoes are heated through.

11 Stir in the coriander leaves and remove from the heat. Divide the potato filling into eight equal portions.

12 Place the griddle used to cook the pancakes over a low heat. Lay a pancake on it, put a portion of the potato filling on one side, roll it up and heat through for about 1 minute.

13 Place the rolled pancake in a very low oven while you finish making all of them, but do not leave them too long or they will become dry.

VARIATION
You could subsitute the potato with sweet potato or parsnip for a sweet and spicy alternative.

Per portion Energy 279kcal/1172kJ; Protein 7.1g; Carbohydrate 49.1g, of which sugars 6g; Fat 7.1g, of which saturates 1.1g; Cholesterol 0mg; Calcium 83mg; Fibre 2.2g; Sodium 29mg.

Spiced lentil-filled pancakes

From the little-known cuisine of the state of Bihar, this recipe for pancakes filled with spiced lentils, *Pittha*, is wholesome and healthy as well as delicious. The pancakes are very versatile – they can be served as an appetizer, a hearty brunch, or as a teatime snack. They can also be frozen, then defrosted and briefly shallow-fried or steamed to reheat when needed.

MAKES 12

Roasted Tomato Chutney (*see* page 195),
  to serve

For the filling:
225g/8oz/1 cup split Bengal gram (channa
  dhal or skinless split chickpeas), washed
2 large garlic cloves, chopped
2.5cm/1in piece fresh root ginger, peeled
  and chopped
2 dried red chillies, chopped
1 fresh green chilli, chopped
2.5ml/½ tsp ground turmeric
2.5ml/½ tsp Asafoetida
50g/2oz/¼ cup natural (plain) yogurt
30ml/2 tbsp fresh coriander (cilantro)
  leaves, chopped
5ml/1 tsp salt, or to taste

For the pastry:
150g/5oz/1¼ cups chapati flour (atta)
  or fine wholemeal (whole-wheat) flour
150g/5oz/1¼ cups plain (all-purpose) flour,
  plus extra for dusting
2.5ml/½ tsp salt
200ml/7fl oz/¾ cup water

1 Soak the split Bengal gram for 4–5 hours. Drain and put into a food processor with the garlic, ginger and chillies. Blend to a paste, adding 30–45ml/2–3 tbsp water if necessary.

2 Put the paste into a non-stick pan with the turmeric and Asafoetida. Cook, stirring, until the mixture is dry and crumbly.

3 Remove from the heat and transfer to a mixing bowl. Add the yogurt, chopped coriander and salt and mix thoroughly. If the mixture is still slightly crumbly, add a little water until it has a paste-like consistency. Allow to cool.

4 Meanwhile, make the pastry. Mix both types of flour and the salt in a mixing bowl, then gradually add the water (the amount needed will depend on the absorbency of the flour), stirring with a spoon or using your fingers.

5 When a dough has formed, transfer it to a floured surface and knead it for about 5 minutes, until soft and pliable.

6 Wrap the dough in clear film (plastic wrap) and allow it to rest for 30 minutes, then divide it into 12 portions and make each portion into a flat cake. Keep them covered with a damp cloth while you are working on one at a time.

7 Using a rolling pin, roll out each cake into roughly a 10cm/4in circle.

8 Divide the filling into 12 equal parts and place a portion to one side of a dough circle, leaving a 1cm/½in border. Repeat until you have used all the filling and all the dough circles.

9 Moisten the edges of the dough circle with water and enclose the filling by folding over the other half, making a half-moon shape. Press to seal and crimp the edges with the back of a fork.

10 Place the pancakes on a piece of oiled baking parchment in a steamer (take care not to completely block the steam vents or the steam won't be able to circulate).

11 Steam over a pan of boiling water for 10 minutes, or until the filling and pancakes are thoroughly cooked. Serve with Roasted Tomato Chutney.

Per portion Energy 148kcal/630kJ; Protein 7.7g; Carbohydrate 29.2g, of which sugars 1.2g; Fat 0.9g, of which saturates 0.2g; Cholesterol 0mg; Calcium 43mg; Fibre 2.4g; Sodium 12mg.

Corn on the cob poached in coconut milk

Fresh corn on the cob is used in India to make this northern Indian recipe, *Nariyal-Makki Masala*, but this version of the classic dish uses frozen corn, so it can be made all year round. It is very quick and easy, and makes an ideal light snack or appetizer or can be served as an accompaniment.

SERVES 4

4 fresh or frozen corn on the cob,
  green skins and any fibres removed
  if fresh
150ml/5fl oz/½ cup coconut milk
2 dried red chillies, chopped
5ml/1 tsp salt, or to taste
30ml/2 tbsp sunflower oil or light
  olive oil
2.5ml/½ tsp black mustard seeds
2.5ml/½ tsp cumin seeds
2 fresh green chillies (deseeded if
  preferred), finely chopped
25ml/1 tbsp fresh coriander (cilantro)
  leaves, finely chopped
22.5ml/1½ tbsp lemon juice

1 Carefully slice the corn on the cob into 2cm/1in thick rounds using a large sharp knife (*see* Cook's Tip if using frozen corn). You will need to apply quite a bit of pressure to cut through, so take care.

2 Put the rounds into a large pan and add the coconut milk, chillies and salt.

3 Add 90ml/3fl oz water and bring to a slow simmer, then cover and cook for 10 minutes, stirring half way through.

4 Meanwhile, heat the oil in a small pan over a medium heat. When it is hot, but not smoking, add the mustard seeds, followed immediately by the cumin seeds. Let the seeds crackle and pop for 5–10 seconds, then pour them over the corn with the oil.

5 Stir to combine, then add the chopped green chillies, chopped coriander and lemon juice.

6 Stir gently to combine thoroughly, then cook, uncovered, for 3–4 minutes, until all the liquid evaporates and the coconut sauce coats the corn.

7 Remove from the heat, transfer to a serving dish and serve immediately.

COOK'S TIP
Thaw frozen corn on the cob slightly in the microwave to make it easier to slice it into rounds. Check the microwave manufacturer's instructions for times.

VARIATION
You can use frozen corn kernels, but you will need to reduce the cooking time in step 3 to 3 minutes, or the corn will be mushy.

Per portion Energy 164kcal/689kJ; Protein 4.2g; Carbohydrate 20.1g, of which sugars 4g; Fat 8g, of which saturates 1.1g; Cholesterol 0mg; Calcium 19mg; Fibre 2g; Sodium 44mg.

Potatoes and chickpeas in lime dressing

There is no cooking involved in making this dish, *Alu Kabli*, except boiling some potatoes, and it makes great use of storecupboard ingredients. It can be eaten as an irresistible snack, which is enjoyed in Bengal at any time of the day, and it is also ideal as an appetizer or as part of a buffet party menu.

2 Boil the potatoes in a pan of salted water for about 10 minutes, until tender, but firm. Drain and leave to cool.

3 Drain the chickpeas in a sieve (strainer) and rinse several times under cold running water. Drain well. Put them in a mixing bowl and add the potatoes.

4 Dry-roast the cumin and peppercorns in a small, heavy pan over a medium heat for about 1 minute, until they release their aroma.

5 Remove the pan from the heat and leave the spices to cool, then crush them in a mortar and pestle or put them in a plastic bag and crush them with a rolling pin. Add the mixture to the potato and chickpeas.

6 Reserve a little onion and add the remainder to the bowl. Add the chilli powder, garam masala, salt, lime juice and chopped coriander. Mix gently and serve topped with the reserved onion.

SERVES 4

450g/1lb waxy potatoes
400g/14oz canned chickpeas, or 400g/14oz
  dried chickpeas, soaked in water overnight
10ml/2 tsp cumin seeds
5ml/1 tsp black peppercorns
1 red onion, finely chopped
2.5ml/½ tsp chilli powder
2.5ml/½ tsp garam masala
2.5ml/½ tsp salt, or to taste
juice of 1 lime
30ml/2 tbsp fresh coriander (cilantro)
  leaves, chopped

1 Peel the potatoes and cut them into 1cm/½in cubes.

Per portion Energy 182kcal/771kJ; Protein 8g; Carbohydrate 24g, of which sugars 3g; Fat 3g, of which saturates 0g; Cholesterol 0mg; Calcium 65mg; Fibre 2.4g; Sodium 418mg.

Poached cabbage rolls

Kobi Na Moothia is a delicious and healthy snack from the state of Gujarat, the home of vegetarian cooking. Cabbage and gram flour (besan) are spiced and made into rolls, then poached, cut into slices and tossed in spice-scented oil. They can be served hot or cold, so can easily be made in advance.

SERVES 4

225g/8oz/2 cups gram flour (besan), sifted
2.5ml/½ tsp bicarbonate of soda
  (baking soda)
5ml/1 tsp salt, or to taste
1.25ml/¼ tsp Asafoetida
5ml/1 tsp dried red chilli flakes
10ml/2 tsp ginger purée
5ml/1 tsp ground turmeric
1 small green cabbage, about 200g/7oz,
  finely shredded

For the tempering:

10ml/2 tbsp sunflower oil or light olive oil
2.5ml/½ tsp black or brown
  mustard seeds
8–10 curry leaves
3–4 whole dried red chillies
1.25ml/¼ tsp Asafoetida
15ml/1 tbsp desiccated (dry unsweetened)
  shredded), coconut, to garnish

1 In a large bowl, mix the gram flour with all the remaining ingredients, except the shredded cabbage.

2 Add the cabbage and 75ml/5 tbsp cold water. Mix together with your hands until a stiff dough is formed.

3 Turn out the dough on to a lightly floured surface and knead for a couple of minutes.

4 Divide the mixture into three equal portions and form each into 5cm/2in-long cylindrical shapes.

5 Wrap the cylinders individually in clear film (plastic wrap), securing the edges so that no water can get inside, then wrap again with foil, securing the edges well to form a tight seal.

6 Bring a large pan of water to the boil and add the rolls. Cook for 25 minutes.

7 Remove from the pan with a slotted spoon and leave to cool. Remove the foil and clear film, then cut them into 1cm/⅛in thick slices.

8 Heat the oil for tempering over a medium heat in a non-stick pan, until almost smoking. Switch off the heat source and add the mustard seeds, followed by the remaining ingredients.

9 Allow the chillies to blacken, then switch on the heat and add the cabbage roll slices.

10 Cook gently until heated through, transfer to a serving dish and garnish with the coconut and chopped coriander.

Per portion Energy 238kcal/1002kJ; Protein 13g; Carbohydrate 31g, of which sugars 4g; Fat 8g, of which saturates 3g; Cholesterol 0mg; Calcium 140mg; Fibre 0.9g; Sodium 379mg.

Egg cutlets

Cutlets of various kinds were a favourite snack item during the period of the British Raj in east and north-east India. *Andey Ka Cutless* are still bestsellers in tea and coffee shops, and are served with afternoon tea, accompanied by tomato ketchup, in the social and sports clubs.

MAKES 12

6 hard-boiled eggs
350g/12oz potatoes, boiled, peeled
  and mashed
45ml/3 tbsp sunflower oil or light olive oil
2.5ml/½ tsp nigella seeds
1 medium onion, finely chopped
10ml/2 tsp ginger purée
2 fresh green chillies, finely chopped
  (deseeded if preferred)
2.5ml/½ tsp ground turmeric
2.5ml/½ tsp chilli powder, or to taste
2.5ml/½ tsp garam masala
15ml/1 tbsp fresh coriander (cilantro)
  leaves, finely chopped
5ml/1 tsp salt, or to taste
sunflower oil, for deep-frying
30ml/2 tbsp plain (all-purpose) flour
1 large (US extra large) egg, beaten
75g/3oz/1½ cups fresh soft breadcrumbs
tomato ketchup or chutney, to serve

1 Remove the shells from the hard-boiled eggs and cut them in half. Scoop out the yolks and mash them. Chop the whites finely and mix the egg yolks and whites with the mashed potatoes in a large bowl.

2 Heat the oil over a medium heat and add the nigella seeds, followed by the onion, ginger and chillies. Fry, stirring, for 5 minutes, until the onion is soft, but not brown.

3 Add the chilli powder, garam masala, coriander and salt. Cook, stirring, for 1–2 minutes, then remove from the heat and add to the potato and egg mixture. Mix until the ingredients are well combined.

4 Divide the mixture into 12 equal portions and form into oval-shaped flat cutlets about 1cm/½in thick. Heat the oil to 180°C/350°F in a large pan suitable for deep-frying.

5 Dip each portion in turn in flour, then in the beaten egg, then roll them in the soft breadcrumbs so they are evenly coated all over.

6 Carefully lower four or five cutlets into the hot oil and fry for 3–4 minutes, until crisp and golden brown.

7 Lift out with a slotted spoon and drain on kitchen paper. Repeat with the other cutlets.

8 Serve immediately with tomato ketchup or chutney.

Per portion Energy 132kcal/550kJ; Protein 5g; Carbohydrate 11g, of which sugars 1g; Fat 8g, of which saturates 1g; Cholesterol 96mg; Calcium 31mg; Fibre 1.0g; Sodium 235mg.

Egg fritters

Konir Bora are great for buffet or drinks parties as well as making a delicious first course with a salad garnish. Hard-boiled eggs are chopped and mixed with breadcrumbs and spices, then fried until crisp – just the sort of snack to eat sitting in front of the fire on a cold, wintry evening.

MAKES 12

2 slices white bread, a day or two old, crusts removed
30–45ml/2–3 tbsp fresh coriander (cilantro) leaves and stalks
1–2 fresh green chillies, chopped (deseeded if preferred)
1cm/½in piece of root ginger, peeled and chopped
5ml/1 tsp fennel seeds
2.5ml/½ tsp salt
1 egg, beaten
4 large (US extra large) hard-boiled eggs
sunflower oil, for deep-frying
15ml/1 tbsp cornflour (cornstarch)
mixed lettuce leaves, red onion rings and diced cucumber, to garnish
chutney, to serve

1 Put the bread in a food processor and process it into crumbs. Add the coriander, chillies, ginger, fennel, salt and beaten egg. Process until the mixture is well blended, then add the hard-boiled eggs and chop them roughly using the pulse action.

2 Transfer the mixture into a bowl and make 12 equal-sized portions. Form each into a ball and flatten to form a smooth round cake.

VARIATION
For a rich treat, use 2 hard-boiled duck eggs instead of hen's eggs.

3 Heat the oil in a pan suitable for deep-frying over medium/high heat. Dust each cake in cornflour, shaking off any excess.

4 Arrange the lettuce leaves, onion rings and cucumber on a serving plate.

5 Fry the cakes in batches for 3–4 minutes, until crisp and golden brown.

6 Lift out with a slotted spoon and drain on kitchen paper. Arrange on the prepared plate and serve with a chutney of your choice.

Per portion Energy 307kcal/1278kJ; Protein 25.1g; Carbohydrate 3.8g, of which sugars 0.1g; Fat 22g, of which saturates 6.1g; Cholesterol 745mg; Calcium 119mg; Fibre 0.1g; Sodium 299mg.

South Indian scrambled eggs

This is a supremely scrumptious dish and can be served in smaller quantities on small crackers with drinks, or as an appetizer spread on hot buttered toast and served with a garnish of salad. A south Indian dish, it is known locally as *Mutta Ulathiyathu*. Freshly grated coconut is the norm, but the desiccated (dry unsweetened shredded) variety is used here for speed and ease of preparation.

2 Add the turmeric, curry leaves and coconut to the pan and stir to combine.

3 Cook for 1 minute, then pour in 120ml/ 4fl oz/½ cup water. Cook over a low heat for about 10 minutes, until the coconut has absorbed most of the water.

SERVES 4

30ml/2 tbsp sunflower oil or light olive oil

1 large onion, finely chopped

2 fresh red chillies, chopped (deseeded if preferred)

2.5ml/½ tsp ground turmeric

6–8 curry leaves

50g/2oz desiccated (dry unsweetened shredded) coconut

4 large (US extra large) eggs, beaten

salt, to taste

small crackers or hot buttered toast, to serve

1 Heat the oil in a medium pan over a moderate heat and fry the onion and chillies for 8–10 minutes, until soft and pale brown.

4 Add the beaten eggs and salt, then cook for 2–4 minutes, stirring constantly until the required consistency is achieved. Remove from the heat and serve on crackers or hot buttered toast.

Per portion Energy 285kcal/1180kJ; Protein 11g; Carbohydrate 11g, of which sugars 8g; Fat 23g, of which saturates 10g; Cholesterol 251mg; Calcium 77mg; Fibre 4.4g; Sodium 297mg.

Parsee spiced omelette

This recipe, *Parsee Poro*, comes from the colourful collection of Parsee cuisine that is prevalent in west India, although its reputation has spread the length and breadth of the country over the years. It is often served at breakfast, but can also be enjoyed as a first course, cut into strips and arranged with alternate layered strips of naan on a plate, and drizzled with a tomato relish.

SERVES 4

4 eggs, separated
salt, to taste
4 spring onions (scallions), very
   finely chopped
2 fresh red chillies, finely chopped
   (deseeded if preferred)
30ml/2 tbsp fresh coriander (cilantro)
   leaves, finely chopped
60ml/4 tbsp sunflower oil or light olive oil
strips of naan and tomato relish, to serve

4 Add a quarter of the beaten egg mixture. Tilt the pan so the egg covers the base in an even layer.

5 Reduce the heat slightly and allow the omelette to brown on the underside.

6 Lift up an edge to check whether it is brown, then, when it is, place the pan under the hot grill and cook until the surface is well browned. Remove and keep warm while you make the remaining omelettes in the same way. Serve with naan and tomato relish.

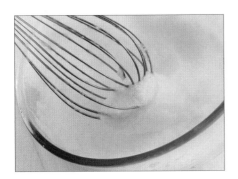

1 Separate the eggs and beat the whites until soft peaks form. Add the yolks and salt and blend well.

2 Divide the spring onions, red chillies and chopped coriander into four equal portions. Preheat the grill (broiler) to medium.

3 Heat 15ml/1 tbsp of the oil in an ovenproof frying pan over a medium heat and add one portion of each of the spring onion, chilli and coriander. Stir-fry for 1 minute.

Per portion Energy 230kcal/950kJ; Protein 8g; Carbohydrate 1g, of which sugars 1g; Fat 22g, of which saturates 4g; Cholesterol 232mg; Calcium 52mg; Fibre 0.3g; Sodium 186mg.

Main Dishes

Colourful, sustaining and packed with flavour, vegetarian main courses form the basis of most meals in many parts of India. With such an array of fresh produce on offer in the vibrant markets, cooks have an almost limitless selection to choose from, and have perfected the art of blending different combinations with various spices and staples such as lentils, beans and potatoes to create healthy and satisfying meals.

Fresh, healthy and flavoursome

A large proportion of the Indian population is vegetarian, primarily for religious reasons. As a result, there is a strong tradition of vegetarian cooking that goes back centuries, and cooks have perfected the art of creating a vast array of tempting, sustaining and nutritious dishes that make fabulous use of whatever produce is available locally. Indeed, the dishes are so delicous that it is quite common practice for meat-eaters to base their meals around vegetarian food and consume only a small amount of meat as an accompaniment.

There is a huge range of fresh vegetables available in Indian street markets and stores, from leafy greens, tomatoes, aubergines (eggplants) and crunchy (bell) peppers to starchy staples such as root vegetables, squashes and plantains. The choice varies from region to region as well as seasonally, resulting in a plethora of different combinations that make use of what is on offer that day. Spicing also changes depending on geographical location, with some regions favouring mild spicing and subtle flavours and others preferring intensely hot and spicy food.

Whatever the preference, cooks always aim to balance both the flavours and the nutritional content of the dishes, ensuring staple carbohydrates are incorporated to provide sustenance and energy. Protein, essential for well-being and particularly important in a vegetarian diet, is often supplied in the form of lentils, beans and peas, which are used on a daily basis. These provide plenty of dietary fibre, vitamins and minerals, and are also cheap and readily available. Gram flour (besan) is also packed with protein, and appears in many guises, from dumplings to sauces, adding flavour as well as acting as a binding and thickening agent. High in calories and full of protein, nuts and seeds are added whole to curries and fried dishes for texture and flavour, or ground and used to make thick, rich sauces.

Dairy products feature strongly on the vegetarian menu, and provide protein as well as calcium and other minerals and vitamins. The Indian cheese, paneer, is packed with as much protein as meat or poultry, and is widely used in curries or formed into balls and served with a sauce. Eggs are similarly important, and provide a delicious and economical alternative to meat in all manner of tasty dishes. Home-made yogurt, containing valuable amounts of protein, calcium and with other beneficial properties, is an integral part of a vegetarian meal. As well as being cooked in dishes and used for making creamy sauces, it can also make a dressing for salads and forms the basis for raitas.

Turnips in cream sauce

This recipe comes from Himachal Pradesh, where, until recently, the only two vegetables used in the local cuisine were potatoes and turnips. The latter play the starring role in this dish, which consists of fried turnips cooked with an array of flavourings and spices and some cream.

SERVES 4

675g/1½lb turnips
60ml/4 tbsp sunflower oil or light olive oil
4 green cardamom pods, bruised
1 large onion, finely sliced
10ml/2 tsp ginger purée
10ml/2 tsp garlic purée
1–2 fresh green chillies, finely chopped
  (deseeded if preferred)
10ml/2 tsp ground coriander
2.5ml/½ tsp ground turmeric
2.5ml/½ tsp chilli powder
2.5ml/½ tsp salt
150ml/¼ pint/⅔ cup double (heavy) cream
2.5ml/½ tsp garam masala
Indian bread, to serve

1 Peel the turnips and and cut them into bitesize pieces.

2 Heat the sunflower or olive oil in a frying pan over a medium heat.

3 Add the turnips in batches and brown them in the oil. Remove with a slotted spoon and drain on kitchen paper.

4 Add the cardamom pods to the remaining oil in the pan and allow them to puff up. Add the onion and fry, stirring regularly, for 5–6 minutes, until it is soft but not brown.

5 Add the ginger, garlic and chillies, and continue to cook for a further 2–3 minutes or until the onion is just beginning to brown.

6 Add the coriander, turmeric and chilli powder. Cook for about 1 minute, then add the fried turnips and 200ml/7fl oz/scant 1 cup lukewarm water. Add salt to taste, bring it to the boil, reduce the heat, cover and simmer for 12–15 minutes, until the turnips are tender.

7 Add the cream and continue to cook, uncovered, until the sauce has thickened. Stir in the garam masala and remove from the heat. Serve with any Indian bread.

Per portion Energy 384kcal/1587kJ; Protein 3g; Carbohydrate 14g, of which sugars 12g; Fat 36g, of which saturates 14g; Cholesterol 51mg; Calcium 127mg; Fibre 5.1g; Sodium 71mg.

Turnips in a spice-laced yogurt sauce

Fresh turnips are available in supermarkets throughout the year. Try to find small ones as they have a delicate, slightly sweet taste, which complements the sour-hot yogurt sauce in this dish. As a main course *Shalgam Ka Salan* merits the use of ghee, which enriches the dish, but you could use oil instead if you prefer.

SERVES 4

5–6 turnips (about 600g/1¼lb)
275g/10oz potatoes
115g/4oz/½ cup full-fat (whole) natural (plain) yogurt
10ml/2 tsp gram flour (besan), sifted
50g/2oz ghee or unsalted butter
1 large onion, finely sliced
10ml/2 tsp ginger purée
1–2 fresh green chillies, finely chopped (deseeded if preferred)
5ml/1 tsp ground coriander
2.5ml/½ tsp ground cumin
2.5ml/½ tsp chilli powder
2.5ml/½ tsp ground turmeric
5ml/1 tsp salt, or to taste
2.5ml/½ tsp sugar
2.5ml/½ tsp garam masala
30ml/2 tbsp fresh coriander (cilantro) leaves, finely chopped

1 Peel the turnips and quarter them. Cut each quarter into four smaller pieces. Peel the potatoes and cut them to the same size as the turnips.

2 Whisk the yogurt and gram flour together and set aside.

COOK'S TIP
If the turnips are really young and tender, with soft skins, then they may not require peeling. If in doubt, however, do peel them.

3 Heat half the ghee or butter over a medium heat and brown the turnips, stirring them frequently, until they have a light crust. Drain on kitchen paper. Brown the potatoes in the same way and drain.

4 Add the remaining ghee or butter to the pan and reduce the heat to low. Fry the onion, ginger and green chillies for about 5 minutes, until the onion is golden brown.

5 Add the coriander, cumin, chilli powder and turmeric, and cook for about 1 minute.

6 Add the vegetables and the yogurt mixture. Add the salt, sugar and 50ml/2fl oz/ 3 tbsp water. Reduce the heat to low, cover and cook for 20 minutes, stirring often.

7 Stir in the garam masala and coriander. Serve with any Indian bread.

Per portion Energy 317kcal/1326kJ; Protein 7.9g; Carbohydrate 39.6g, of which sugars 17g; Fat 15.6g, of which saturates 6.7g; Cholesterol 3mg; Calcium 194mg; Fibre 6.3g; Sodium 61mg.

Potatoes in aromatic yogurt sauce

In Indian cooking, the humble potato is given gourmet status in many different dishes, and *Dum Aloo Kashmiri* is one of the most delicious. Here, whole potatoes are fried before being simmered in a yogurt sauce. The people of Kashmir cook these potatoes in mustard oil, which needs to be heated until smoking hot to reduce its pungency and give the dish a superbly nutty, mellow flavour.

4 Place the pan back over a low heat. Add the chilli powder, followed by 30ml/2 tbsp water. Cook for 1 minute, then add the remaining spices. Cook for a further minute.

5 Add the browned potatoes, salt and yogurt. Cover the pan tightly and reduce the heat to low. Cook for 5–6 minutes, until the sauce thickens and coats the potatoes.

6 Remove from the heat and serve with naan or chapatis.

SERVES 4

60ml/4 tbsp mustard oil
700g/1½lb small potatoes, boiled and peeled
2.5–5ml/½–1 tsp chilli powder
2 brown cardamom pods, bruised
4 green cardamom pods, bruised
2.5ml/½ tsp ground ginger
5ml/1 tsp ground coriander
5ml/1 tsp ground fennel
5ml/1 tsp salt, or to taste
150g/5oz/½ cup full-fat (whole) natural
  (plain) yogurt, whisked
naan or chapatis, to serve

1 In a medium-sized pan, heat the oil until smoking, add half the potatoes and fry until they are well browned.

2 Remove from the heat and drain on kitchen paper. Repeat with the remaining potatoes.

3 When they are cool enough to handle, prick the potatoes all over to allow the flavours to penetrate.

Per portion Energy 261kcal/1092kJ; Protein 5.8g; Carbohydrate 33.2g, of which sugars 5.1g; Fat 12.7g, of which saturates 1.8g; Cholesterol 1mg; Calcium 93mg; Fibre 1.8g; Sodium 53mg.

Spinach in clove-infused yogurt sauce

The strong flavour of spinach is perfectly matched by the pungent sweetness of cloves in this unusual dish, *Palak-Dahi Ki Kari*, which can be served hot or at room temperature. The yogurt should be thick set, preferably Greek (US strained plain), so it doesn't split when heated. It makes a healthy meal when accompanied by plain basmati rice and served with a lentil dish.

SERVES 4

400g/14oz spinach, fresh or frozen
(thawed if frozen)
200g/7oz/scant 1 cup Greek
(US strained plain) yogurt
5ml/1 tsp gram flour (besan)
45ml/3 tbsp sunflower oil or light olive oil
2.5cm/1in piece cinnamon stick
5 cardamom pods, bruised
1 large onion, finely sliced
4 cloves garlic, crushed to a pulp
10ml/2 tsp fresh root ginger, finely grated
2 fresh red chillies, chopped
(deseeded if preferred)
3.75ml/¾ tsp salt, or to taste
10ml2 tsp ghee or unsalted butter
5 whole cloves
Plain Boiled Rice (*see* page 36) and a lentil
dish, to serve

1 Put the spinach in a large heatproof bowl, pour over boiling water and stir until the leaves have wilted.

2 Drain the spinach and rinse in cold water, then squeeze out as much water as possible. If you are using thawed frozen spinach, simply squeeze out the excess water. Chop the spinach finely.

3 Whisk the yogurt and the gram flour together in a small bowl and set aside.

4 Heat the oil in a frying pan over a low heat and add the cinnamon and cardamom.

5 When the cardamom pods puff up, add the onion, garlic, ginger and chillies, and increase the heat. Fry for 8–10 minutes, until the ingredients are medium-brown, stirring regularly.

6 Add the spinach and salt and cook for 4–5 minutes, until heated through. Add the yogurt and 75ml/2½fl oz/⅓ cup water. Stir well, cover the pan cook for 3–4 minutes.

7 Switch off the heat source and keep the pan covered.

8 Melt the ghee or butter and add the cloves. When they start sizzling, switch off the heat and cook for 25–30 seconds.

9 Pour the oil over the spinach, stir and cover. Let it stand for 10–15 minutes, then serve with Plain Boiled Rice and a lentil dish.

Per portion Energy 237kcal/980kJ; Protein 7g; Carbohydrate 8g, of which sugars 6g; Fat 20g, of which saturates 7g; Cholesterol 15mg; Calcium 256mg; Fibre 0.9g; Sodium 379mg.

Corn kernels in yogurt and gram flour sauce

Golden gram flour (besan) sauce, spiced with cumin and coriander and accentuated with chillies, mingles with the sweet, milky taste of corn kernels to create this enticing dish, *Makki Ke Dane Ki Kari*. Canned corn kernels can be used instead of frozen ones, but drain and rinse them well beforehand.

SERVES 4

150g/5oz/⅔ cup full-fat (whole) natural (plain) yogurt
30ml/2 tbsp gram flour (besan), sifted
45ml/3 tbsp sunflower oil or light olive oil
2.5ml/½ tsp black mustard seeds
2.5ml/½ tsp cumin seeds
1 medium onion, finely chopped
5ml/1 tsp ginger purée
5ml/1 tsp garlic purée
10ml/2 tsp ground coriander
2.5ml/½ tsp ground turmeric
2.5–5ml/½–1 tsp chilli powder
400g/14oz/2¼ cups frozen corn, thawed
5ml/1 tsp salt, or to taste
10ml/2 tsp ghee or unsalted butter
2.5ml/½ tsp garam masala
30ml/2 tbsp fresh coriander (cilantro) leaves, finely chopped
julienne strips of fresh tomato, to garnish
Ginger and Cumin Puffed Bread with Spinach (*see* pages 216–17), or Butter-flavoured Rice with Spiced Stock (*see* page 152), to serve

1 Mix the yogurt and gram flour together well in a large bowl and set aside.

2 Heat the oil in a frying pan over a medium heat and add the mustard seeds. As soon as they begin to pop, add the cumin seeds and let them sizzle for a few seconds.

3 Add the onion and stir-fry for 5–6 minutes, until translucent. Add the ginger and garlic and stir-fry for about 1 minute.

4 Reduce the heat to low and add the coriander, turmeric and chilli powder. Fry gently for 30–40 seconds, then add the yogurt mixture and cook for 3–4 minutes, stirring constantly.

5 Add the corn, salt and 200ml/7fl oz/¾ cup warm water. Cook until the sauce begins to bubble, then cover the pan and simmer over a low heat for 15–20 minutes.

6 In a small pan or a steel ladle, melt the ghee or butter over a low heat and add the garam masala.

VARIATION
You can use fresh corn when it is in season. Remove the green outer leaves, stand the corn on its end and run a sharp knife down the side to slice off the kernels. You will need 6–8 corn cobs, depending on their size.

7 Stir and cook for about 30 seconds, then pour the spiced butter over the corn, making sure that none of the garam masala is left behind.

8 Stir in the coriander and remove from the heat. Transfer to a serving dish and garnish with julienne strips of tomato. Serve with Ginger and Cumin-scented Puffed Bread with Spinach or Butter-flavoured Rice with Spiced Stock.

Per portion Energy 258kcal/1068kJ; Protein 6.9g; Carbohydrate 16.7g, of which sugars 7.6g; Fat 18.7g, of which saturates 5.6g; Cholesterol 5mg; Calcium 84mg; Fibre 3.2g; Sodium 1165mg.

Royal corn curry

Corn is an extremely popular vegetable in northern India, where the cornfields of Punjab make a wonderful sight as the crops sway in the breeze. In India, the corn kernels for this dish, *Shahi Bhutta*, would be meticulously removed from the cob just before preparing the dish, but frozen or canned kernels save time and work equally well when the fresh cobs are not in season.

3 Fry for 8–9 minutes, until the onion is lightly browned, stirring frequently to encourage even cooking.

4 Add the turmeric and ground ingredients. Cook for 1 minute, then add the corn, milk and salt. Simmer for 8–10 minutes, until thickened, stirring occasionally.

5 Stir in the tomatoes and garam masala, and transfer to a serving dish. Serve with bread and/or Saffron-scented Pilau Rice.

SERVES 4

15ml/1 tbsp white poppy seeds
15ml/1 tbsp desiccated (dry unsweetened shredded) coconut
5ml/1 tsp coriander seeds
60ml/4 tbsp sunflower oil or light olive oil
60ml/4 green cardamom pods, bruised
1 large onion, finely chopped
10ml/2 tsp ginger purée
2 fresh green chillies, finely chopped (deseeded if preferred)
2.5ml/½ tsp ground turmeric
450g/1lb/2½ cups frozen corn, thawed and drained, or canned corn, drained and rinsed
225ml/8fl oz/scant 1 cup full-fat (whole) milk
5ml/1 tsp salt, or to taste
110g/4oz tomatoes, skinned and chopped
2.5ml/½ tsp garam masala
bread and/or Saffron-scented Pilau Rice (*see* pages 156–7), to serve

1 Grind the poppy seeds, desiccated coconut and coriander seeds in a coffee grinder until fine, then set aside.

2 Heat the oil in a large pan over a low heat and fry the cardamom pods gently for 25–30 seconds, until they puff up, then increase the heat to medium and add the onion, ginger and chillies.

Per portion Energy 368kcal/1539kJ; Protein 7.7g; Carbohydrate 43.6g, of which sugars 21.6g; Fat 19.4g, of which saturates 5.2g; Cholesterol 8mg; Calcium 128mg; Fibre 4.4g; Sodium 343mg.

Plantain curry

Plantains are used in this delightful recipe from Tamil Nadu, *Vazhakkai Kari*, and these are often sold by Asian grocers and larger supermarkets. Unripe bananas with a dark green skin also work well, although the flavour is different. Cook them on the day of purchase so that they do not get a chance to ripen. The food of this region is generally blisteringly hot, but the quantity of chilli can be adjusted to taste.

SERVES 4

4 plantains
15ml/1 tbsp full-fat (whole) natural
    (plain) yogurt
400ml/14fl oz/1⅔ cups canned coconut milk
7.5ml/1½ tsp chilli powder
2.5ml/½ tsp ground turmeric
5ml/1 tsp salt, or to taste
45ml/3 tbsp sunflower oil or light olive oil
2.5ml/½ tsp black or brown mustard seeds
2.5ml/½ tsp cumin seeds
6–8 curry leaves
2 red onions, finely sliced
1–2 fresh green chillies, chopped
    (deseeded if preferred)
Plain Boiled Rice (*see* page 36), to serve

1 Peel the plantains and halve them lengthways. Cut each into 2.5cm/1in chunks.

2 Rub the plantain with the yogurt, then soak in a bowl of cold water for 15–20 minutes. This removes any stickiness.

COOK'S TIP
Freshly made coconut-based curries thicken considerably upon cooling, so do not worry if the curry looks a little watery when you have finished cooking. Either leave it to cool slightly before serving, or cook the sauce for a little longer to reduce it to the desired consistency.

3 Drain the plantain chunks and rinse. Put them in a medium pan and add the coconut milk, chilli powder, turmeric and salt.

4 Add 200ml/7fl oz/scant 1 cup water to the pan and place over a low heat. Cover and simmer for 20–25 minutes or until the plantain is tender, but still firm.

5 Meanwhile, heat the oil in a small pan over a medium heat and add the mustard seeds.

6 As soon as the mustard seeds begin to pop, add the cumin and the curry leaves.

7 Add the onion and chillies and fry for 8–10 minutes, stirring regularly, until the onion begins to colour. Reduce the heat slightly halfway through the cooking time.

8 Pour the onion and spices over the curry, stir and simmer for 4–5 minutes. Serve with Plain Boiled Rice.

Per portion Energy 283kcal/1192kJ; Protein 3g; Carbohydrate 44g, of which sugars 16g; Fat 2g, of which saturates 2g; Cholesterol 0mg; Calcium 73mg; Fibre 3.7g; Sodium 620mg.

Cauliflower, peas and potatoes in tomato sauce

Phulkcopir Dalna is classic family fare, in which crisp white cauliflower florets join hands with cubed browned potatoes and green, tender peas in a rich chilli-tomato sauce. Mustard oil is the traditional choice, but sunflower or light olive oil can be used instead if preferred.

SERVES 4

1 small cauliflower, about 350g/12oz
60ml/4 tbsp mustard oil
450g/1lb potatoes, peeled and cut
   into 2.5cm/1in chunks
10ml/2 tsp sugar
2.5ml/½ tsp mustard seeds
5ml/1 tsp cumin seeds
5ml/1 tsp ginger purée
5ml/1 tsp garlic purée
2.5ml/½ tsp ground turmeric
5ml/1 tsp ground coriander
5ml/1 tsp ground cumin
2.5–5ml/½–1 tsp chilli powder
150g/5oz fresh tomatoes, chopped
5ml/1 tsp salt, or to taste
150g/5oz frozen garden peas
2.5ml/½ tsp garam masala
15ml/1 tbsp chopped fresh coriander
   (cilantro) leaves
Indian bread or Plain Boiled Rice
   (*see* page 36), and a yogurt-based
   salad or drink, to serve

1 Divide the cauliflower into 2.5cm/1in florets. Blanch them in a pan of salted boiling water for 2 minutes, then plunge into cold water to prevent further cooking.

2 Heat half the oil in a large, non-stick pan over a medium-high heat until smoking point is reached.

3 Add the potatoes and brown them for 3–4 minutes in several batches. Drain on kitchen paper.

4 Add the remaining oil to the pan and sprinkle the sugar evenly over the base. As soon as it starts to caramelize, add the mustard seeds, followed by the cumin. Let them crackle and pop for a few seconds and reduce the heat to low.

5 Add the ginger and garlic and cook, stirring, for 2–3 minutes.

6 Add the turmeric, coriander and cumin, cook for 1 minute, then add the tomatoes, fried potatoes and salt.

7 Pour in 400ml/14fl oz/1⅔ cups warm water. Bring it to the boil, reduce the heat to low, cover and cook for 15 minutes.

8 Drain the cauliflower and add to the potatoes. Add the peas, cook for 5 minutes, then stir in the garam masala and coriander.

9 Remove from the heat and serve with Indian bread or Plain Boiled Rice, and a yogurt-based salad or drink.

Per portion Energy 293kcal/1221kJ; Protein 8g; Carbohydrate 29g, of which sugars 8g; Fat 17g, of which saturates 2g; Cholesterol 0mg; Calcium 78mg; Fibre 6.3g; Sodium 554mg.

Crushed parsnips in spiced mustard oil

Parsnip is not an Indian ingredient, but the sweet flesh of this root vegetable provides an exciting contrast in flavour when seasoned the north Indian way with pungent mustard oil, and can be used to create delicious variations on classic dishes, including this favourite, *Parsnip Bharta*.

SERVES 4

675g/1½lb parsnips, peeled and cut into
  even dice
salt and ground black pepper
30ml/2 tbsp mustard oil
2.5ml/½ tsp black or brown
  mustard seeds
30ml/2 tbsp finely chopped red onion
1 fresh green chilli, finely chopped
  (deseeded if preferred)
30ml/2 tbsp fresh coriander (cilantro)
  leaves, finely chopped
Plain Boiled Rice (*see* page 36) and
  a lentil or paneer dish, to serve

1 Put the parsnips into a pan and pour in enough water to cover them. Add a pinch of salt and boil for 7–8 minutes, until tender but firm. Drain in a colander.

2 Heat the oil in a wok or a non-stick frying pan over a high heat, until smoking. Add the mustard seeds and immediately add the parsnips and the remaining ingredients. Stir-fry for 3 minutes. Remove from the heat.

3 Lightly mash a few pieces of parsnip with the back of the spoon. Stir everything well, then serve with Plain Boiled Rice, accompanied by a lentil or paneer dish.

VARIATION
If you can't get mustard oil, use vegetable oil and add a dash of English mustard.

COOK'S TIP
Make sure that you heat the oil until it is smoking, because it is at this point that mustard oil mellows and transforms into a deliciously nutty ingredient.

Per portion Energy 182kcal/760kJ; Protein 3g; Carbohydrate 22g, of which sugars 10g; Fat 10g, of which saturates 1g; Cholesterol 0mg; Calcium 78mg; Fibre 7.5g; Sodium 116mg.

Smoked aubergine with ginger and chilli

The delicious smoky flavour of aubergine (eggplant) is matched with a few well-chosen whole spices and chillies to create this Punjabi dish, *Baingan Bharta*. Traditionally, the aubergine was cooked on the smouldering ashes of a *tandoor* before the flesh was removed and mashed and then blended with spices. In a Western kitchen it can be cooked on the barbecue or grilled (broiled).

3 Cook for 15–20 minutes, turning them over frequently, until the aubergines are tender and the skin is slightly charred. Remove from the heat and let them cool.

4 Cut the aubergines in half. Scrape the flesh into a bowl and mash with a fork.

5 Heat the oil over a medium heat. Add the fennel. Cook for 30 seconds, until browned.

6 Add the onion, ginger, garlic and chillies. Fry for 5–6 minutes, until the onion is soft but not brown, stirring often. Stir in the turmeric.

7 Reserve some of the tomato and add the remainder to the onions. Cook for 4 minutes, stirring, then add the mashed aubergine and salt. Continue to cook for 2–3 minutes.

8 Reserve a few of the coriander leaves and stir the remainder into the aubergine mixture. Serve garnished with the reserved tomatoes and coriander.

SERVES 4

2 large aubergines (eggplants), about
  675g/1½lb
45ml/3 tbsp sunflower oil or light olive oil
2.5ml/½ tsp fennel seeds
1 onion, finely chopped
2.5cm/1in piece of fresh root ginger,
  peeled and finely grated
2–3 large cloves garlic, peeled
  and crushed
2 fresh green chillies, finely chopped
  (deseeded if preferred)
2.5ml/½ tsp ground turmeric
2 fresh tomatoes, skinned and chopped
5ml/1 tsp salt, or to taste
30ml/2 tbsp fresh coriander (cilantro)
  leaves, finely chopped, plus extra sprigs,
  to garnish

1 Preheat the grill (broiler) to high. Make two lengthways slits on the surface of each aubergine, without cutting through.

2 Rub a little oil on the skins. Place the aubergines on a grill pan and grill (broil) about 15cm/6in below the heat source.

Per portion Energy 142kcal/588kJ; Protein 2g; Carbohydrate 7g, of which sugars 6g; Fat 12g, of which saturates 2g; Cholesterol 0mg; Calcium 32mg; Fibre 3.6g; Sodium 499mg.

Aubergine in peanut and sesame seed sauce

The state of Maharashtra is well known for its vegetarian dishes, which combine simple cooking methods and complex flavours. Both peanuts and sesame seeds add an opulent taste to this dish, *Baingan Ki Subzi*, and it more than merits its place as a main course. This is a quicker and healthier version of the traditional recipe, but is just as delicious. Serve it with plain rice or a bread of your choice.

SERVES 4

50g/2oz sesame seeds
25g/1oz desiccated (dry unsweetened shredded) coconut
25g/1oz dry-roasted peanuts
2 aubergines (eggplants), about 500g/1¼lb
45ml/3 tbsp sunflower oil or light olive oil
1 large onion, finely chopped
3 cloves garlic, crushed
2.5ml/½ tsp ground turmeric
5ml/1 tsp chilli powder, or to taste
5ml/1 tsp ground cumin
5ml/1 tsp salt, or to taste
2.5ml/½ tsp garam masala
15ml/1 tbsp tamarind or lime juice
15ml/1 tbsp fresh coriander (cilantro) leaves, chopped
rice or bread, to serve

5 Heat the oil over a medium heat and fry the onion for 5 minutes, until soft but not brown. Add the garlic and cook for 1 minute, then add the turmeric, chilli powder and cumin. Cook for about 2 minutes.

6 Drain the aubergine and add to the pan. Add the salt and pour in 500ml/17fl oz/ generous 2 cups warm water.

7 Bring to the boil, reduce the heat to low, and cook for 10 minutes.

8 Add the sesame seeds and coconut and cook for 2–3 minutes, or until the aubergine is tender. Add the garam masala, tamarind or lime juice and the coriander, stir and remove from the heat. Sprinkle over the peanuts and serve with rice or bread.

1 In a heavy pan, dry-roast the sesame seeds over a medium heat for 1 minute, until they are just a shade darker. Remove from the heat and leave to cool.

2 In the same pan, dry-roast the coconut for 1–2 minutes, until it turns a pale creamy colour. Leave to cool, then mix with the sesame seeds. Grind the mixture in batches in a coffee grinder and set aside.

3 Crush the roasted peanuts to a coarse texture and set aside.

4 Cut the aubergine into 5cm/2in cubes and soak them in a bowl of cold water.

Per portion Energy 306kcal/1268kJ; Protein 7g; Carbohydrate 12g, of which sugars 9g; Fat 26g, of which saturates 6g; Cholesterol 0mg; Calcium 135mg; Fibre 05.6g; Sodium 558mg.

Clove-infused stuffed aubergines

Small, slim aubergines (eggplants) are used to make this traditional dish, *Baingan Ke Lonj*. The aubergines are sliced along most of their length, leaving them joined at the top, and these cavities are stuffed with a spicy onion paste tempered with clove and cinnamon. The aubergines are then tied shut and gently simmered in an onion sauce. This dish goes well with rice, bread or lentils.

SERVES 4

400g/14oz small, slim aubergines (eggplants)

60ml/4 tbsp sunflower oil or light olive oil

1 large onion, finely chopped

10ml/2 tsp ginger purée

1–2 fresh green chillies, finely chopped (deseeded if preferred)

5ml/1 tsp salt, or to taste

5ml/1 tsp ground turmeric

2.5ml/½ tsp chilli powder

5ml/1 tsp ground coriander

2.5ml/½ tsp ground cumin

2.5ml/½ tsp garam masala

4 cloves

1cm/½in piece of cinnamon stick

1 fresh tomato

sprigs of fresh coriander (cilantro), to garnish

wedges of lime, to garnish

rice and/or *Phulkas* (*see* page 205) and a lentil dish, to serve

1 Trim off the stalks from the aubergines. Cut them lengthways from the bottom to the top, leaving about 1cm/½in uncut at the top end so there are two conjoined slices that can be opened up and stuffed. Take care not to slice all the way along the length or the dish will not work.

2 Carefully place the aubergines in a large bowl of salted water and soak for 15–20 minutes. This helps remove any bitterness.

3 Meanwhile, heat half the oil over a medium heat and add the onion, ginger and chillies. Stir-fry for 4–5 minutes, until the onion is soft.

4 Reduce the heat to low and add half the salt, along with the turmeric, chilli powder, coriander and cumin. Cook for 1 minute, then stir in the garam masala and remove from the heat.

5 Drain the aubergines, rinse them and dry with a clean dish towel.

6 Stuff the aubergines with the onion mixture, using about 5ml/1 tsp of mixture per aubergine. Tie them up with a piece of thread in a criss-cross fashion. Reserve any remaining onion mixture.

7 Heat the remaining oil in a large pan over a low heat. Add the cloves and cinnamon. Let them sizzle for a few seconds, then add the aubergines and the remaining salt.

8 Increase the heat to medium and cook the aubergines, stirring, for 3–4 minutes. Add any reserved onion mixture and pour in 500ml/18fl oz/2 cups warm water. Bring it to the boil, reduce the heat to low, cover the pan and cook for 20 minutes.

9 Cut the tomato into quarters, remove the seeds and finely slice each piece into julienne strips, for a garnish.

10 At the end of the cooking time, remove the lid and cook, uncovered, for a few minutes longer, if necessary, to reduce the sauce. There should be very little liquid left and the thickened spice paste should coat the aubergines.

11 Remove the pan from the heat and carefully remove the threads holding the aubergines together, keeping them intact. Serve each aubergine with some of the sauce, accompanied by rice and/or *Phulkas* and a lentil dish of your choice.

Per portion Energy 188kcal/779kJ; Protein 3.9g; Carbohydrate 15.6g, of which sugars 9g; Fat 13g, of which saturates 1.6g; Cholesterol 0mg; Calcium 59mg; Fibre 3.8g; Sodium 9mg.

Stuffed sweet peppers

Sweet (bell) peppers are grown extensively in the hilly terrain of Kashmir and Shimla, and in India they are known as *pahadi mirch*, meaning 'mountain chillies'. In this recipe, *Bharwan Shimla Mirch*, the peppers are stuffed with a mixture of crushed boiled potatoes, cashew nuts and spices. Green (bell) peppers are used, but for a more colourful dish, you can also use red and yellow ones, which will vary the taste.

SERVES 4–6

275g/10oz potatoes
75ml/5 tbsp sunflower oil or light olive oil
2.5ml/½ tsp black mustard seeds
2.5ml/½ tsp cumin seeds
1 large onion, finely chopped
1 fresh green chilli, finely chopped
  (deseeded if preferred)
2.5ml/½ tsp ground turmeric
2.5ml/½ tsp chilli powder
5ml/1 tsp garam masala
50g/2oz/½ cup raw cashew nuts, chopped
5ml/1 tsp salt, or to taste
30ml/2 tbsp fresh coriander (cilantro)
  leaves, finely chopped
15ml/1 tbsp lemon juice
4 medium-sized green (bell) peppers
Roasted Tomato Chutney (*see* page 195),
  to serve

1 Boil the potatoes in their skins (this is important as the potatoes, when mashed, should not be mushy), in a large pan of salted boiling water for 10–12 minutes, or until cooked and soft.

2 Leave the potatoes to cool, then peel. Crush them lightly with a fork or potato masher so that some larger pieces remain.

3 Heat 45ml/3 tbsp of the oil in a frying pan over a medium heat and, when it is quite hot but not smoking, throw in the mustard seeds, followed by the cumin seeds. Let the seeds pop for 10–15 seconds.

4 Add the onion and green chilli. Fry, stirring regularly, for 5–6 minutes, until the onion is soft.

5 Add the turmeric, chilli powder, garam masala and cashew nuts to the pan, cook for 1 minute, then remove from the heat.

6 Add this mixture to the mashed potato, and stir in the salt, chopped coriander and lemon juice. Mix thoroughly and set aside. Preheat the oven to 190°C/375°F/Gas 5.

7 Wash the peppers and slice off the tops. Using a small knife, carefully remove the white pith and the seeds.

VARIATION
You can use the potato filling to stuff other vegetables, such as courgettes (zucchini), marrows (large zucchini) and even tomatoes.

8 Fill the peppers with the potato mixture, pressing the filling down into the cavity. Smooth the surface with the back of a spoon.

9 Heat the remaining 30ml/2 tbsp oil in a pan over a medium heat and add the peppers. Using tongs, turn to coat with oil.

10 Stand the peppers in an ovenproof dish or roasting pan and bake for 25–30 minutes, turning and basting them occasionally. Serve with Roasted Tomato Chutney.

Per portion Energy 224kcal/933kJ; Protein 4.6g; Carbohydrate 20.2g, of which sugars 10.1g; Fat 14.5g, of which saturates 2.2g; Cholesterol 0mg; Calcium 29mg; Fibre 3.1g; Sodium 36mg.

Stuffed baked marrow

This elegant dish, *Lazeez Ghia Mussallam*, is from Lucknow in north India. It involves hollowing out a marrow (large zucchini) and stuffing it with a filling made of paneer, the ubiquitous Indian cheese; the filling is deliciously spiced with onion, fresh root ginger, chilli and fresh coriander (cilantro). When buying marrows, look for ones with skins that are an even green colour with no hint of brown or yellow.

SERVES 4–6
a good pinch of saffron threads, pounded
30ml/2 tbsp hot milk
1 medium marrow (large zucchini)
5ml/1 tsp salt
60ml/4 tbsp sunflower oil or light olive oil
1 large onion, roughly chopped
10ml/2 tsp ginger purée
10ml/2 tsp garlic purée
115g/4oz/½ cup full-fat (whole) natural
　(plain) yogurt
50g/2oz/½ cup roasted cashew nuts
115g/4oz paneer (Indian cheese), grated
2 fresh green chillies, finely chopped
15ml/1 tbsp fresh coriander (cilantro) leaves
　and stalks, finely chopped
30ml/2 tbsp fresh mint leaves, finely
　chopped, or 5ml/1 tsp dried mint
2.5–5ml/½–1 tsp chilli powder
5ml/1 tsp ground coriander
2.5ml/½ tsp garam masala
30ml/2 tbsp tomato purée (paste)
2.5ml/½ tsp sugar
2.5ml/½ tsp salt, or to taste
Indian bread, to serve

1 Put the pounded saffron and the hot milk in a small bowl and set aside.

2 Slice off both ends of the marrow and, using an apple corer or a medium-sized knife with a narrow blade, scoop out the seeds. Do this with a rotating movement. Use a long-handled spoon to scrape out any remaining seeds.

3 Peel the marrow, then prick it all over with a fork and rub in the salt. Place in a colander in the sink and leave to drain.

4 Preheat the oven to 190°C/375°F/Gas 5. Heat half the oil in a large frying pan, add the onion and fry over a medium heat for 4–5 minutes. Add the ginger and garlic and fry for a further 2–3 minutes.

5 Remove the onion, ginger and garlic with a slotted spoon, leaving behind the oil, and put into a blender with the yogurt, saffron-infused milk and the saffron, and the cashew nuts. Blend to form a coarse paste.

6 Transfer half the yogurt paste to a mixing bowl and add the cheese, half the chillies, half the fresh coriander and half the mint. Season to taste and mix thoroughly.

7 Wipe the marrow with kitchen paper and stuff it with the cheese mixture, leaving a 1cm/½in gap at both ends.

8 Add the remaining oil to the pan and heat over a high heat. Add the marrow and brown it on all sides. Transfer to a roasting pan.

9 In the frying pan, cook the chilli powder, coriander and garam masala for 30 seconds, then add the tomato purée and sugar.

10 Cook for 1–2 minutes, then stir in the reserved yogurt paste, the remaining chillies and coriander, the mint, 120ml/4fl oz/½ cup lukewarm water and the salt.

11 Pour the mixture over the marrow and spread it down the sides. Cover the roasting pan with a piece of foil and bake in the centre of the oven for 20–25 minutes.

12 Remove from the oven and allow to rest for 10 minutes. Transfer to a serving dish. Mix the spice paste with the cooking juices and spread it all over the marrow, then carve the marrow into thick slices. Serve with any Indian bread.

Per portion Energy 241kcal/998kJ; Protein 5g; Carbohydrate 10g, of which sugars 8g; Fat 21g, of which saturates 6g; Cholesterol 13mg; Calcium 92mg; Fibre 1.7g; Sodium 236mg.

Cauliflower braised with chilli and fenugreek

Snow-white florets of cauliflower are simmered in rich coconut milk, teamed with lightly browned red onion and flavoured with only two spices in this dish, *Ambat*, which is a classic example of the delicious, healthy cuisine of Karnataka. It goes well with plain boiled basmati rice.

4 Add the coconut milk and salt. Leave it to bubble without a lid over a very low heat.

5 Heat the remaining oil over a medium heat and fry the onion for 5 minutes, until golden. Add the onion, together with the oil, to the cauliflower. Stir and increase the heat slightly.

6 Add the fenugreek and chilli paste to the cauliflower with the tamarind or lime juice. Simmer for 1–2 minutes, remove from the heat and serve with Plain Boiled Rice.

SERVES 4

45ml/3 tbsp sunflower oil or light olive oil

2.5ml/½ tsp fenugreek seeds

1–2 dried red chillies, chopped

1 cauliflower, divided into 1cm/½in florets

400ml/14fl oz/1½ cups canned
   coconut milk

5ml/1 tsp salt, or to taste

1 red onion, finely sliced

22.5ml/1½ tbsp tamarind juice or
   lime juice

Plain Boiled Rice (*see* page 36),
   to serve

1 In a small pan, heat 10ml/2 tsp of the oil over a low heat and add the fenugreek and chillies. Stir them around until they are just a shade darker. Leave to cool.

2 Meanwhile, blanch the cauliflower in a large pan of lightly salted boiling water for 2 minutes, then drain and return to the pan.

3 Crush the fenugreek and chillies to a paste with the oil in which they were fried using a mortar and pestle.

Per portion Energy 153kcal/636kJ; Protein 5.9g; Carbohydrate 10.6g, of which sugars 9.5g; Fat 9.9g, of which saturates 1.5g; Cholesterol 0mg; Calcium 64mg; Fibre 2.9g; Sodium 124mg.

Spiced vegetables over rice

This recipe, *Tarkari Bhate*, is just one of a variety of tasty Bengali rice dishes made using steamed vegetables and lentils, which are spiced up and simply served with plain boiled rice. You can use any combination of vegetables you like. The distinctive taste in Bengali cuisine comes from mustard oil.

SERVES 4

115g/4oz carrots, peeled and cut into
  bitesize pieces
1 small turnip, peeled and cut into
  bitesize pieces
½ small green cabbage
45ml/3 tbsp mustard oil, plus extra for
  drizzling (optional)
2.5ml/½ tsp black or brown
  mustard seeds
2.5ml/½ tsp cumin seeds
2 whole dried red chillies
1–2 fresh green chillies, chopped
  (deseeded if preferred)
115g/4oz baby spinach leaves
2.5ml/½ tsp salt, or to taste
Plain Boiled Rice (*see* page 36),
  to serve

2 Heat the oil in a frying pan until smoking point is reached. Switch off the heat, then add the mustard seeds followed by the cumin, dried chillies and fresh chillies.

3 Cook for 25–30 seconds, then add the steamed vegetables, spinach and salt.

4 Stir until the spinach has wilted, then remove from the heat.

5 Put the cooked rice in a serving dish and serve topped with the spiced vegetables. Bengalis sprinkle extra mustard oil on the vegetables, but this is optional.

1 Place the carrots, turnip and cabbage in an electronic steamer, or in a steamer basket placed over a pan of simmering water, and steam until tender but firm.

Per portion Energy 345kcal/1452kJ; Protein 6g; Carbohydrate 55g, of which sugars 6g; Fat 13g, of which saturates 1g; Cholesterol 0mg; Calcium 109mg; Fibre 5.5g; Sodium 305mg.

Mixed vegetable stew

This dish, *Laganshala*, would traditionally form part of a Parsi wedding feast, which is famous for its elaborate and extensive range of dishes – in fact it is so lavish that the invitees often fast before attending so they can eat more! The recipe has a complex yet subtle flavour with a sweet-and-sour undertone that reflects the influence of Gujarati cooking on the region.

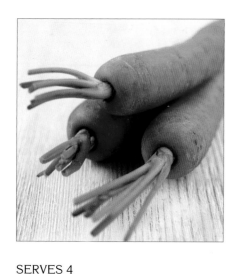

SERVES 4

45ml/3 tbsp sunflower oil or light olive oil

1 large onion, finely chopped

10ml/2 tsp ginger purée

10ml/2 tsp garlic purée

5ml/1 tsp chilli powder, or to taste

5ml/1 tsp ground turmeric

5ml/1 tsp ground cumin

5ml/1 tsp ground coriander

225g/8oz potatoes, peeled and cut into
  2.5cm/1in cubes

225g/8oz sweet potatoes, peeled and cut
  into 2.5cm/1in cubes

225g/8oz carrots, scraped and cut into
  thick rounds

150g/5oz green beans

2 ripe tomatoes, chopped

15ml/1 tbsp Worcestershire sauce

15ml/1 tbsp vinegar

5ml/1 tsp salt, or to taste

5ml/1 tsp sugar

30ml/2 tbsp fresh coriander (cilantro)
  leaves, chopped

Indian bread or Plain Boiled Rice
  (*see* page 36), to serve

VARIATION
Use 45ml/3 tbsp canned chopped tomatoes in place of fresh ones.

1 Heat the oil over a medium heat and add the onion. Fry for about 5 minutes, until the onion is soft.

2 Add the ginger and garlic and stir. Cook for 2 minutes, then add the chilli powder, turmeric, cumin and coriander. Cook for 1 minute, then add 15ml/1 tbsp water. Continue to cook for 2 minutes, then add a further 15ml/1 tbsp water.

3 Add all the vegetables, except the green beans and tomatoes.

4 Add 425ml/15fl oz water and bring it to the boil. Reduce the heat to medium, cover and cook for 15 minutes.

5 Add the beans and tomatoes, Worcestershire sauce, vinegar, salt and sugar. Cook, uncovered, for 5–6 minutes or until the sauce has thickened.

6 Stir in the chopped coriander and remove from the heat. Serve with any bread or Plain Boiled Rice.

COOK'S TIP
This dish can easily be made in advance and chilled in the refrigerator for a couple of days. To reheat, either transfer the stew to a pan and heat until simmering, or place it in the microwave and cook for about 3 minutes, or until piping hot.

Per portion Energy 260kcal/1088kJ; Protein 4g; Carbohydrate 36g, of which sugars 15g; Fat 12g, of which saturates 2g; Cholesterol 0mg; Calcium 78mg; Fibre 6.2g; Sodium 584mg.

Mixed vegetables with five-spice mix

This Assamese vegetable dish, *Meeholi Bhaji*, is made either with freshly picked produce or with odds and ends that are already in the kitchen. It has a wonderful confetti of colours and a fabulous mingling of flavours, which are imparted by the different types of vegetables and the five-spice mix that is typical of this region. It produces a thin sauce, which the Assamese people serve with rice and a lentil dish.

SERVES 4

60ml/4 tbsp mustard oil
175g/6oz potatoes, cut into 2.5cm/1in cubes
115g/4oz carrots, cut into 2.5cm/1in cubes
150g/5oz cauliflower, divided into
  2.5cm/1in florets
2 bay leaves
5ml/1 tsp ground coriander
5ml/1 tsp ground cumin
2.5ml/½ tsp ground turmeric
2.5ml/½ tsp chilli powder
½ a small cabbage (about 200g/7oz),
  finely shredded
115g/4oz garden peas, fresh or frozen
  (boiled until tender, if fresh)
5ml/1 tsp salt, or to taste
4–5 whole fresh green chillies
2 ripe tomatoes, cut into 2.5cm/1in chunks
30ml/2 tbsp fresh coriander (cilantro)
  leaves, chopped
Plain Boiled Rice (*see* page 36) or Plain
  Flour Flat Bread (*see* page 202)

For the five-spice mix:
2.5ml/½ tsp black or brown mustard seeds
2.5ml/½ tsp cumin seeds
2.5ml/½ tsp fennel seeds
2.5ml/½ tsp nigella seeds
6 fenugreek seeds

1 Heat 45ml/3 tbsp of the oil in a non-stick or cast iron pan until it reaches smoking point, then reduce the heat slightly and add the potatoes and carrots.

2 Stir-fry for about 4 minutes, until they begin to brown, then remove with a slotted spoon and drain on kitchen paper. Brown the cauliflower in the remaining oil for about 3 minutes, then remove and drain.

3 Add the remaining oil to the pan and heat until smoking point is reached. Switch off the heat source and add the five-spice mix. Let it crackle and pop for about 30 seconds.

4 Add the bay leaves, coriander, cumin, turmeric and chilli powder.

5 Place the pan over a low heat and fry the spices for about 1 minute.

6 Add the browned potatoes and carrots and pour in 300ml/½ pint/1¼ cups lukewarm water. Bring it to the boil, reduce the heat to low and cover the pan.

7 Cook for 5–6 minutes, then add the cauliflower, cabbage, peas and salt.

8 Cover and simmer for 4–5 minutes, then add the chillies, tomatoes and coriander.

9 Cook, uncovered for 2–3 minutes, remove from the heat and serve with Plain Boiled Rice or Plain Flour Flat Bread.

> ## VARIATION
> You can either buy pre-mixed five-spice mix or make your own, as in this recipe.

Per portion Energy 161kcal/668kJ; Protein 3g; Carbohydrate 10g, of which sugars 4g; Fat 13g, of which saturates 2g; Cholesterol 0mg; Calcium 38mg; Fibre 2.2g; Sodium 413mg.

Medley of vegetables with dumplings

Oondhiu is a fabulous mixture of fresh vegetables such as potatoes, green beans, aubergines (eggplants), sweet potatoes and bananas, cooked with spicy gram flour (besan) dumplings and enhanced by dried fenugreek leaves (kasuri methi). This recipe provides a healthy and substantial vegetarian main course.

SERVES 4

For the dumplings:
125g/4½oz/generous 1 cup gram flour (besan)
1.25ml/¼ tsp salt
a pinch of bicarbonate of soda (baking soda)
2.5ml/½ tsp aniseed
30ml/2 tbsp dried fenugreek leaves
1 fresh green chilli, finely chopped
   (deseeded if preferred)
15ml/1 tbsp fresh coriander (cilantro)
   leaves, finely chopped
15ml/1 tbsp hot sunflower oil
15ml/1 tbsp lime juice
15ml/1 tbsp water
sunflower oil, for deep-frying

For the vegetable curry:
50g/2oz desiccated (dry unsweetened
   shredded) coconut
10ml/2 tsp ground coriander
20ml/4 tsp garlic purée
20ml/4 tsp ginger purée
20ml/4 tsp chilli powder, or to taste
5ml/1 tsp ground turmeric
30ml/2 tbsp sunflower oil or light olive oil
1.25ml/¼ tsp Asafoetida
200g/7oz potatoes, cut into 2.5cm/1in cubes
200g/7oz aubergine (eggplant), cut into
   2.5cm/1in chunks
150g/5oz sweet potato, cut into
   2.5cm/1in cubes
125g/4½oz green beans, cut into
   2.5cm/1in lengths
2 unripe bananas, thickly sliced
Indian bread, to serve

1 For the dumplings: put the gram flour into a mixing bowl and add the remaining dumpling ingredients, up to and including the chopped coriander.

2 Mix thoroughly and add the hot oil, lime juice and water. Mix until a stiff dough is formed and knead it for about 1 minute. Divide the dough into 10 equal balls.

3 Heat the oil in a wok or other suitable pan for deep-frying over a medium heat. Fry the dumplings until they are crisp and golden brown. Drain on kitchen paper and set aside.

4 For the vegetable curry: grind the coconut in a coffee grinder and mix in a bowl with the coriander, 10ml/2 tsp of the garlic, 10ml/2 tsp of the ginger, the chilli powder and turmeric. Add 150ml/4fl oz/½ cup water and stir until it forms a paste. Alternatively, put the coconut in 150ml/4fl oz/½ cup water, bring to the boil and allow to cool, then purée in a blender along with the spices. Set the purée aside.

5 Heat the oil over a medium heat and add the Asafoetida and the remaining garlic and ginger, and cook until they begin to brown.

6 Add the coconut spice paste to the pan, increase the heat slightly, and cook for 3–4 minutes, stirring.

7 Add the potatoes to the pan and pour in 450ml/16fl oz/1¾ cups warm water. Bring the mixture to the boil, reduce the heat to low, cover the pan and cook for 7–8 minutes.

8 Add the aubergine and sweet potato, bring back to the boil, reduce the heat to medium, cover and cook for 5–6 minutes.

9 Add the green beans and the banana slices, cover and cook for 4–5 minutes. Add the dumplings to the pan and cook for 3–4 minutes longer.

10 Remove from the heat and serve with any Indian bread.

Per portion Energy 523kcal/2182kJ; Protein 7.8g; Carbohydrate 47.6g, of which sugars 5.8g; Fat 35.1g, of which saturates 9.8g; Cholesterol 0mg; Calcium 98mg; Fibre 5.8g; Sodium 30mg.

Gram flour dumplings in a tomato sauce

This protein-rich dish, *Ghoomni,* is from the state of Bihar, where vegetarian food is prevalent. Gram flour (besan) is mixed with chillies and spices and made into a dough, which is poached until set and cut into slices known as *gatte.* These are then fried and simmered in a spicy sauce. Asafoetida is added to the sauce for its curative quality as gram flour is sometimes difficult to digest.

SERVES 4

For the dumplings:

300g/10½oz/generous 2½ cups gram flour (besan), sifted

2.5ml/½ tsp bicarbonate of soda (baking soda)

2.5ml/½ tsp ground turmeric

5ml/1 tsp cumin seeds

5ml/1 tsp fennel seeds

5ml/1 tsp dried red chilli flakes

2.5cm/1in piece of fresh root ginger, grated

30ml/2 tbsp fresh coriander (cilantro) leaves, chopped

5ml/1 tsp salt, or to taste

150g/5oz/generous ½ cup full-fat (whole) natural (plain) yogurt

sunflower oil, for deep-frying

For the sauce:

45–60ml/3–4 tbsp sunflower oil or light olive oil

2.5cm/1in piece of cinnamon stick

4 cloves

1.25ml/¼ tsp Asafoetida

1 large onion, finely sliced

10ml/2 tsp ground coriander

2.5–5ml/½–1 tsp chilli powder

2.5ml/½ tsp ground turmeric

250g/9oz canned chopped tomatoes, with their juice

5ml/1 tsp salt, or to taste

2.5ml/½ tsp garam masala

30ml/2 tbsp fresh coriander (cilantro) leaves, chopped, to garnish

Indian bread, to serve

1 Put the gram flour in a mixing bowl and add the remaining dumpling ingredients except the yogurt and oil. Mix well to combine, then add the yogurt.

COOK'S TIP
Ensure the parcels are completely sealed or they will be spoiled.

2 Add 50–75ml/2–2½fl oz/¼–⅓ cup water and mix until a soft dough is formed. The amount of water you use will depend on the type of yogurt and its water content.

3 Brush two pieces of foil with oil and place one half of the dough on it. Wrap and roll it into a cylindrical shape and seal by twisting the two ends to form a tight parcel. Repeat with the remaining dough.

4 Bring a large pan of water to the boil and place the parcels in it. Reduce the heat to medium, cover and cook for 20 minutes.

5 Remove the parcels from the water using tongs and set aside until they are cool enough to handle.

6 Remove the foil and allow the rolls to cool, then cut them in half. Cut each half into 1cm/½in slices. These could now be stored, covered, in the refrigerator for 24 hours, if you like.

7 Heat the oil in a wok or other suitable pan for deep-frying over a medium heat. Fry the dumpling slices for 3–4 minutes, until well browned. Drain on kitchen paper. Keep hot.

8 To make the sauce, heat the oil over a low heat and add the cinnamon, cloves and Asafoetida. Allow to sizzle for 20 seconds, then add the onion. Increase the heat to medium and fry the onion for 7 minutes, until soft. Add the coriander, chilli and turmeric.

9 Cook for 1 minute, then add the tomatoes. Continue to cook until the tomato juice evaporates, then add 30ml/2 tbsp water. Cook for 2 minutes, then add a further 30ml/2 tbsp water and cook for 2 minutes.

10 Add 500ml/17fl oz/generous 2 cups lukewarm water and simmer, uncovered, for 8–10 minutes. Switch off the heat and add the fried dumpling slices. Stir gently, transfer to a serving dish and garnish with coriander. Serve with any Indian bread.

Per portion Energy 457kcal/1915kJ; Protein 19g; Carbohydrate 47g, of which sugars 10g; Fat 24g, of which saturates 3g; Cholesterol 4mg; Calcium 268mg; Fibre 11.5g; Sodium 1217mg.

Chickpeas in onion-scented tomato sauce

Ghughni is the most popular street food in Kolkata. Street vendors serve it to hundreds of people every day, topped with a flat bread of some kind. It is wonderfully aromatic and packed full of protein and fibre. Traditionally, dried chickpeas are soaked and boiled until tender before cooking them in the spiced sauce, but canned chickpeas give an excellent result if you rinse them thoroughly before use.

3 Add the coriander, cumin, turmeric and chilli powder. Continue to cook for about 2 minutes, then add the tomatoes.

4 Cook for 7–8 minutes, until the tomatoes reach a paste-like consistency. Add 30–45ml/ 2–3 tbsp water during the cooking time.

SERVES 4

45ml/3 tbsp mustard oil, sunflower oil or
   light olive oil
1 large onion, finely chopped
2.5cm/1in piece of cinnamon stick
10ml/2 tsp ginger purée
10ml/2 tsp garlic purée
10ml/2 tsp ground coriander
10ml/2 tsp ground cumin
2.5ml/½ tsp ground turmeric
2.5ml/½ tsp chilli powder
150g/5oz canned chopped tomatoes
   with their juice
5ml/1 tsp salt, or to taste
675g/1½lb canned chickpeas, drained
   and well rinsed
julienne strips of fresh tomato and fresh
   red chillies, and sprigs of fresh coriander
   (cilantro), to garnish
Plain Boiled Rice (*see* page 36) and Indian
   bread, to serve

1 Heat the mustard oil over a medium heat until smoking point is reached (if using sunflower or olive oil, heat until hot) and add the onion and cinnamon stick. Stir-fry for about 15 minutes, until the onion is well browned, taking care not to burn it. Reduce the heat slightly halfway through.

2 Add the ginger and garlic and cook for 2–3 minutes.

5 Add 150ml/¼ pint/⅔ cup lukewarm water, salt and the chickpeas. Reduce the heat, cover and simmer for 5 minutes. Garnish with tomato, chilli and coriander. Serve with Plain Boiled Rice and Indian bread.

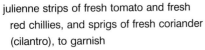

Per portion Energy 274kcal/1146kJ; Protein 10g; Carbohydrate 26g, of which sugars 5g; Fat 15g, of which saturates 2g; Cholesterol 0mg; Calcium 89mg; Fibre 1.2g; Sodium 788mg.

Vegetables and split chickpeas in spinach sauce

Sai Bhaji is the national dish of Sindh, in the Indus Valley, which is the site of the world's most ancient civilization. A selection of different vegetables mixed with split Bengal gram (channa dhal or skinless split chickpeas) are cooked together until they reach a soft, pulpy texture. A final tadka (seasoning) of browned onion, ginger, garlic and chillies completes the dish, which is served with rice and bread.

SERVES 4

125g/4½oz/¾ cup split Bengal gram
  (channa dhal or skinless split chickpeas)
225g/8oz potatoes, peeled and cut into
  2.5cm/1in cubes
125g/4½oz carrots, scraped and cut into
  2.5cm/1in chunks
1 large aubergine (eggplant), cut into
  2.5cm/1in chunks
30ml/2 tbsp dill leaves, roughly chopped
250g/9oz fresh spinach, roughly chopped
5ml/1 tsp salt, or to taste
225g/8oz canned chopped tomatoes with
  their juice
60ml/4 tbsp sunflower oil or light olive oil
1 medium onion, finely chopped
10ml/2 tsp ginger purée
10ml/2 tsp garlic purée
2 fresh green chillies, finely chopped
  (deseeded if preferred)
2.5ml/½ tsp ground turmeric
1 small tomato, cut into julienne strips,
  to garnish
Plain Boiled Rice (*see* page 36) and Indian
  bread, to serve

3 Add the spinach and salt and stir for 1–2 minutes, until the spinach has wilted. Cover the pan and cook for 10–15 minutes, then remove from the heat.

4 Mash the vegetables lightly, making sure that the potatoes are mashed well in order to thicken the sauce. Add the chopped tomatoes and return the pan to the heat. Cook for 2–3 minutes, then set aside.

5 In a separate pan, heat the oil over a medium heat and fry the onion, ginger, garlic and green chillies, stirring regularly, until the mixture begins to brown. Stir in the turmeric and add this spice mixture to the vegetables. Stir to mix thoroughly.

6 Transfer to a serving dish. Garnish with the julienne strips of tomato and serve with Plain Boiled Rice or any Indian bread.

1 Wash the split Bengal gram, transfer to a large bowl and soak in cold water for 30–60 minutes. Drain well, then put them into a pan with the potatoes, carrots, aubergine and dill.

2 Pour in 425ml/15fl oz/1¾ cups water and bring it to the boil. Reduce the heat to low, cover and simmer for 15 minutes.

Per portion Energy 336kcal/1406kJ; Protein 12.2g; Carbohydrate 42.7g, of which sugars 16g; Fat 14.1g, of which saturates 1.7g; Cholesterol 0mg; Calcium 214mg; Fibre 9.6g; Sodium 124mg.

Spiced chickpeas with cumin and coriander

The people of Punjab have mastered the art of cooking chickpeas and combining them with a fragrant mixture of spices. This dish, *Chole*, is a true delight and, served garnished with tomato, raw onion, green chilli and mint, makes a sumptuous, balanced and healthy meal.

SERVES 4

60ml/4 tbsp sunflower oil or light olive oil
10ml/2 tsp ginger purée
10ml/2 tsp garlic purée
1 large onion, finely sliced
5ml/1 tsp ground cumin
5ml/1 tsp ground coriander
2.5ml/½ tsp ground turmeric
5ml/1 tsp chilli powder
125g/4oz canned chopped tomatoes,
   with their juice
400g/14oz/3 cups canned chickpeas,
   drained and rinsed
175g/6oz boiled potatoes, cut into
   2.5cm/1in cubes
5ml/1 tsp salt or to taste
5ml/1 tsp sun-dried mango powder
   (amchur), or 22.5ml/1½ tbsp lemon juice
2.5ml/½ tsp garam masala
15ml/1 tbsp fresh coriander (cilantro)
   leaves, finely chopped
15ml/1 tbsp fresh mint leaves, chopped
Deep-fried Leavened Bread (*see* page 220)
   or any other bread, to serve

To garnish:
1 small tomato, seeded and cut into
   julienne strips
1 small onion, coarsely chopped
1 fresh green chilli, deseeded and cut into
   julienne strips
sprigs of fresh mint

1 Heat the oil over a low heat in a heavy pan and add the ginger and garlic; stir-fry for 30 seconds.

COOK'S TIP
Dried mango powder, or amchur, is made from ground dried unripe mangoes and is used in Indian cooking as a souring agent. It is much sourer than other acidity regulators, such as lemon juice, so far less is required.

2 Add the sliced onion, increase the heat to medium and fry for 6–7 minutes or until the onion is soft and beginning to colour.

3 Add the cumin, coriander, turmeric and chilli powder and stir-fry for 1 minute, then add the tomatoes. Cook for 3–4 minutes or until the oil begins to separate from the spiced tomato mixture.

4 Add the chickpeas, potatoes, salt and 150ml/5fl oz/½ cup warm water. Bring it to the boil and reduce the heat to low. Cover and simmer for 10–12 minutes.

5 Blend the sun-dried mango powder with a little water and add to the chickpeas, or add the lemon juice.

6 Stir in the garam masala, chopped coriander and mint leaves and remove the pan from the heat.

7 Transfer to a serving dish and garnish with the ingredients listed. Serve immediately with Deep-fried Leavened Bread or any other bread.

VARIATION
You could use dried chickpeas instead of canned ones, if preferred. Simply rinse, then soak in cold water overnight. Drain, then simmer in a pan of water for 1–2 hours, until tender, then use in the same way as canned ones.

Per portion Energy 300kcal/1256kJ; Protein 10.1g; Carbohydrate 33.7g, of which sugars 7.5g; Fat 15g, of which saturates 1.8g; Cholesterol 0mg; Calcium 82mg; Fibre 6.2g; Sodium 232mg.

Spiced split chickpeas with fried bread

This recipe, *Dal Pakwan*, is from Sindh, across the north-western border, a former part of India which is now in Pakistan. Comprising spiced split Bengal gram (channa dhal or skinless split chickpeas), accompanied by deep-fried bread with cumin and nigella seeds, this vegetarian meal can easily match any meat dish.

SERVES 4

For the spiced chickpeas:

250g/9oz split Bengal gram (channa dhal or skinless split chickpeas)

30ml/2 tbsp sunflower oil or light olive oil

5ml/1 tsp cumin seeds

2–3 fresh green chilies, chopped (deseeded if preferred)

5ml/1 tsp ground turmeric

2.5ml/½ tsp chilli powder

5ml/1 tsp salt, or to taste

2.5ml/½ tsp garam masala

30ml/2 tbsp fresh coriander (cilantro) leaves, chopped

For the bread:

275g/10oz/2½ cups plain (all-purpose) flour, plus extra for dusting

2.5ml/½ tsp salt

2.5ml/½ tsp sugar

2.5ml/½ tsp cumin seeds

2.5ml/½ tsp nigella seeds

30ml/2 tbsp sunflower oil or light olive oil

150ml/¼ pint/⅔ cup lukewarm water

sunflower oil, for deep-frying

1 Wash the split Bengal gram thoroughly in a sieve (strainer) under cold running water, then soak in a bowl of water for 2–3 hours. Drain well.

2 Heat the oil over a medium heat and add the cumin, chilli, turmeric and chilli powder, followed by the drained Bengal gram. Stir-fry for 2–3 minutes, then pour in 750ml/1¼ pints/3 cups warm water.

3 Bring it to the boil, cover the pan and reduce the heat to low. Simmer for 35–40 minutes or until the peas are tender.

4 Add the salt, garam masala and chopped coriander, stir to combine, then remove from the heat.

5 To make the bread: mix the flour, salt, sugar, cumin and nigella seeds in a large mixing bowl. Rub in the oil and gradually add the water, then mix until a dough is formed. You may need a little less or more water as the absorbency level of flour can differ.

6 Transfer the dough to a lightly floured surface and knead for 3–4 minutes, then cover with a damp dish towel and set aside for 30 minutes.

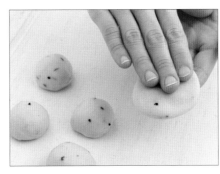

7 Divide the dough into 16 equal portions and shape them into balls, then flatten them into cakes by pressing them between your palms.

8 Heat the oil in a wok or other suitable pan for deep-frying over a medium heat. Check that the temperature is right by dropping a little of the dough into the oil. If it floats to the surface immediately without turning brown, then the temperature is just right. Alternatively, check the temperature on a thermometer; it should be at least 180°C/350°F.

9 Dust each flattened cake lightly in the flour and roll out to about a 7.5cm/3in disc. Using a fork, pierce the surface all over so that it does not puff during frying.

10 Carefully lower one bread into the hot oil using a slotted spoon and fry for about 2 minutes, until it is well browned.

11 Lift out and drain on kitchen paper. Keep warm by covering with foil while you repeat with the remaining breads.

12 Serve the breads immediately with the spiced chickpeas.

Per portion Energy 647kcal/2725kJ; Protein 21g; Carbohydrate 91g, of which sugars 25g; Fat 3g, of which saturates 25g; Cholesterol 0mg; Calcium 135mg; Fibre 9.2g; Sodium 769mg.

Chickpeas in a spice-laced yogurt sauce

The people of the Himalayan state of Himachal Pradesh are predominantly meat-eaters, but they also have some delicious vegetarian dishes, and *Channa Madra* is one of the most popular. Chickpeas are simmered in yogurt infused with cardamom and cloves, producing a beautifully fragrant sauce.

3 Add the cinnamon, green and brown cardamom, cloves, black pepper, cumin, turmeric and ginger. Stir-fry for 30 seconds.

4 Add the yogurt, increase the heat slightly and cook, stirring regularly, for 4–5 minutes.

5 Add the chickpeas, salt and sugar. Cover the pan and reduce the heat to low. Simmer for 10–12 minutes, then stir in the garam masala and remove from the heat.

6 Transfer to a serving dish, garnish with mint and serve with chapatis or *Phulkas*.

SERVES 4

300g/10oz/1¼ cups full-fat (whole) natural (plain) yogurt
10ml/2 tsp gram flour (besan)
50g/2oz/4 tbsp ghee
1.25ml/¼ tsp Asafoetida
2.5cm/1in piece cinnamon stick
4 green cardamom pods, bruised
2 brown cardamom pods, bruised
4 cloves
2.5ml/½ tsp black pepper, crushed
5ml/1 tsp ground cumin
2.5ml/½ tsp ground turmeric
15ml/1 tsp ginger purée
600g/1¼lb/4 cups canned chickpeas, drained and rinsed
5ml/1 tsp salt, or to taste
3.75ml/¾ tsp sugar
2.5ml/½ tsp garam masala
sprigs of fresh mint, to garnish
chapatis or *Phulkas* (*see* page 205), to serve

1 Whisk the yogurt and gram flour together in a bowl, then set aside.

2 Melt the ghee over a low heat and add the Asafoetida.

VARIATION
This recipe uses ghee, but sunflower oil or light olive oil would work too.

Per portion Energy 367kcal/1540kJ; Protein 15.9g; Carbohydrate 34.3g, of which sugars 7.5g; Fat 19.6g, of which saturates 7.7g; Cholesterol 8mg; Calcium 225mg; Fibre 6.2g; Sodium 392mg.

Lentils with spiced butter

North India's most famous lentil dish, *Dhal Makhani*, is made with black lentils, known as urid dhal. They are available in Indian stores and some large supermarkets. No north Indian wedding banquet or special occasion meal is complete without this fragrant and satisfying dish.

SERVES 4

175g/6oz/¾ cup whole black lentils
  (urid dhal)
10ml/2 tsp garlic purée
10ml/2 tsp ginger purée
2.5–5ml/½–1 tsp chilli powder
2–3 whole fresh green chillies
50g/2oz/⅓ cup canned red kidney beans,
  drained and rinsed
30ml/2 tbsp tomato purée (paste)
150g/5oz tomatoes, skinned and chopped
5ml/1 tsp salt, or to taste
2.5ml/½ tsp sugar
50g/2oz/4 tbsp butter
150ml/5fl oz/⅔ cup double (heavy) cream
fine julienne strips of fresh root ginger and
  fresh tomato, to garnish
naan or *Phulkas* (*see* page 205), to serve

> ## VARIATION
> If you cannot get urid dhal, try split Bengal gram (channa dhal) instead.

1 Wash the lentils in several changes of water and soak them for 3–4 hours, or overnight. Drain well and put them into a heavy pan with 600ml/1 pint/2½ cups water.

2 Bring to the boil. Add the garlic, ginger, chilli powder and chillies. Reduce the heat to low, cover and simmer for 30 minutes.

3 Mash about a quarter of the lentils with the back of a spoon in the pan.

4 Add the kidney beans, tomato purée, fresh tomatoes, salt and sugar. Stir to combine thoroughly, then cover the pan and simmer for 5–6 minutes.

5 Add the butter and cream, then simmer gently for a further 5 minutes. Serve, garnished with strips of ginger and tomato, accompanied by naan or *Phulkas*.

Per portion Energy 420kcal/1750kJ; Protein 13g; Carbohydrate 27.9g, of which sugars 4.9g; Fat 31.4g, of which saturates 18.1g; Cholesterol 78mg; Calcium 71mg; Fibre 5.5g; Sodium 184mg.

Red split lentils with mustard and cumin

In a country where the vast majority of the population is vegetarian, lentils provide all the nutrients required for a healthy diet, and regularly form part of a meal. Called dhal, dal or daail, they are cooked in different corners of the country with their own distinctive combination of spices to produce an utterly satisfying dish.

SERVES 4

115g/4oz/½ cup red split lentils
115g/4oz/½ cup yellow split lentils
  (moong or mung dhal)
2.5ml/½ tsp ground turmeric
5ml/1 tsp salt, or to taste
25g/1oz/2 tbsp ghee or unsalted butter
30ml/2 tbsp sunflower oil
2.5ml/½ tsp mustard seeds
2.5ml/½ tsp cumin seeds
2 dried red chillies, whole
2 bay leaves
1 small onion, finely chopped
30ml/2 tbsp coriander (cilantro) leaves,
  finely chopped
julienne strips of fresh tomato, to garnish
Wholemeal Flat Bread (*see* page 203)
  and/or Plain Boiled Rice (*see* page 36)

1 Wash both types of lentils thoroughly in a sieve (strainer) under cold water, then drain. Put them in a pan with the turmeric and add 1 litre/1¾ pints/4 cups water.

2 Bring to the boil and remove any froth with a spoon. Boil for 3–5 minutes.

3 Skim off any further froth, reduce the heat to low and cover the pan. Simmer for 30–35 minutes, then stir in the salt. Stir the lentils once or twice during cooking.

4 Heat the ghee or butter and oil in a pan over a medium heat until almost smoking. Turn the heat off and add the mustard and cumin seeds, followed by the chillies and bay leaves. Allow the chillies to blacken slightly, then turn the heat back up to medium.

5 Add the onion and stir-fry until the onion turns golden brown. Add all the cooked spices to the lentils and mix well.

6 Stir in the chopped coriander and remove from the heat. Serve with Wholemeal Flat Bread and/or Plain Boiled Rice.

> **COOK'S TIP**
> Don't add salt earlier in the cooking time or the lentils will be tough.

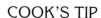

Per portion Energy 263kcal/1110kJ; Protein 15.2g; Carbohydrate 36.6g, of which sugars 2.2g; Fat 7.4g, of which saturates 1g; Cholesterol 0mg; Calcium 49mg; Fibre 3g; Sodium 24mg.

Lentils in chilli-infused coconut milk

Flavoursome lentils are combined with deep green spinach and rich coconut milk to create this simple but unforgettable dish, *Dali Ambat*. Plenty of protein and fibre in the lentils make it an excellent vegetarian main course. Serve this with boiled basmati rice for a satisfying meal.

SERVES 4

200g/7oz red split lentils

250g/9oz spinach, fresh or frozen, chopped

5ml/1 tsp ground turmeric

45ml/3 tbsp sunflower oil or light olive oil

2 dried red chillies, snipped

2.5ml/½ tsp fenugreek seeds

200ml/7fl oz/scant 1 cup canned
  coconut milk

30ml/2 tbsp tamarind juice

1 small onion, finely chopped

Plain Boiled Rice (*see* page 36), to serve

1 Wash the lentils in a sieve (strainer) in several changes of water. Drain, transfer to a pan and pour over 750ml/1¼ pints/3 cups water. Place over a high heat and bring it to the boil.

2 Boil, uncovered, for 8–9 minutes, then reduce the heat to low. Cover and simmer for 25–30 minutes, until the lentils are soft.

3 Add the spinach and turmeric, cover and simmer for 10–12 minutes.

4 Meanwhile, heat 15ml/1 tbsp of the oil in a frying pan over a low heat and fry the chillies and fenugreek seeds gently until they are a shade darker. Take care not to burn them or they will taste bitter.

5 Remove the spices from the heat, leave to cool, then crush them to a fine paste with a mortar and pestle or the back of a spoon, along with the flavoured oil.

6 Add the spice paste to the lentils and pour in the coconut milk. Add the tamarind juice, stir well and simmer for 5–7 minutes. Remove from the heat and keep hot.

7 In a separate pan, heat the remaining oil over medium heat and fry the onion for 8–10 minutes, until it begins to brown. Stir the onion into the lentils, remove from the heat and serve with Plain Boiled Rice.

Per portion Energy 319kcal/1342kJ; Protein 15g; Carbohydrate 39g, of which sugars 11g; Fat 13g, of which saturates 2g; Cholesterol 0mg; Calcium 166mg; Fibre 8.1g; Sodium 163mg.

Spicy lentils with whole-wheat rolls

From the desert region of Rajasthan, this recipe, *Dhal Baatis*, uses ghee and yogurt instead of water to make the rolls. These are then served with spiced lentils and generous amounts of ghee, which is the best choice for a traditional flavour, although sunflower oil or light olive oil can be used instead.

SERVES 4

For the baatis*:*

300g/10½oz/2½ cups wholemeal (whole-wheat) flour
50g/2oz/⅓ cup semolina
2.5ml/½ tsp baking powder
2.5ml/½ tsp salt
50g/2oz/4 tbsp ghee or unsalted butter, melted
75g/3oz/⅓ cup full-fat (whole) natural (plain) yogurt
sunflower oil, for roasting

For the dhal:

150g/5oz/scant 1 cup whole mung beans (sabut mung dhal)
75g/3oz/½ cup split Bengal gram (channa dhal or skinless split chickpeas)
5ml/1 tsp salt, or to taste
25g/1oz/2 tbsp ghee or unsalted butter
1 medium onion, finely chopped
10ml/2 tsp ginger purée
10ml/2 tsp garlic purée
2.5ml/½ tsp ground turmeric
2.5–5ml/½–1 tsp chilli powder
5ml/1 tsp ground coriander
5ml/1 tsp ground cumin
2.5ml/½ tsp garam masala
juice of 1 lime
30ml/2 tbsp fresh coriander (cilantro) leaves, chopped

1 To make the dhal: wash the mung beans and the split Bengal gram and soak them separately for 4–5 hours. Drain well.

2 To make the *baatis*: put the flour, semolina, baking powder and salt in a large mixing bowl and stir to mix. Beat the melted ghee or butter and the yogurt together and add to the flour.

3 Mix with your fingertips and gradually add 150ml/5fl oz/⅔ cup water. Mix until a dough is formed.

4 Transfer the dough to a flat surface and knead until it has absorbed all the moisture – it will be quite sticky at first.

5 Cover the dough with a damp dish towel and leave for 30 minutes. Preheat the oven to 190°C/375°F/Gas 5.

6 Shape the dough into marble-sized balls. Pour enough oil into a roasting pan to cover the base to about 5mm/¼in depth, heat it over a medium heat and add the dough balls in a single layer, spacing them apart slightly. Shake the pan so that all the balls are coated with the fat.

7 Roast in the centre of the oven for about 20 minutes, until crisp and well-browned, turning them often so they brown evenly.

8 Place the mung beans in a large pan with 1.2 litres/2 pints/5 cups water. Bring to the boil, reduce the heat to medium and partially cover the pan.

9 Cook for 10–12 minutes, then add the gram. Bring back to the boil, cover and simmer for 20–25 minutes longer. Add the salt, mash some of the beans and peas with the back of a spoon and mix well. Switch off the heat.

10 Melt the ghee or butter over a low heat and fry the onion, stirring, for 4–5 minutes until softened. Add the ginger and garlic and cook for 1 minute. Add the turmeric, chilli powder, coriander and cumin, stir-fry for about a minute and add to the cooked dhal with the garam masala, lime juice and chopped coriander. Stir to mix well and serve with the *baati*.

Per portion Energy 820kcal/3439kJ; Protein 27.6g; Carbohydrate 101.3g, of which sugars 10g; Fat 36.8g, of which saturates 11.1g; Cholesterol 2mg; Calcium 136mg; Fibre 11.2g; Sodium 300mg.

Vegetables with roasted split mung beans

A delightful dish from Tripura with definite influences from Bengal, *Shukto* is a dish in which different types of vegetables and the roasted mung beans themselves act as the main flavouring agents. Its superb taste belies the simplicity of the spicing and cooking method. Mustard oil is preferred, but other types of cooking oil can be used if liked, though the same flavour profile will not be achieved.

SERVES 4

115g/4oz skinless split mung beans
  (mung dhal)
60ml/4 tbsp mustard oil
175g/6oz carrots, peeled and cut into batons
1 turnip, peeled and cut into bitesize pieces
115g/4oz cauliflower, divided into
  2.5cm/1in florets
3–4 whole dried red chillies
2.5ml/½ tsp ground turmeric
5ml/1 tsp salt, or to taste
2.5ml/½ tsp sugar
250g/9oz baby spinach leaves
Plain Boiled Rice (*see* page 36), to serve

For the five-spice mix:

2.5ml/½ tsp black or brown mustard seeds
2.5ml/½ tsp cumin seeds
2.5ml/½ tsp nigella seeds
2.5ml/½ tsp fennel seeds
6 fenugreek seeds

1 Wash the mung beans in a sieve (strainer), then transfer to a large bowl and soak in cold water for 1–2 hours. Drain well.

2 Heat 15ml/1 tbsp of the oil in a non-stick pan over a medium heat until it reaches smoking point, then add the mung beans. Roast for 2–3 minutes, stirring regularly.

3 Reduce the heat to low and continue to roast for a further 3–4 minutes or until the mung beans are a shade darker. Transfer to a plate and set aside.

4 In the same pan, heat 30ml/2 tbsp of the remaining oil until smoking point is reached, then add the carrots and turnip.

5 Stir-fry the vegetables for 3–4 minutes, until they begin to brown, then remove with a slotted spoon and transfer to a plate, leaving behind the oil.

6 In the same oil, stir-fry the cauliflower florets for 3–4 minutes, until brown patches appear, then remove with a slotted spoon and add to the other browned vegetables on the plate.

7 Add the remaining oil to the pan and heat until smoking point is reached.

8 Switch off the heat source and add the five-spice mix, immediately followed by the dried red chillies and the ground turmeric. Cook for 2–3 minutes, until the chillies blacken and the five-spice mix releases its aroma.

9 Add the roasted mung beans, salt, sugar, carrots and turnips and pour in 400ml/14fl oz/1¾ cups water and bring it to the boil.

10 Reduce the heat to low, cover the pan and simmer for 10 minutes. Add the cauliflower, cover and simmer for 5 minutes.

11 Add the spinach and stir over a medium heat until the spinach has wilted. Cook, uncovered, for 2–3 minutes. Remove from the heat and serve with Plain Boiled Rice.

Per portion Energy 196kcal/809kJ; Protein 5g; Carbohydrate 9g, of which sugars 8g; Fat 16g, of which saturates 2g; Cholesterol 0mg; Calcium 156mg; Fibre 6.4g; Sodium 600mg.

Garlic-flavoured mung beans

Khar is made in a variety of ways in Assam and is always served at the beginning of a meal, as it is believed to aid digestion. However, it is not really an appetizer, but part of the main meal. Bicarbonate of soda (baking soda) is used here to replace the traditional ingredient of banana tree trunk ashes, known as *kharoni*.

2 Heat 45ml/3 tbsp of the mustard oil over a medium heat, until it reaches smoking point. Switch off the heat and add the fenugreek. When the seeds go a shade darker, add the garlic, half the ginger and the red and green chillies.

3 Turn the heat back on to medium and stir-fry the ingredients for 1–2 minutes.

4 Drain the soaked mung beans and add them to the pan. Stir-fry for 3–4 minutes, then add the bicarbonate of soda and salt.

5 Pour in 600ml/1 pint/2½ cups warm water and bring the mixture to the boil. Reduce the heat and cook for 12–15 minutes or until the beans are tender.

6 Add the diced courgette and cook for a further 4–5 minutes. Remove the pan from the heat and add the remaining mustard oil and ginger. Stir well to combine thoroughly, then transfer to a serving dish and serve with Plain Boiled Rice.

SERVES 4

225g/8oz/1½ cups whole mung beans
(sabut mung dhal)
60ml/4 tbsp mustard oil
8–10 fenugreek seeds
4–5 large garlic cloves, crushed
8cm/3in piece of fresh root ginger, grated
1 fresh red chilli, sliced diagonally
(deseeded if preferred)
1 fresh green chilli, sliced diagonally
(deseeded if preferred)
2.5ml/½ tsp bicarbonate of soda
(baking soda)
5ml/1 tsp salt, or to taste
1 courgette (zucchini), finely diced
Plain Boiled Rice (*see* page 36), to serve

1 Wash the mung beans in several changes of water, then transfer them to a large bowl, cover with cold water and soak them for 6–8 hours or overnight.

Per portion Energy 268kcal/1125kJ; Protein 13.5g; Carbohydrate 27g, of which sugars 1.5g; Fat 12.6g, of which saturates 1.6g; Cholesterol 0mg; Calcium 70mg; Fibre 8.8g; Sodium 13mg.

Mung beans with mustard, ginger and yogurt

This dish, *Khatte Sabut Mung*, comprises green mung beans with flecks of red chillies, spiced with mustard, fresh root ginger and cumin, and served with a creamy yogurt sauce. The sauce is made with just yogurt, with no added water or stock, and it is important that it is whisked well beforehand to prevent it curdling.

SERVES 4

225g/8oz/1¼ cups whole mung beans (sabut mung dhal)
60ml/4 tbsp sunflower oil or light olive oil
5ml/1 tsp cumin seeds
2 whole dried red chillies
1 medium onion, finely chopped
2.5cm/1in piece of fresh root ginger, grated
1 fresh green chilli, finely chopped (deseeded if preferred)
2.5ml/½ tsp ground turmeric
5ml/1 tsp salt, or to taste
200g/7oz/scant 1 cup Greek (US strained plain) yogurt
30ml/3 tsp English (hot) mustard
15ml/1 tbsp lime juice
Ginger and Cumin Puffed Bread with Spinach (*see* pages 216–17), to serve

1 Wash the mung beans, then drain and soak in water for 6–8 hours or overnight. Drain the beans and put them in a pan with 450ml/15fl oz/scant 2 cups water. Bring to the boil and skim off any froth.

2 Cook on a medium heat for 12–15 minutes. Stir as the water evaporates, reduce the heat to low and cook for 5 minutes longer. The beans should remain whole and about 30–45ml/2–3 tbsp liquid should remain. Remove from the heat and set aside.

3 Heat the oil over a medium heat and add the cumin seeds and red chillies. Allow the chillies to blacken. Add the onion, ginger and green chilli.

4 Stir-fry for 5–7 minutes, until the onion begins to brown. Add the turmeric, salt and the beans, and stir to combine thoroughly.

5 Whisk the yogurt until smooth, then add to the bean mixture.

6 Reduce the heat to low, add the mustard and cook for 4–5 minutes. Stir in the lime juice and remove from the heat.

7 Serve with Ginger and Cumin-flavoured Puffed Bread with Spinach.

Per portion Energy 334kcal/1403kJ; Protein 17.3g; Carbohydrate 39.1g, of which sugars 10.8g; Fat 13.5g, of which saturates 1.8g; Cholesterol 1mg; Calcium 190mg; Fibre 10.2g; Sodium 57mg.

Black-eyed beans in coconut and tamarind sauce

This recipe, *Feijoada*, originates from the Christian community of Goa. The black-eyed beans (peas) are packed with protein and other nutrients that provide a well-balanced vegetarian diet. Ginger, garlic, chilli and onions make up the flavours of the sauce, which is enriched with coconut milk and the tart taste of tamarind.

SERVES 4

700g/1¼lb/4½ cups canned black-eyed
  beans (peas), rinsed and drained
400ml/14fl oz/1½ cups coconut milk
5ml/1 tsp salt, or to taste
5ml/1 tsp tamarind concentrate or
  22.5ml/1½ tbsp lemon juice
5ml/1 tsp gram flour (besan)
60ml/4 tbsp sunflower oil or light olive oil
1 large onion, finely chopped
10ml/2 tsp ginger purée
10ml/2 tsp garlic purée
10ml/2 tsp ground coriander
5ml/1 tsp ground turmeric
5–7.5ml/1–1½ tsp chilli powder
toasted flaked coconut, to garnish
Plain Boiled Rice (*see* page 36), to serve

1 Put the rinsed, drained black-eyed beans in a large pan and pour in the coconut milk, salt and tamarind concentrate, if using. If you are using lemon juice instead of tamarind concentrate, do not add it yet. Stir to combine.

2 Blend the gram flour with 10ml/2 tsp water, making sure there are no lumps, and add it to the beans. Stir over a low heat and let it simmer for 5–6 minutes.

3 Meanwhile, heat the oil in a small pan over a medium heat and add the onion. Fry, stirring often, for 5–7 minutes, until the onion begins to brown.

4 Add the ginger and garlic and continue to cook for a further 2–3 minutes, stirring frequently. Add the coriander, turmeric and chilli powder and cook for 1 minute longer.

5 Add the onion and spice mixture to the beans. If you are using lemon juice instead of tamarind concentrate, add it at this stage. Stir well to combine everything thoroughly.

6 Remove the pan from the heat and transfer the mixture to a serving dish. Garnish with the toasted flaked coconut and serve with Plain Boiled Rice.

Per portion Energy 354kcal/1487kJ; Protein 14.3g; Carbohydrate 48.9g, of which sugars 19.6g; Fat 12.7g, of which saturates 1.7g; Cholesterol 0mg; Calcium 193mg; Fibre 13g; Sodium 797mg.

Savoury sago with chilli, coconut and peanut

Sago is a very underused ingredient, and this recipe, known as *Sabudana Khichdi*, will surprise as well as delight your palate. It is delicious and very quick to make once you have soaked, drained and rinsed the sago. It makes a very satisfying main meal and the peanuts add plenty of protein to the dish.

SERVES 4

275g/10oz sago
200g/7oz potatoes
25g/1oz/2 tbsp unsalted butter
15ml/1 tbsp sunflower oil or light olive oil
5ml/1 tsp cumin seeds
1 medium onion, finely chopped
2 fresh green or red chillies, chopped
  (deseeded if preferred)
50g/2oz desiccated (dry unsweetened
  shredded) coconut
salt, to taste
115g/4oz roasted, unsalted peanuts, crushed
30ml/2 tbsp fresh coriander (cilantro)
  leaves, chopped

1 Soak the sago in water for 45 minutes, then drain and rinse. Leave to drain.

2 Peel the potatoes, then cut them into 2.5cm/1in dice. Soak for about 10 minutes, then drain and dry with a clean dish towel.

3 Heat the butter and oil over a medium heat and add the cumin seeds.

4 When they pop, add the potatoes and onion. Cook them for about 8 minutes, until they begin to brown slightly. Add the chillies and coconut, and cook, stirring, for about 1 minute.

5 Pour in 120ml/4fl oz/½ cup water and cook for 6 minutes, until the potatoes are tender.

6 Add the sago and salt to the pan. Stir and cook for 5 minutes, stirring frequently until the sago is heated through.

7 Add the crushed peanuts and the chopped coriander. Stir to mix well, remove from the heat and transfer to a serving dish. Serve immediately.

Per portion Energy 567kcal/2384kJ; Protein 10g; Carbohydrate 81g, of which sugars 5g; Fat 25g, of which saturates 10g; Cholesterol 0mg; Calcium 47mg; Fibre 6.1g; Sodium 111mg.

Egg, potato and green pea curry

In this classic dish, *Dimer Dalna*, hard-boiled eggs and cubed boiled potatoes are flavoured with turmeric and chilli powder, then shallow-fried to a rich golden colour before being simmered in an aromatic sauce. The jade-green peas, golden eggs and potato cubes doused in a rich-red sauce create a strikingly beautiful dish. Luchi are the traditional accompaniment to this curry, but you can use any Indian bread.

SERVES 4

4 hard-boiled eggs
350g/12oz medium-sized potatoes, peeled and quartered
60ml/4 tbsp sunflower oil or light olive oil
2.5ml/½ tsp ground turmeric
2.5ml/½ tsp chilli powder
2.5cm/1in piece of cinnamon stick
4 green cardamom pods, bruised
4 cloves
2 bay leaves
1 large onion, finely chopped
5ml/1 tsp ground coriander
2.5ml/½ tsp ground cumin
1 ripe tomato, skinned and chopped
5ml/1 tsp salt, or to taste
2.5ml/½ tsp sugar
115g/4oz/1 cup frozen peas
2.5ml/½ tsp garam masala
Indian bread, to serve

1 Shell the eggs and make four small slits in each without cutting them right through.

2 Wash the potatoes to remove the starch and dry them with a cloth.

3 Heat the oil over a low heat and add 1.25ml/¼ tsp each of the turmeric and chilli powder, followed by the whole eggs.

4 Stir the eggs around for 3–4 minutes, until they are coloured by the spices and develop a light golden crust.

5 Remove the eggs with a slotted spoon and set them aside on a piece of kitchen paper to absorb any excess oil.

6 Add the potatoes to the same oil and increase the heat to medium. Stir-fry them for 4–5 minutes, until they are well browned and develop a light golden crust. Remove them with a slotted spoon, leaving behind as much oil as possible in the pan, and drain on kitchen paper.

7 Reduce the heat to low and add the cinnamon, cardamom, cloves and bay leaves to the oil remaining in the pan, and fry them for a few seconds.

8 Add the onion, increase the heat to medium, and fry for 9–10 minutes, until the onion is golden brown.

9 Reduce the heat to low, then add the ground coriander and cumin and the remaining turmeric and chilli powder.

10 Stir-fry for 1 minute, then add the tomato and continue to cook for 1–2 minutes.

11 Add the browned potatoes, salt and sugar and pour in 250ml/9fl oz/1 cup warm water. Bring the mixture to the boil, cover the pan and reduce the heat to low. Cook for 8–10 minutes, until the potatoes are almost cooked.

12 Add the peas, cover the pan and cook for 5–6 minutes longer, until the potatoes are tender and the peas are cooked.

13 Stir in the garam masala and remove from the heat. Serve with your favourite Indian bread.

COOK'S TIP
To save time, omit skinning the tomato before chopping it, although the dish will not look as good.

Per portion Energy 316kcal/1317kJ; Protein 11.9g; Carbohydrate 29g, of which sugars 9.3g; Fat 18g, of which saturates 3.1g; Cholesterol 190mg; Calcium 79mg; Fibre 4.2g; Sodium 87mg.

Eggs on spiced potatoes

The inspiration for this recipe, *Sali Pur Eeda*, comes from the wonderful culinary repertoire of the Parsis, a people who migrated to India centuries ago from their homeland in Persia. This is a healthier version of the original recipe as the potatoes are shallow-fried rather than deep-fried.

SERVES 4

700g/1½lb potatoes

60ml/4 tbsp sunflower oil or light olive oil

1 medium onion, finely chopped

1–2 fresh green chillies, finely chopped (deseeded if preferred)

5ml/1 tsp salt, or to taste

15g/½oz fresh coriander (cilantro) leaves and stalks, finely chopped

4 large (US extra large) eggs

1.25ml/¼ tsp chilli powder or paprika

1.25ml/¼ tsp ground cumin

chapatis or pooris, to serve

VARIATION

For a really luxurious treat, use duck eggs instead of hen's eggs.

1 Peel the potatoes and slice them thinly. Cut the slices into strips about the size of thin French fries. Rinse, then dry with a cloth.

2 In a non-stick pan with a lid, heat the oil over a medium heat and fry the onion and chillies for 5–7 minutes, until the onions begin to brown.

3 Add the potatoes and salt to the onion mixture. Stir and mix well.

4 Cover and cook for 10–12 minutes. Stir occasionally and reduce the heat for the last 2–3 minutes. The potatoes should brown slightly.

5 Stir in the chopped coriander. Spread out the mixture and smooth the surface by gently pressing down with a spoon.

6 Break the eggs on top of the potatoes, spacing them out evenly.

7 Reduce the heat to low, cover the pan and cook for 6–7 minutes or until the eggs are set. Remove the pan from the heat and sprinkle the chilli powder or paprika and cumin over the surface.

8 Serve with a wide spatula or fish slice so that you can pick up a portion of potato and one egg together. Serve with chapatis or pooris.

Per portion Energy 303kcal/1270kJ; Protein 9.6g; Carbohydrate 29.7g, of which sugars 3.2g; Fat 17.2g, of which saturates 3.1g; Cholesterol 190mg; Calcium 52mg; Fibre 2.2g; Sodium 91mg.

Spiced aubergine with hard-boiled egg

Khagina is similar to the north-Indian dish *bharta*, but the addition of hard-boiled eggs makes all the difference in taste, texture and appearance. In days gone by, it graced many tables of the British-influenced clubs in Kolkata (formerly Calcutta) and it remains a favourite dish in most of these establishments.

SERVES 4

1 aubergine (eggplant), about 350g/12oz
45ml/3 tbsp sunflower oil or light olive oil
2.5ml/½ tsp mustard seeds
2.5ml/½ tsp fennel seeds
2.5ml/½ tsp nigella seeds
1 medium onion, finely chopped
5ml/1 tsp ginger purée
1 fresh green chilli, chopped
2.5ml/½ tsp ground turmeric
2.5ml/½ tsp ground cumin
1 ripe tomato, skinned and chopped
2 hard-boiled eggs, roughly chopped
15g/½oz fresh coriander (cilantro) leaves
  and stalks, roughly chopped
2.5ml/½ tsp salt
strips of naan or crackers, to serve

1 Preheat the grill (broiler) to high and make two small incisions in the aubergine. Rub with oil, place 15cm/6in below the heat source and grill (broil) for 8–10 minutes, turning it over halfway through. Remove from the heat and leave to cool.

2 When the aubergine is cool enough to handle, slit it lengthways into two halves and scrape out the flesh with a knife or a spoon. Discard the skin and chop the flesh finely.

VARIATION
Top the dish with stir-fried cubes of paneer (Indian cheese).

3 Heat the oil over a medium heat and add the mustard seeds; as soon as they start popping, add the fennel and nigella seeds. Sizzle for 15–20 seconds.

4 Add the onion, ginger and chilli. Stir-fry for 5–7 minutes, until the onion browns.

5 Add the turmeric and cumin and stir-fry for 30–40 seconds.

6 Add the aubergine and the tomato, and stir-fry for 1–2 minutes, then add the eggs, coriander and salt. Cook for 1 minute. Serve with strips of naan or on crackers.

Per portion Energy 173kcal/719kJ; Protein 6g; Carbohydrate 10.6g, of which sugars 6.6g; Fat 12.4g, of which saturates 2g; Cholesterol 95mg; Calcium 62mg; Fibre 3.2g; Sodium 44mg.

South Indian fried eggs

This delicious vegetarian dish, *Dakshini Andey*, originates from Kerala and is based on a recipe known locally as 'egg roast'. The 'roast' is, in fact, hard-boiled eggs, which are fried with spices until browned. This version includes potatoes to make a more substantial meal.

3 Heat the oil over a low heat in a non-stick frying pan, and add the cumin, chilli powder and turmeric, followed by the eggs. Stir for 2–3 minutes, until the eggs have developed a light crust. Add salt and remove from the pan. Keep hot while you fry the potatoes.

4 In the same oil, fry the potatoes over a medium heat, stirring regularly until they begin to brown. Add salt to taste.

5 Return the eggs to the pan and stir in the coriander. Remove from the heat and serve.

SERVES 4

350g/12oz waxy potatoes
4 hard-boiled eggs, shelled
30ml/2 tbsp sunflower oil or light olive oil
2.5ml/½ tsp ground cumin
1.25ml/¼ tsp chilli powder
1.25ml/¼ tsp ground turmeric
salt, to taste
30ml/2 tbsp fresh coriander (cilantro) leaves, finely chopped

COOK'S TIP
Slitting the eggs enables the spices to permeate them fully.

1 Parboil the potatoes without skinning them, then cool, peel and cut them into wedges.

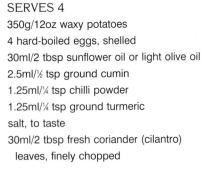

2 Make four slits lengthways on each egg, taking care not to cut them right through.

Per portion Energy 199kcal/831kJ; Protein 8.5g; Carbohydrate 15.8g, of which sugars 1.1g; Fat 12g, of which saturates 2.4g; Cholesterol 190mg; Calcium 43mg; Fibre 0.9g; Sodium 81mg.

Duck eggs with cauliflower

Duck eggs are very popular in the north-east of India, but hen's eggs are also perfectly suitable here. This dish, *Hahor Koni Aru Phoolkobi*, was created by my mother and includes lightly spiced cauliflower florets and golden eggs accentuated with fresh chillies and coriander (cilantro) leaves.

SERVES 4

1 medium-sized cauliflower, about 450g/1lb, divided into 2.5cm/1in florets

iced water

45ml/3 tbsp sunflower oil or light olive oil

2.5ml/½ tsp black mustard seeds

5ml/1 tsp cumin seeds, lightly crushed

5ml/1 tsp coriander seeds, lightly crushed

2.5ml/½ tsp nigella seeds

1 medium onion, finely sliced

1–2 fresh green chillies, finely chopped (deseeded if preferred)

5ml/1 tsp ground turmeric

2.5ml/½ tsp salt, or to taste

30ml/2 tbsp fresh coriander (cilantro) leaves, finely chopped

4 duck eggs, beaten

Wholemeal Flat Bread (*see* page 203) and/or Plain Boiled Rice (*see* page 36) and Red Split Lentils with Mustard and Cumin (*see* page 124), to serve

1 Blanch the cauliflower florets in boiling salted water for 3 minutes, drain, then immediately plunge in iced water.

2 Heat the oil in a non-stick wok or a frying pan over a medium heat. When hot, but not smoking, add the mustard seeds, and as soon as they pop, add the cumin, coriander and nigella seeds.

3 Let the seeds crackle for a few seconds, then add the onion and chillies and stir-fry for about 5 minutes, until the onion is soft, but not brown. Add the turmeric.

4 Drain the cauliflower florets and add them to the pan along with the salt. Stir-fry for 3–4 minutes, until the cauliflower is heated through, then add the chopped coriander and stir to combine.

5 Pour over the egg and leave it to set for 2 minutes, then stir to coat the cauliflower. Serve immediately with Wholemeal Flat Breads and/or Plain Boiled Rice and Red Split Lentils with Mustard and Cumin.

Per portion Energy 264kcal/1095kJ; Protein 16.1g; Carbohydrate 7.9g, of which sugars 4.5g; Fat 19g, of which saturates 3.5g; Cholesterol 509mg; Calcium 90mg; Fibre 2.5g; Sodium 103mg.

Indian cheese balls

The Indian cheese known as paneer in the rest of the country is called sana in north-east India and Bengal. In this recipe, *Sanar Kofta*, grated Indian cheese is mixed with mashed potatoes and a few chosen spices, formed into small balls and browned before being simmered in a spicy sauce.

SERVES 4

225g/8oz/2 cups paneer (Indian cheese), coarsley grated
200g/7oz/1 cup cooked potatoes, mashed
10ml/2 tsp ginger purée
1 fresh green chilli, chopped
2.5ml/½ tsp garam masala
1 egg, beaten
30ml/2 tbsp fresh coriander (cilantro) leaves, finely chopped
7.5ml/1½ tsp salt, or to taste
60ml/4 tbsp sunflower oil or light olive oil
4 green cardamom pods, bruised
2.5cm/1in piece of cinnamon stick
1 large onion, finely chopped
5ml/1 tsp garlic purée
2.5ml/½ tsp ground turmeric
2.5–5ml/½–1 tsp chilli powder
5ml/1 tsp ground coriander
5ml/1 tsp ground cumin
150g/5oz frozen garden peas
3–4 whole fresh green chillies
Plain Boiled Rice (*see* page 36), to serve

1 Mix together the paneer, potatoes, 5ml/1 tsp of the ginger, the chilli, garam masala, egg, coriander and half the salt in a bowl.

2 With dampened hands, make about 16 equal-sized balls from the mixture.

COOK'S TIP
Paneer provides as much protein per portion as meat, fish and poultry.

3 Heat 30ml/2 tbsp of the oil in a non-stick pan over a medium heat and brown the cheese balls. Drain on kitchen paper.

4 Add the remaining oil to the pan and stir in the cardamom and cinnamon. Let them sizzle for a few seconds, then add the onion and fry until it is beginning to brown.

5 Add the ginger and the garlic. Cook for 1 minute. Add the turmeric, chilli powder, coriander and cumin. Fry for 1 minute.

6 Pour in 300ml/10fl oz/1¼ cups warm water and add the remaining salt. Bring the mixture to the boil and cook over a medium heat for 2–3 minutes.

7 Add the browned cheese balls in a single layer and spoon over some of the sauce. Add the peas and whole chillies, reduce the heat to low, and cook for 5–6 minutes or until the sauce has thickened to the desired consistency. Serve with Plain Boiled Rice.

Per portion Energy 263kcal/1097kJ; Protein 12.2g; Carbohydrate 20.4g, of which sugars 8.8g; Fat 15.5g, of which saturates 3g; Cholesterol 55mg; Calcium 89mg; Fibre 2.3g; Sodium 242mg.

Sweet peppers with Indian cheese and cumin

Paneer (Indian cheese) has a bland taste, but it absorbs other flavours well and adds much-needed protein as well as texture to a dish. In this north Indian recipe, *Shimla Mirch Aur Paneer Ka Salan*, it is combined with the warmth of roasted cumin, and further enhanced by the taste and aroma of roasted (bell) peppers and garlic.

SERVES 4

1 large green (bell) pepper
1 large red pepper
7.5ml/1½ tsp cumin seeds
30ml/2 tbsp sunflower oil or light olive oil
3–4 large cloves of garlic, crushed
2.5ml/½ tsp chilli powder
2.5ml/½ tsp salt, or to taste
225g/8oz paneer (Indian cheese), cut into
  2.5cm/1in cubes
30ml/2 tbsp chives, snipped
Indian bread or Plain Boiled Rice (*see* page
  36) and a vegetable curry, to serve

1 Preheat the grill (broiler) to high. Place the peppers on a grill pan and position it 15cm/6in below the heat source. Grill (broil) the peppers for 8–10 minutes, until the skin is charred, turning them over frequently. Put them in a plastic bag and set aside for 20–25 minutes.

4 Heat the oil over a low heat and fry the garlic for 2 minutes, until it is just beginning to brown. Add the chilli powder, salt and paneer. Stir gently and cook for 2–3 minutes.

5 Add the crushed cumin and the prepared peppers along with any reserved juice. Stir until the peppers are heated through, then stir in the chives. Serve with any bread or Plain Boiled Rice and a vegetable curry.

2 Pull off the skin, deseed the the peppers and remove the pith. Cut the flesh into 2.5cm/1in strips. Reserve any juices.

3 Meanwhile, dry-roast the cumin seeds in a small, heavy pan over a medium heat for 1 minute, until they are a shade darker and release their aroma. Leave to cool, then crush in a mortar and pestle or with the back of a wooden spoon.

VARIATION

You could use halloumi instead of paneer (Indian cheese), if preferred. If using, omit the salt in step 4.

Per portion Energy 259kcal/1067kJ; Protein 3g; Carbohydrate 5g, of which sugars 4g; Fat 26g, of which saturates 12g; Cholesterol 36mg; Calcium 58mg; Fibre 1.9g; Sodium 368mg.

Indian cheese curry in milk

This recipe, *Sana Thongba*, comes from the state of Manipur and makes a satisfying meal when served with rice. It contains garden peas and potatoes along with cubes of cheese and the entire dish is cooked in milk, making it protein-rich, creamy and nutritious as well as delicious.

SERVES 4

30ml/2 tbsp sunflower oil or light olive oil
2 bay leaves
10ml/2 tsp ginger purée
10ml/2 tsp garlic purée
1 fresh green chilli, finely chopped
2.5ml/½ tsp ground turmeric
5ml/1 tsp ground coriander
2.5ml/½ tsp ground cumin
2.5ml–5ml/½–1 tsp chilli powder
200g/7oz paneer (Indian cheese)
150g/5oz frozen peas or fresh peas
250g/9oz potatoes
2.5cm/1in piece of cinnamon stick
2.5ml/½ tsp salt, or to taste
600ml/1 pint/2½ cups full-fat (whole) milk
2.5ml/½ tsp garam masala
a mixture of wild and basmati rice,
  to serve

1 Heat the oil in a large, non-stick pan over a low heat and add the bay leaves, ginger, garlic and chilli. Fry gently for 3–4 minutes, until the garlic softens but does not brown.

2 Add the turmeric, coriander, cumin and chilli powder. Stir and cook for 2 minutes.

3 Meanwhile, cut the paneer into 2.5cm/1in cubes. Set aside.

VARIATION
For a richer version, substitute half the milk with double (heavy) cream.

4 Put the peas in a bowl, cover with boiling water and leave until tender. Drain.

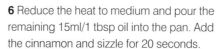

5 Peel the potatoes, then cut them into 2.5cm/1in chunks.

6 Reduce the heat to medium and pour the remaining 15ml/1 tbsp oil into the pan. Add the cinnamon and sizzle for 20 seconds.

7 Add the potatoes, salt and milk and stir to combine. Bring to the boil, reduce the heat to low and simmer, uncovered, for 20 minutes, stirring often.

8 Add the paneer and peas and simmer for 6–7 minutes. Stir in the garam masala and remove from the heat. Serve with a mixture of wild and basmati rice.

COOK'S TIP
Wild rice is particularly beneficial in a vegetarian diet because it is high in protein, unlike true rice, which contains incomplete proteins. It provides useful amounts of the essential amino acid, lysine, which is a building block of protein in the body. It also aids calcium absorption and is involved in the production of various hormones, enzymes and antibodies.

Per portion Energy 378kcal/1566kJ; Protein 10g; Carbohydrate 22g, of which sugars 8g; Fat 29g, of which saturates 14g; Cholesterol 50mg; Calcium 235mg; Fibre 3.6g; Sodium 413mg.

Cinnamon and clove-scented cheese curry

Paneer (Indian cheese) is a great source of protein and the vast majority of the Indian population thrive on this versatile ingredient. In this dish, *Channer Dalna*, melt-in-the-mouth cubes of cheese and tender pieces of potato are bathed in a fragrant spiced sauce to create a memorable vegetarian curry.

SERVES 4

60ml/4 tbsp sunflower oil or light olive oil
225g/8oz/2 cups paneer (Indian cheese),
    cut into 2.5cm/1in cubes
400g/14oz potatoes, peeled and cut into
    2.5cm/1in cubes
2.5cm/1in piece of cinnamon stick
4 green cardamom pods, bruised
4 cloves
1 large onion, finely chopped
5ml/1 tsp ginger purée
5ml/1 tsp garlic purée
2.5ml/½ tsp ground turmeric
2.5–5ml/½–1 tsp chilli powder
2.5ml/½ tsp ground cumin
5ml/1 tsp salt, or to taste
2.5ml/½ tsp garam masala
15ml/1 tbsp fresh coriander (cilantro)
    leaves, chopped
Indian bread, to serve

4 Cook for 5–6 minutes until the onion has softened, then add the ginger and garlic and fry until the onion is beginning to brown. Add the turmeric, chilli powder and cumin and cook for about 1 minute.

5 Add 30ml/2 tbsp water, and cook until the mixture is dry and the water has evaporated. Repeat this process twice more, adding 30ml/2tbsp water each time (90ml/6 tbsp water in all).

8 Add the browned paneer, stir gently to combine and increase the heat to medium. Cook, uncovered, for 6 minutes or until the sauce has thickened.

9 Stir in the garam masala and coriander. Transfer to a serving dish and serve with any Indian bread.

1 Heat half the oil in a non-stick pan over a medium heat and brown the cubes of paneer. Stand well away from the pan while frying the paneer as it tends to splutter. Drain the cubes on kitchen paper.

2 Dry the cubes of potato with a cloth and brown them in the same oil. Drain on kitchen paper.

3 Add the remaining oil to the pan. Reduce the heat to low. Add the cinnamon, cardamom and cloves. Sizzle for 30 seconds, until the cardamom pods have puffed up. Add the onion and increase the heat slightly.

6 Add the potatoes, salt and 250ml/9fl oz/ 1 cup warm water to the pan.

7 Bring to the boil, reduce the heat to low, cover the pan and simmer for 10 minutes, stirring occasionally.

VARIATION

This curry is also delicious served with Plain Boiled Rice (*see* page 36) or Yellow Rice (*see* page 150).

Per portion Energy 280kcal/1170kJ; Protein 11.5g; Carbohydrate 28.5g, of which sugars 9.5g; Fat 14.2g, of which saturates 2.9g; Cholesterol 7mg; Calcium 85mg; Fibre 2.8g; Sodium 230mg.

Rice Dishes

A very important part of the Indian diet, rice is eaten daily in many parts of the country – as an accompaniment to curries, with a range of small side dishes and as the main dish itself. Cooked with combinations of spices and the addition of fresh vegetables, nuts and even dried fruits, there is a huge range of different variations on offer, from simple steamed side dishes to sustaining and colourful pilau dishes.

Fragrant, filling and versatile

Rice originated as a form of grass in Thailand and north-east India where, over time, it was cultivated, harvested and transported to other parts of south-east Asia. Initially, in India, its production was mainly confined to monsoon-fed areas or near rivers and delta areas, where conditions were best suited to its requirements. Today, however, with the advent of modern farming methods, rice is grown all over India, although the country's diverse geographical and climatic conditions still have a profound influence on the type of crop grown in each region. In the snow-fed foothills of the Himalayas in northern India, for instance, the exquisite basmati rice (meaning 'the fragrant one') is grown in abundance, while in southern India a variety called *ambey mohur*, which means 'mango-like fragrance', is more commonly cultivated and used.

Rice is considered sacred in India and is required for every religious ritual. A symbol of wealth, it is thrown at a newly wed couple in much the same way that confetti is strewn in the West, wishing them great riches in their married life. In addition, before a new bride enters her husband's home, a bowl of rice is placed at the door. The bride has to gently kick it so that the grains are scattered on the floor, symbolizing the good fortune she is bringing to her new house.

Half the population of India eats rice on a daily basis, usually simply served boiled and accompanied by curries of various types. Pilaus and biryanis are generally cooked only for celebrations and other special occasions. Long grain rice, of which there are several varieties, is the usual choice for serving with curries and for making savoury dishes. Among the long grain types, basmati is universally popular. Short grain rice is used to make desserts, or ground to create rice flour, which is used in batters and sweet dishes.

Rice always requires a little preparation before it is cooked in order to achieve perfect results. Firstly, weigh the rice accurately and then wash it in cold water, rubbing the grains gently, until the water runs clear. Secondly, soak the rice in cold water for 20–30 minutes, then leave it to drain completely in a sieve (strainer). Next, transfer the rice to a large, heavy pan with a tight-fitting lid. The slender grains expand considerably once cooked, so to allow for this, use a pan that will be two-thirds full when the rice is cooked. Measure the water accurately, following the recipe guidelines, and once the lid is on, set the timer, and never lift the lid. Finally, when the rice is cooked, switch off the heat and let the pan sit undisturbed for 15–20 minutes. After this time, simply fork through the rice and serve.

Yellow rice

Tinged with turmeric, this golden rice, *Peela Bhat*, is delicately spiced with a small quantity of cinnamon and cloves. The earthy taste and musky aroma of turmeric, combined with its health benefits, make this rice a wonderful, nutritious change from boiled rice, and it is the perfect accompaniment to any dish.

SERVES 4

225g/8oz/generous 1 cup basmati rice
15ml/1 tbsp ghee or 10ml/2 tsp butter and
  10ml/2 tsp light olive oil
2.5cm/1in piece of cinnamon stick
5 cloves
2.5ml/½ tsp ground turmeric
2.5ml/½ tsp salt, or to taste

COOK'S TIP
Be careful when using turmeric, as it can easily stain clothing.

1 Wash the rice until the water runs clear. Put it in a large bowl, cover with cold water and leave to soak for 20 minutes, then drain.

2 Heat the ghee or butter and oil over a low heat and add the cinnamon and cloves. Sizzle for 25–30 seconds, then stir in the turmeric and rice. Stir-fry for 2 minutes.

3 Pour in 450ml/16fl oz/1¾ cups warm water and add the salt. Bring it to the boil and allow to boil steadily for 2 minutes.

4 Reduce the heat to low, cover and cook for 8 minutes. Switch off the heat and let it stand undisturbed for 20–25 minutes. Fluff up the rice with a fork and serve.

Per portion Energy 239kcal/995kJ; Protein 4.3g; Carbohydrate 45.2g, of which sugars 0g; Fat 4.2g, of which saturates 1.8g; Cholesterol 0mg; Calcium 13mg; Fibre 0g; Sodium 1mg.

Turmeric-tinged rice with fried onion

Originating in the state of Karnataka, *Birinji* is a fairly uncomplicated rice dish comprising fragrant spiced rice and sweet caramelized onions. Southern Indians thrive on rice, unlike the people in the north, where the staple is bread. This rice recipe is ideal with any vegetable curry or lentil dish.

SERVES 4

225g/8oz/generous 1 cup basmati rice
45ml/3 tbsp sunflower oil or light olive oil
4 green cardamom pods, bruised
4 cloves
2.5cm/1in piece of cinnamon stick
5ml/1 tsp ground turmeric
5ml/1 tsp salt, or to taste
1 large onion, finely sliced
2.5cm/1in piece of fresh root ginger,
   finely grated
2 cloves garlic, crushed
2–3 fresh green chillies, sliced at
   an angle

1 Wash the rice in a sieve (strainer) in several changes of water, until the water runs clear, then soak in a bowl of water for 20–30 minutes. Drain and set aside.

2 Heat 15ml/1 tbsp of the oil over a low heat in a heavy pan. Add the cardamom, cloves and cinnamon and let them sizzle for 15–20 seconds.

3 Stir in the turmeric and immediately follow with the drained rice. Stir-fry the rice for 2–3 minutes, then pour in 450ml/¾ pint/ scant 2 cups lukewarm water.

4 Add the salt and bring the water to the boil. Reduce the heat to very low, cover the pan with a lid and cook very gently for 8–9 minutes.

5 Meanwhile, heat the remaining oil in a separate pan over a medium heat. Add the onion, ginger, garlic and chillies. Fry for 9–10 minutes, until the onion is caramel-brown, stirring regularly.

6 When the rice is cooked, switch off the heat and allow it to stand undisturbed for 10 minutes. Stir in the fried onion and serve.

Per portion Energy 307kcal/1290kJ; Protein 4g; Carbohydrate 49g, of which sugars 0g; Fat 12g, of which saturates 1g; Cholesterol 0mg; Calcium 15mg; Fibre 1.2g; Sodium 497mg.

Butter-flavoured rice with spiced stock

Rice is eaten throughout India, but is most popular in areas where heavy rainfall results in thriving rice crops. This wonderful dish, *Ghee Bhat*, is cooked in ghee along with a few aromatic spices. The flavour of this rice is rich, but still mild enough to go with any vegetable curry.

3 Add the remaining ghee or butter to the pan and add the onion. Increase the heat to medium and fry, stirring, until well browned.

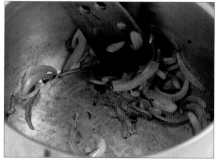

4 Remove any excess fat by pressing the onions to the side of the pan, then lift them out and drain them on kitchen paper.

5 Reduce the heat to low and add the cinnamon, cloves and bay leaves. Sizzle for 10–15 seconds, then add the drained rice and cook for 2 minutes. Pour in 450ml/ 16fl oz/ scant 2 cups hot water, add the salt, bring to the boil and cook for 2 minutes.

6 Reduce the heat to very low, cover and cook for 7–8 minutes. Switch off the heat and leave, undisturbed, for 7–8 minutes.

SERVES 4

225g/8oz/generous 1 cup basmati rice
50g/2oz/4 tbsp ghee or unsalted butter
25g/1oz raw cashew nuts
15ml/1 tbsp seedless raisins
1 large onion, finely sliced
2.5cm/1in piece of cinnamon stick
4 cloves
2 bay leaves
5ml/1 tsp salt, or to taste

1 Put the rice in a sieve (strainer) and wash it thoroughly under cold runinng water, then transfer it to a large bowl, cover with cold water and leave to soak for 20 minutes. Leave to drain in the sieve.

2 Melt half the ghee or butter over a low heat, then brown the cashew nuts. Drain on kitchen paper and set aside. Add the raisins to the pan and stir until they are plump. Drain on kitchen paper and set aside.

7 Fluff up the rice with a fork and mix in half the fried onions. Reserve a few cashews and raisins and mix the remainder into the rice.

8 Transfer to a serving dish and garnish with the remaining onion, cashews and raisins.

Per portion Energy 369kcal/1537kJ; Protein 5.8g; Carbohydrate 57.4g, of which sugars 9.6g; Fat 13g, of which saturates 5.9g; Cholesterol 0mg; Calcium 44mg; Fibre 1.8g; Sodium 6mg.

Lemon-laced rice with cardamom

Bengali lemon-laced rice, *Lebur Bhat*, is rather different from the version that is cooked in southern India. It has a more prominent lemon flavour, which smells and tastes wonderfully refreshing. Bay leaves, cardamom, cinnamon and cloves are commonly used in east India to flavour rice dishes.

SERVES 4

225g/8oz/generous 1 cup basmati rice
30ml/2 tbsp mustard oil
2.5ml/½ tsp black mustard seeds
2.5cm/1in piece of cinnamon stick
4 cardamom pods, bruised
2 cloves
1 bay leaf
25g/1oz seedless raisins
5ml/1 tsp salt, or to taste
5ml/1 tsp sugar
45ml/3 tbsp freshly squeezed
  lemon juice

3 Place the pan back over a medium heat and add the drained rice and raisins. Add the salt and sugar and cook, stirring, for 2 minutes. Pour in 450ml/16fl oz/scant 2 cups hot water and bring it to the boil.

4 Add the lemon juice, stir and reduce the heat to low. Cover and cook for 7–8 minutes without lifting the lid. Switch off the heat and leave, undisturbed, for 8–10 minutes. Fluff up the rice with a fork and serve.

1 Wash the rice until the water runs clear and then soak it for 20 minutes. Leave to drain in a sieve (strainer).

2 In a heavy pan, heat the oil until it is smoking. Remove from the heat and add the mustard seeds (covering the pan if necessary to prevent the mustard seeds from jumping out of the pan). Add the cinnamon, cardamom, cloves and bay leaf and let them sizzle for a few seconds.

Per portion Energy 294kcal/1228kJ; Protein 5.4g; Carbohydrate 52.9g, of which sugars 5.4g; Fat 6.8g, of which saturates 0.7g; Cholesterol 0mg; Calcium 28mg; Fibre 0.1g; Sodium 498mg.

Rice with aubergine, coconut and cashew nuts

This recipe, *Vangi Bhat*, is from the coastal state of Karnataka where people generally eat a range of vegetarian and seafood dishes cooked with coconut. This makes a delicious and substantial vegetarian main course. Serve with cucumber raita for a balanced meal.

SERVES 4

225g/8oz/generous 1 cup basmati rice
1 large aubergine (eggplant)
50g/2oz/4 tbsp ghee or unsalted butter
2.5cm/1in piece of cinnamon stick
5 cloves
1 large onion, finely sliced
5ml/1 tsp salt, or to taste
5ml/1 tsp garam masala
30ml/2 tbsp fresh coriander (cilantro)
  leaves, finely chopped
30ml/2 tbsp desiccated (dry unsweetened
  shredded) coconut, ground until fine
30ml/2 tbsp cashew nuts
cucumber raita, to serve

1 Wash the rice until the water runs clear. Soak in a bowl of cold water for 20 minutes and leave to drain in a sieve (strainer).

2 Cut the aubergine into quarters lengthways, then cut each quarter into 1cm/½in chunks. Soak in a bowl of cold salted water for 15–20 minutes, then rinse well.

3 Melt the ghee or butter in a heavy pan over a low heat, then add the cinnamon and cloves. Let them sizzle for 25–30 seconds.

4 Add the onion. Increase the heat slightly to medium and fry for 9–10 minutes, stirring occasionally, until the onion begins to turn a golden-brown colour.

5 Add the drained rice, aubergine, salt, garam masala and half the chopped coriander. Stir-fry gently for 2–3 minutes, then add 450ml/¾ pint/scant 2 cups lukewarm water.

6 Bring the water to the boil, reduce the heat to low, cover the pan tightly and cook for 8–9 minutes.

7 Remove the pan from the heat and gently spread the coconut and cashew nuts on top of the rice mixture, then replace the lid and leave the pan to stand, off the heat, for a further 8–10 minutes.

8 Fluff up the rice with a fork and transfer it to a serving dish. Serve garnished with the remaining chopped coriander and with some raita to accompany it.

Per portion Energy 461kcal/1932kJ; Protein 8g; Carbohydrate 62g, of which sugars 9g; Fat 22g, of which saturates 13g; Cholesterol 35mg; Calcium 72mg; Fibre 5.9g; Sodium 1000mg.

Coconut rice

This snow-white basmati rice dish, speckled with black mustard seeds and dotted with red chilli pieces, looks quite stunning, and it tastes as good as it looks. *Thengai Sadam* is best served with a simple lentil dish or a vegetable curry, as it is quite rich and very flavoursome.

SERVES 4

225g/8oz/generous 1 cup basmati rice
5ml/1 tsp salt, or to taste
50g/2oz/⅔ cup desiccated (dry unsweetened shredded) coconut
125ml/4fl oz/½ cup milk
30ml/2 tbsp sunflower oil or light olive oil
50g/2oz/½ cup raw cashew nuts
2.5ml/½ tsp black mustard seeds
15ml/1 tbsp split Bengal gram (channa dhal or skinless split chickpeas)
2–3 dried red chillies
8–10 curry leaves

1 Wash the rice until the water runs clear. Transfer to a bowl, cover with cold water and leave to soak for 20 minutes, then leave to drain in a sieve (strainer).

2 Put the rice into a heavy pan. Pour in 450ml/16fl oz/scant 2 cups hot water. Stir in the salt and bring it to the boil. Let it boil for 2 minutes, then turn the heat down to very low, cover and cook for 8 minutes.

3 Remove from the heat and let the pan stand undisturbed for 8–10 minutes.

4 Meanwhile, put the coconut into a small pan and add the milk. Stir over a low-medium heat for about 5 minutes, until the coconut has absorbed all the milk.

5 Heat the oil in a small pan over a low heat and brown the cashew nuts. Drain on kitchen paper.

6 In the same pan, increase the heat to medium and, when the oil is hot but not smoking, add the mustard seeds, split Bengal gram, chillies and curry leaves. Cook until the chillies blacken slightly.

7 Pour the entire contents of the pan over the cooked rice and add the coconut and cashew nuts. Gently mix with a fork to fluff up the rice and combine the ingredients, then serve.

Saffron-scented pilau rice

Pilau rice, sometimes studded with dried fruits such as apricots and raisins and often with nuts such as almonds, is a delicacy enjoyed in the hilly terrain of northern India. *Kesar Pulao* is a basic recipe for spicy saffron-scented rice, which provides a delicate accompaniment to so many main dishes.

SERVES 4

225g/8oz/1 cup basmati rice
a good pinch of saffron threads, pounded
30ml/2 tbsp hot milk
25g/1oz/4 tbsp ghee or unsalted butter
4 green cardamom pods, bruised
2.5cm/1in piece of cinnamon stick
4 cloves
2 star anise
2.5ml/½ tsp salt
22.5ml/1½ tbsp rose water
45ml/3 tbsp blanched almonds
chapatis or *Phulkas* (*see* page 205), to serve

1 Wash the rice in several changes of water until the water runs clear, then soak for 20–30 minutes.

2 Soak the saffron in the milk for 10 minutes.

COOK'S TIP
Pounding the saffron helps release maximum flavour and colour.

3 Melt the ghee or butter over a low heat, then add the cardamom, cinnamon, cloves and star anise. Sizzle for 30 seconds.

4 Drain the rice and add to the spiced butter. Add the salt and stir to mix well, then pour in 450ml/16fl oz/2 cups hot water and bring to the boil. Let it boil for 1–2 minutes, then reduce the heat to low, cover the pan and cook for 7–8 minutes.

5 Remove the pan from the heat, then sprinkle the saffron-infused milk and the rose water over the top.

6 Cover the pan again and let it stand for 10 minutes, without removing the lid.

7 Meanwhile, heat a heavy frying pan over a medium heat. When hot, add the almonds and toast, stirring often, for 2–3 minutes, until golden. Take care not to let the almonds burn.

8 Fluff up the rice with a fork, transfer it to a serving dish and garnish with the almonds. Serve with chapatis or *Phulkas*.

VARIATION
Add stir-fried cubes of paneer (Indian cheese) and garden peas, or rinsed canned chickpeas tossed with garlic and root ginger purée.

Per portion Energy 262kcal/1090kJ; Protein 4.4g; Carbohydrate 45.3g, of which sugars 0.4g; Fat 6.7g, of which saturates 3g; Cholesterol 0mg; Calcium 20mg; Fibre 0g; Sodium 4mg.

Vegetable pilau

Local climate and soil conditions mean that rice flourishes in Bengal, and it has become the staple diet of the people who live there. This colourful creation, *Torkarir Pulao*, made with basmati rice and fresh produce, is ideal as a vegetarian main meal. The choice of vegetables can be varied according to seasonal availability.

SERVES 4

225g/8oz/generous 1 cup basmati rice
60ml/4 tbsp sunflower oil or light olive oil
25g/1oz raw cashew nuts
25g/1oz seedless raisins
4 green cardamom pods, bruised
2.5cm/1in piece of cinnamon stick
4 cloves
2 bay leaves
1 large onion, finely sliced
5ml/1 tsp ginger purée
5ml/1 tsp garlic purée
1–2 fresh green chillies, chopped
   (deseeded if preferred)
2.5ml/½ tsp ground turmeric
75g/3oz/½ cup carrots, cut into sticks
110g/4oz baby corn, halved
75g/3oz/½ cup green beans, cut into
   2.5cm/1in lengths
5ml/1 tsp salt, or to taste
50ml/2fl oz/3 tbsp single (light) cream

1 Wash the rice in a sieve (strainer) in several changes of water until it runs clear, then soak in a bowl of cold water for 20–30 minutes. Drain and set aside.

2 In a heavy pan, heat the oil over a medium/low heat and brown the cashew nuts. Drain on kitchen paper.

> ### VARIATION
> Try blanched almonds or unsalted peanuts instead of cashew nuts.

3 Add the raisins to the oil in the pan and fry until puffed up. Drain on kitchen paper.

4 Add the cardamom, cinnamon, cloves and bay leaves to the oil and let them sizzle until the cardamoms have puffed up.

5 Add the onion, ginger, garlic and chillies, increase the heat and fry for 10 minutes, until the onion is brown, stirring regularly.

6 Stir in the turmeric and add all the vegetables and the salt. Stir and cook for 2–3 minutes.

7 Add the rice and stir-fry for 2–3 minutes, then pour in 450ml/16fl oz/1¾ cups hot water and bring it to the boil. Boil steadily for 2 minutes, then reduce the heat to low.

8 Pour the cream evenly over the rice and cover the pan tightly. Cook for 10–12 minutes. Remove from the heat and leave, undisturbed, for 8–10 minutes.

9 Fluff up the rice and serve, garnished with the nuts and raisins.

Per portion Energy 410kcal/1705kJ; Protein 8.1g; Carbohydrate 60.9g, of which sugars 12.5g; Fat 14.9g, of which saturates 2g; Cholesterol 0mg; Calcium 55mg; Fibre 3g; Sodium 343mg.

Carrot and green pea pilau

Central Indian food is an amalgamation of recipes from the neighbouring states. This recipe, *Gajjar-Mattar Ke Pulao*, though cooked elsewhere, is richer than others, perhaps as a result of the influence of a Royal household. Because of this it is more suitable as a main course than as an accompaniment.

SERVES 4

225g/8oz/generous 1 cup basmati rice
a good pinch of saffron threads, pounded
15ml/1 tbsp hot milk
2.5cm/1in piece of cinnamon stick
2 star anise
175ml/6fl oz/¾ cup full-fat (whole) milk
5ml/1 tsp salt, or to taste
5ml/1 tsp cumin seeds
10ml/2 tsp coriander seeds
5ml/1 tsp black peppercorns
50g/2oz/4 tsp ghee or unsalted butter
10ml/2 tsp ginger purée
1 fresh green chilli, chopped
  (deseeded if preferred)
175g/6oz carrots, cut into batons
110g/4oz frozen garden peas
4 cloves
4 green cardamom pods, bruised
15ml/1 tbsp seedless raisins
15ml/1 tbsp slivered almonds
raita, to serve

3 Put the rice in a heavy pan and add the steeped saffron with its soaking milk, along with the cinnamon stick and star anise.

4 Add the milk and pour in 300ml/½ pint/1¼ cups water and half the salt. Bring it to the boil, reduce the heat to very low, cover and cook for 7-8 minutes. Remove from the heat and let it stand, undisturbed, for 10 minutes.

8 Stir-fry the carrots over a medium heat for 3–4 minutes, then add 50ml/2fl oz/¼ cup water. Cover and cook over a low heat until the carrots are almost tender.

9 Add the peas, the remaining salt and the ground spices, then cover and cook for 5–6 minutes. Remove from the heat.

1 Wash the rice until the water runs clear, then soak for 20–30 minutes. Drain well.

2 Soak the saffron in the hot milk and leave to infuse for 10 minutes.

VARIATIONS
• Replace the carrot batons with thick strips of pumpkin.
• Garnish with fried onions instead of cardamom, raisins and almonds.

5 Meanwhile, heat a small, heavy pan over a medium heat, then add the cumin, coriander and peppercorns and dry-roast for about 1 minute, until they release their aroma, stirring constantly.

6 Remove from the pan and leave to cool, then crush them to a fine powder with a mortar and pestle. Set aside.

7 Heat half the ghee or butter in a frying pan over a low heat and add the ginger and green chilli. Cook for 1 minute, then add the carrots.

10 Fluff up the rice with a fork and add the cooked vegetables. Using a fork or a flat wooden spoon, stir them around gently to mix the vegetables without breaking them up, then cover the pan.

11 Melt the remaining ghee or butter over a low heat and add the cloves, cardamom, raisins and almonds. Stir and cook until the cardamom pods and the raisins swell up and the nuts are a light brown colour.

12 Transfer the pilau to a serving dish and sprinkle the spiced butter evenly on top. Garnish with the cardamom, raisins and almonds. Serve with a raita.

Per portion Energy 422kcal/1772kJ; Protein 8g; Carbohydrate 63g, of which sugars 12g; Fat 17g, of which saturates 10g; Cholesterol 42mg; Calcium 104mg; Fibre 5.2; Sodium 534mg.

Pilau rice with coconut and coriander pesto

A fabulous flavour triangle is created when fresh coriander (cilantro), mint leaves and green chillies combine in this sumptuous pilau, *Chatni Pulao*, which can be a vegetarian meal in itself when served with a raita. The pesto sauce used here is not dissimilar to the Italian version, although the Indian recipe does not contain pine nuts, and includes coconut to add richness.

SERVES 4

225g/8oz/generous 1 cup basmati rice

25g/1oz/⅓ cup desiccated (dry unsweetened shredded) coconut

3 garlic cloves, roughly chopped

2.5cm/1in piece of fresh root ginger, roughly chopped

15g/½oz fresh coriander (cilantro) leaves and stalks, roughly chopped

15g/½oz fresh mint leaves and stalks, roughly chopped

1–2 fresh green chillies, roughly chopped (deseeded if preferred)

50g/2oz/4 tbsp ghee, or 25g/1oz/2 tbsp unsalted butter and 30ml/2 tbsp sunflower oil or light olive oil

25g/1oz raw cashew nuts

2.5cm/1in piece of cinnamon stick

4 cardamom pods, bruised

4 cloves

1 medium onion, finely sliced

75g/3oz/½ cup green beans, cut into 2.5cm/1in pieces

75g/3oz/½ cup peas, frozen and thawed, or pre-cooked fresh ones

5ml/1 tsp salt, or to taste

3 Transfer the rehydrated coconut to a blender or food processor with the water in which it was soaked. Add the garlic, ginger, coriander, mint and chillies, and blend until smooth. Alternatively, you can pound the ingredients to a smooth paste using a large mortar and pestle. Set aside.

4 Melt the ghee or butter and oil in a heavy pan over a low heat. Add the cashew nuts and stir-fry for about 2 minutes, until browned. Take care not to let them burn. Drain on kitchen paper.

5 In the same pan, stir-fry the cinnamon, cardamom and cloves for 30 seconds.

8 Add the ground coconut mixture. Stir-fry for 2–3 minutes.

9 Add the beans, peas and salt. Pour in 450ml/16fl oz/scant 2 cups warm water, bring to the boil, cover and reduce the heat to low.

10 Cook for 8–9 minutes without lifting the lid and then switch off the heat. Let the pan stand undisturbed for 10 minutes, fluff up the rice with a fork and serve.

1 Wash the rice in a sieve (strainer) in several changes of water until it runs clear, then soak in a bowl of cold water for 20–30 minutes. Drain and set aside.

2 Put the coconut in a large heatproof bowl, then pour over 150ml/5fl oz/½ cup boiling water. Leave to soak for 10 minutes.

6 Add the onion to the pan, increase the heat to medium and fry the onions for about 10 minutes, until they are golden brown, stirring regularly.

7 Add the drained rice, stir to combine and cook for 1–2 minutes.

Per portion Energy 418kcal/1736kJ; Protein 8.2g; Carbohydrate 56g, of which sugars 5.8g; Fat 18g, of which saturates 9.4g; Cholesterol 0mg; Calcium 76mg; Fibre 3.8g; Sodium 10mg.

Pilau rice with aromatic spices and mixed fruits

This north Indian pilau rice recipe, *Kashmiri Pulao*, is quite different from any other made around the country. It is cooked in milk instead of water and is further enriched with the addition of cream. The rice is then given an exotic appearance by folding in locally grown fruits such as apricots, cherries and plums. It makes an exquisite and very satisfying vegetarian main dish that is perfect for a dinner party.

SERVES 4

225g/8oz/generous 1 cup basmati rice
a good pinch of saffron threads, pounded
30ml/2 tbsp hot milk
25g/1oz glacé cherries
50g/2oz/¼ cup unsalted butter
30ml/2 tbsp sunflower oil or light
  olive oil
4 green cardamom pods, bruised
4 cloves
5cm/2in piece cinnamon stick, halved
5ml/1 tsp Royal cumin (shahi zeera)
5ml/1 tsp salt, or to taste
450ml/¾ pint/scant 2 cups lukewarm milk
50ml/2fl oz/¼ cup single (light) cream
25g/1oz/¼ cup walnut pieces
25g/1oz/¼ cup blanched and
  slivered almonds
25g/1oz/⅙ cup dried ready-to-eat
  apricots, sliced
25g/1oz/⅙ cup dried ready-to-eat
  plums, sliced

4 Heat half the butter and half the oil in a heavy pan over a low heat and add the cardamom, cloves, cinnamon and Royal cumin. Stir-fry gently for 25–30 seconds, then add the drained rice.

5 Stir and fry for 2–3 minutes, until the rice grains are coated with the butter/oil mixture.

6 Stir in the salt and pour in the milk. Increase the heat to medium and bring the mixture to the boil.

10 Add the walnut pieces and fry for about 2 minutes, or until lightly browned. Drain on kitchen paper. Fry the almonds until lightly browned, then drain on kitchen paper.

11 Rinse the cherries and cut them in half. Add the apricots, plums and cherries to the pan and cook for 3–4 minutes, until softened.

12 Pile the fruits over the cooked rice and add the nuts. Mix well and serve immediately.

1 Wash the rice in several changes of water by tossing and turning the grains gently in a sieve (strainer) until the water runs clear. Soak in a bowl of cold water for 30 minutes, then leave to drain in the sieve.

2 Place the pounded saffron in a small bowl, pour over the hot milk and set aside.

3 Put the cherries in a separate bowl of lightly salted water and leave to soak for 10 minutes.

7 Add the steeped saffron along with all the milk it was soaked in and stir well. Add the cream, reduce the heat to very low, cover the pan tightly and cook for 10 minutes.

8 Switch off the heat and let the pan stand undisturbed for a further 10 minutes.

9 Meanwhile, heat the remaining butter and oil together in a frying pan over a low heat.

Per portion Energy 551kcal/2310kJ; Protein 62g; Carbohydrate 23g, of which sugars 9g; Fat 24g, of which saturates 4g; Cholesterol 205mg; Calcium 22mg; Fibre 0.9g; Sodium 1699mg.

Indian cheese pilau

The bland taste of paneer (Indian cheese) makes it an extremely versatile ingredient, as it can absorb any flavour quite easily. The cheese is used in both sweet and savoury dishes, and in each recipe it takes on a completely different taste and flavour. This pilau rice, *Sanar Pulao*, with wonderfully fragrant yet subtle spicing, really tingles your taste buds and satisfies your soul.

SERVES 4

225g/8oz/generous 1 cup basmati rice
50g/2oz/4 tbsp ghee, or 15ml/1 tbsp
  sunflower oil and 25g/1oz/2 tbsp
  unsalted butter
225g/8oz paneer (Indian cheese), cut into
  bitesize pieces
6 green cardamom pods, bruised
4 cloves
2.5cm/1in piece of cinnamon stick
2 bay leaves
1 large onion, finely sliced
1–2 fresh green chillies, finely chopped
  (deseeded if preferred)
2.5ml/½ tsp ground turmeric
5ml/1 tsp salt, or to taste
115g/4oz frozen garden peas
25g/1oz raisins
15ml/1 tbsp toasted flaked (sliced)
  almonds, to garnish

1 Wash the rice in several changes of water by tossing and turning the grains gently in a sieve (strainer) until the water runs clear. Soak in a bowl of cold water for 30 minutes, then leave to drain in the sieve.

2 In a heavy pan, heat the ghee or oil and butter over a medium heat. Add the paneer and sauté for 2–3 minutes, until browned. Remove with a slotted spoon and drain on kitchen paper.

3 Add the cardamom, cloves, cinnamon and bay leaves to the remaining fat in the pan.

4 Allow to sizzle for a few minutes, then add the onion and green chillies. Fry for 9–10 minutes, until the onion is a caramel-brown colour, stirring regularly.

5 Add the rice and turmeric and reduce the heat to low. Stir-fry gently for 1–2 minutes, then and add the salt, browned paneer, peas and raisins.

6 Pour in 450ml/¾ pint/scant 2 cups water and bring it to the boil. Allow to boil for about 1 minute, then reduce the heat to low.

7 Cover the pan tightly and cook the pilau for 8–9 minutes. Remove from the heat and allow to stand undisturbed for 10 minutes.

8 Fluff up the rice with a fork and transfer to a serving dish. Serve, garnished with the roasted almonds.

VARIATIONS
• You can replace the paneer (Indian cheese) with an equal amount of halloumi cheese, but omit the salt in step 5.
• Replace the frozen peas with fresh broad (fava) beans, sliced green (French) beans or fresh peas, when they are in season. Or you can use other frozen vegetables, such as corn or soya beans.

Per portion Energy 55kcal/2318kJ; Protein 8g; Carbohydrate 61g, of which sugars 9g; Fat 33g, of which saturates 20g; Cholesterol 71mg; Calcium 83mg; Fibre 4.9g; Sodium 615mg.

Side Dishes

From rich, satisfying vegetable dishes and light, zesty salads to creamy, cooling yogurt raitas and all manner of flavoursome chutneys, side dishes are perhaps the most important element of many Indian meals. Served simply with bread or poppadums to whet the appetite, as accompaniments to a main course, or with other side dishes, the versatility of these flavour sensations knows no bounds.

Vibrant, zesty and soothing

Indian cuisine is famous for its colourful side dishes and no meal is complete without at least two different vegetable accompaniments, which often steal the limelight from the main dish. Choosing side dishes requires great care and attention, as they must complement rather than compete with the flavours of the main meal. For this reason, rich and complex main courses are best served with the simplest sides. Similarly, if you plan to provide a rich side dish, and some of the Indian side dishes can indeed be rich, then serve a simple main course. Following this basic principle will help you to maintain the overall balance of flavours.

A useful carbohydrate that carries other flavours well, potatoes display their versatility by appearing in numerous dishes, whether fried with different spices or bathed in innumerable sauces and partnered with other vegetables. Beans, peas and lentils are also popular, not least because they are very sustaining and nutritious, but also because their often bland flavour makes them the perfect foil for complex main dishes.

Other, less sustaining vegetables such as okra, courgettes (zucchini), cauliflowers and carrots, and even some fruits, are generally used to make simple side dishes, especially in the east and north-east of the country. Elsewhere, the addition of cream, nuts or coconut milk result in more complex flavours and, when several of these richer tidbits are served together with rice or bread, they make a complete meal.

In addition to cooked vegetable and fruit dishes, Indian cuisine has a wide repertoire of cold accompaniments, including fresh and zesty salads that cleanse the palate, cool and creamy yogurt dressings and raitas, and of course the ubiquitous chutneys and pickles that are served all over the country, as well as most of the rest of the world. Salads are generally made from cooling ingredients such as ccucumbers and pears, or tangy, refreshing fruits such as pineapple. Raitas, made with creamy yogurt, usually include chopped raw vegetables such as cucumber, but can also contain more unusual additions such as bananas, the sweetness of which balances the spice of other dishes.

Chutneys and pickles are often eaten with bread, but are delectable with kebabs and all kinds of snacks. Souring agents are very important in making chutneys as they balance the spices and chillies. Lime juice, tamarind, dried mango powder (*amchur*) and pomegranate seeds are often used as in this capacity, helping to create wonderful flavours.

Crushed potatoes with hard-boiled eggs

This classic dish, *Alu-Konir Pitika*, can be enjoyed any time of day as a snack, side dish or light meal. It is very easy to make, being a simple combination of mashed potatoes and chopped hard-boiled eggs flavoured with mustard oil, finely chopped shallots, green chilli and fresh coriander (cilantro) leaves.

SERVES 4

700g/1½lb potatoes

4 hard-boiled eggs, peeled

5ml/1 tsp salt, or to taste

30ml/2 tbsp mustard oil

2 shallots, finely chopped

1 fresh green chilli, finely chopped
(deseeded if preferred)

30ml/2 tbsp fresh coriander (cilantro)
leaves, finely chopped

julienne strips of fresh red chillies,
to garnish

Garlic-flavoured Mung Beans (*see* page
130) and Plain Boiled Rice (*see* page 36),
to serve

1 Peel the potatoes, cut them into chunks, then boil them in a large pan of salted water for about 10 minutes, until they are soft. Drain well, then mash until smooth.

2 Cut the eggs in half and separate the whites from the yolks. Chop the whites.

3 Mash the yolks to a paste in a large bowl using a fork.

4 Add the potato and egg whites with all the remaining ingredients. Stir to combine.

5 Spoon the mixture in four ring moulds or small bowls, then turn out onto serving plates and garnish with the red chilli strips. Serve with Garlic-flavoured Mung Beans and Plain Boiled Rice.

Per portion Energy 150kcal/622kJ; Protein 7.2g; Carbohydrate 5.9g, of which sugars 4.2g; Fat 11.2g, of which saturates 2.1g; Cholesterol 190mg; Calcium 47mg; Fibre 1.1g; Sodium 72mg.

Potatoes sautéed with five-spice and poppy seeds

The east and north east Indian five-spice mix transforms the simplest ingredient into a stunning dish. In this dish, *Afu Guti Diya Alu*, cubed potatoes are sautéed with aromatic five-spice and are tinged with turmeric. Opulent poppy seed paste coats the potatoes, giving them a luxurious taste.

SERVES 4

30ml/2 tbsp white poppy seeds
675g/1½lb potatoes
60ml/4 tbsp mustard oil
4–5 large garlic cloves, crushed
1–2 fresh green chillies, finely chopped
2.5ml/½ tsp ground turmeric
5ml/1 tsp salt, or to taste
rotis and a curry, to serve

For the five-spice mix:
2.5ml/½ tsp black or brown mustard seeds
2.5ml/½ tsp cumin seeds
2.5ml/½ tsp fennel seeds
2.5ml/½ tsp nigella seeds
6 fenugreek seeds

1 Dry-roast the poppy seeds in a heavy pan over a medium heat. Stir constantly for about 1 minute or until they are just a shade darker. Do not allow them to become too dark.

2 Remove the poppy seeds from the pan and let them cool, then grind them in a spice or coffee mill, or in a mortar and pestle.

3 Peel the potatoes and cut them into 1cm/½in cubes. Soak them in water for 15 minutes, then drain and dry with a cloth.

4 Heat half the oil in a heavy, non-stick frying pan over a medium-high heat until smoking point is reached. Add the potatoes and fry for 3–4 minutes, stirring regularly, until browned. Drain on kitchen paper.

5 Add the remaining oil to the pan and reduce the heat. Add the five-spice mix and let it crackle and pop for 15–20 seconds.

6 Reduce the heat to low and add the garlic and chilli. Continue to fry for 2–3 minutes, until the garlic has turned light brown.

7 Stir in the turmeric, potatoes and salt. Mix, then add 120ml/4fl oz/½ cup water and reduce the heat to low. Cover and cook for 8–10 minutes, until the potatoes are tender.

8 Add the poppy seeds and increase the heat. Stir-fry until the potatoes have absorbed any excess liquid and are coated with the poppy seeds. Serve with rotis and a curry.

Per portion Energy 265kcal/1106kJ; Protein 5g; Carbohydrate 30g, of which sugars 1g; Fat 18g, of which saturates 2g; Cholesterol 0mg; Calcium 115mg; Fibre 2.7g; Sodium 506mg.

Golden potato cubes with chilli and coriander

This is a very simple, but gloriously delicious potato dish, which is often accompanied by Deep-fried Soft Puffed Bread (*see* pages 218–19) for breakfast or high tea. *Alu Bhaji* can also be served as an accompaniment to a lentil dish and with any other type of bread for a satisfying vegetarian meal.

2 Stir in the turmeric and cumin and cook for about 1 minute.

3 Add the potatoes, salt and water. Bring to the boil, reduce the heat to low, cover and cook for 12 minutes, until the potatoes are tender and have absorbed most of the water.

4 Stir in the coriander leaves and remove from the heat. Transfer to a serving dish and serve with Deep-fried Soft Puffed Bread and/or a lentil dish.

SERVES 4

60ml/4 tbsp mustard oil or sunflower oil

1 medium onion, finely chopped

1–2 fresh green chillies, finely chopped (deseeded if preferred)

5ml/1 tsp ground turmeric

5ml/1 tsp ground cumin

450g/1lb potatoes, peeled and cut into bitesize pieces

3.75ml/¾ tsp salt, or to taste

250ml/8fl oz/1 cup lukewarm water

15ml/1 tbsp fresh coriander (cilantro) leaves, chopped

Deep-fried Soft Puffed Bread (*see* pages 218–19), and/or a lentil dish, to serve

1 Heat the oil over a medium heat until smoking point is reached. Add the onion and chilli and fry for 7–8 minutes, stirring often, until the onion is beginning to colour.

Per portion Energy 234kcal/973kJ; Protein 3g; Carbohydrate 22g, of which sugars 3g; Fat 15g, of which saturates 2g; Cholesterol 0mg; Calcium 22mg; Fibre 2.4g; Sodium 305mg.

Potatoes in coconut milk with garlic-infused butter

These potatoes, *Batata Ghashi*, are so fabulously tasty that you won't believe how simple they are to make. The only thing to remember is that you will need to pre-boil the potatoes in their skins and leave to cool completely before adding them to the sauce. Serve with flat bread for scooping up the juices.

SERVES 4

500g/1lb 2oz waxy potatoes
30ml/2 tbsp sunflower oil or light olive oil
30ml/2 tbsp ground coriander
2.5ml/½ tsp ground turmeric
2.5–5ml/½–1 tsp chilli powder
400ml/14fl oz/1½ cups canned coconut milk
5ml/1 tsp salt, or to taste
22.5ml/1½ tbsp tamarind juice or lime juice
15ml/1 tbsp ghee or unsalted butter
4–5 large garlic cloves, crushed
flat bread, to serve

1 Boil the potatoes in their skins. Cool and peel them, then cut into 2.5cm/1in cubes.

2 Heat the oil over a low heat and add the coriander, turmeric and chilli powder. Stir and cook for about 1 minute.

3 Add the potatoes, coconut milk and salt. Stir well and bring to a slow simmer. Cook for 6–8 minutes. Add the tamarind or lime juice.

4 Meanwhile, melt the ghee or butter over a low heat and add the garlic. Fry until it is lightly browned but do not allow it to darken.

5 Stir the garlic butter mixture into the potatoes, remove from the heat and serve immediately with any flat bread.

Per portion Energy 207kcal/870kJ; Protein 3.2g; Carbohydrate 26.8g, of which sugars 6.5g; Fat 10.6g, of which saturates 2.9g; Cholesterol 0mg; Calcium 46mg; Fibre 1.3g; Sodium 617mg.

New potatoes in yogurt and poppy seed sauce

Dum Aloo is a rich side dish, which can also be served as a main course with any Indian bread. The potatoes are boiled first, but not fully cooked, then combined with a purée of yogurt, poppy seeds and fried onions. The final cooking is done using the dum (steam cooking) method, which involves tightly sealing the pan with foil and a lid and cooking over a very low heat, either on the stove or in a low oven.

SERVES 4

15ml/1 tbsp white poppy seeds
60ml/4 tbsp sunflower oil or light olive oil
700g/1½lb new potatoes, par-boiled
  and peeled
1 large onion, finely sliced
75g/3oz/⅓ cup full-fat (whole) natural
  (plain) yogurt
5ml/1 tsp ginger purée
2.5–5ml/½–1 tsp chilli powder
5ml/1 tsp ground coriander
5ml/1 tsp ground cumin
5ml/1 tsp salt, or to taste
2.5ml/½ tsp garam masala
Indian bread, to serve

1 Grind the poppy seeds in a coffee grinder or mortar and pestle and set aside.

2 In a heavy pan, heat the oil over a medium heat and fry the potatoes in two batches until they are well browned. Drain them on kitchen paper.

3 When they are cool enough to handle, prick the potatoes with a cocktail stick (toothpick).

4 In the same oil, fry the onion until it is a pale golden colour. Press the onion to the side of the pan to remove any excess oil, then transfer to kitchen paper to drain.

5 Blend the yogurt, poppy seeds and fried onion in a blender to form a smooth purée, then set aside.

6 In the remaining oil in the pan, fry the ginger over a low heat for 1 minute, then add the chilli powder, coriander and cumin. Stir-fry for 30–40 seconds, then add the purée.

7 Cook until the mixture begins to bubble, then add the browned potatoes, salt and garam masala. Cover the pan with a piece of foil and press it all the way round the edge to seal. Put the lid on and reduce the heat to very low.

8 Cook for about 30 minutes, until the potatoes are tender and the sauce has thickened. Serve with any Indian bread.

Per portion Energy 322kcal/1346kJ; Protein 7.2g; Carbohydrate 41.7g, of which sugars 10.8g; Fat 15.3g, of which saturates 2.3g; Cholesterol 2mg; Calcium 116mg; Fibre 3.8g; Sodium 41mg.

Potatoes with coriander and sun-dried mango

In this recipe, *Aloo Chokha*, cubed potatoes are adorned with crushed coriander seeds, red and green chillies and fresh coriander (cilantro) leaves. Sun-dried mango powder, known as amchur, is commonly used in Indian recipes and is sold in Asian shops. It has an unmistakably distinctive sour taste, but if amchur proves difficult to find, lime juice can be substituted, although you will need to use more of it.

SERVES 4

60ml/4 tbsp sunflower oil or light olive oil

1 large onion, finely sliced

1–2 fresh green chillies, chopped
  (deseeded if preferred)

1–2 dried red chillies, sliced into 2–3 pieces

10ml/2 tsp coriander seeds, crushed

5ml/1 tsp ground cumin

2.5ml/½ tsp ground turmeric

450g/1lb potatoes, cut into 2.5cm/1in cubes

5ml/1 tsp salt, or to taste

5ml/1 tsp sun-dried mango powder
  (amchur) or 15ml/1 tbsp lime juice

30ml/2 tbsp fresh coriander (cilantro)
  leaves, chopped

a lentil dish and/or a vegetable curry, and
  any Indian bread, to serve

1 Heat the oil over a medium heat. Fry the onion with the chillies for 6–7 minutes, until the onion is beginning to brown.

2 Add the coriander and fry for 1 minute. Add the cumin and turmeric and fry for 1 minute.

3 Add the potato cubes and the salt and stir to combine everything thoroughly. Pour in 250ml/9fl oz/1 cup warm water and bring it to the boil.

4 Reduce the heat to low, cover the pan with a tight-fitting lid and cook for 12–15 minutes, until the potatoes are tender and all the water has been absorbed.

5 Stir in the mango powder or lime juice and chopped coriander, and remove from the heat. Serve with a lentil dish and/or a vegetable curry, accompanied by any Indian bread.

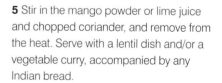

Per portion Energy 237kcal/990kJ; Protein 4.2g; Carbohydrate 29.7g, of which sugars 8.5g; Fat 12.2g, of which saturates 1.5g; Cholesterol 0mg; Calcium 47mg; Fibre 2.9g; Sodium 509mg.

Peas and potatoes in tomato sauce

The Bengali community takes great pride in this simple but exquisite dish, *Alu Matarer Dalna*, in which plump fresh peas with turmeric-tinged potatoes float in a rich tomato sauce. The sharp lemony taste of cardamom, musky ginger and warm cumin produce an unforgettable flavour combination.

3 Place the pan over a low heat and allow the cardamom pods to puff up, then add the cumin, coriander, turmeric and chilli powder.

4 Cook for about 1 minute, then add the tomatoes. Increase the heat slightly and cook until the tomato pieces are broken up.

5 Sprinkle over 30ml/2 tbsp water and continue to cook for 2–3 minutes. Repeat this process once more and cook until the tomatoes reach a paste-like consistency and the oil begins to float on the surface.

6 Add the potatoes, salt and 250ml/8fl oz/ 1 cup water. Bring to the boil, reduce the heat to low and cook for 10 minutes.

7 Add the peas and cook for 5–7 minutes or until the potatoes are tender and the sauce has thickened.

8 Stir in the garam masala and lemon juice, and garnish with the ginger and fresh coriander. Serve with bread or rice.

SERVES 4

60ml/4 tbsp mustard oil or sunflower oil
450g/1lb potatoes, peeled and cut into
 2.5cm/1in cubes
10ml/2 tsp sugar
4 green cardamom pods, bruised
2 cloves
10ml/2 tsp ground cumin
5ml/1 tsp ground coriander
2.5ml/½ tsp ground turmeric
2.5–5ml/½–1 tsp chilli powder
115g/4oz canned chopped tomatoes,
 with their juice
5ml/1 tsp salt, or to taste
115g/4oz frozen garden peas
2.5ml/½ tsp garam masala
15ml/1 tbsp lemon juice
fresh root ginger, peeled and cut into
 julienne strips, and sprigs of fresh
 coriander (cilantro), to garnish
Indian bread or boiled rice, to serve

1 Heat half the mustard oil in a frying pan over a medium-high heat until smoking point is reached (if using sunflower oil, heat until hot). Add the potatoes and fry for 4–5 minutes, until the edges brown. Drain on kitchen paper.

2 Heat the remaining oil until it begins to smoke. Remove from the heat and add the sugar. As soon as it begins to caramelize, add the cardamom pods and cloves.

Per portion Energy 254kcal/1061kJ; Protein 5g; Carbohydrate 26g, of which sugars 5g; Fat 16g, of which saturates 2g; Cholesterol 0mg; Calcium 28mg; Fibre 4.0g; Sodium 519mg.

Potatoes in chilli-tamarind sauce

In this dish, *Batata Saung*, boiled and cubed potatoes are tossed in a chilli-hot tamarind sauce that is flavoured with onion and a generous amount of crushed garlic. It makes a delicious accompaniment to any meal. It is essential to boil the potatoes in their skin in order to preserve the starch content.

SERVES 4

450g/1lb potatoes

60ml/4 tbsp sunflower oil or light
   olive oil

2.5ml/½ tsp black mustard seeds

1 large onion, finely chopped

4–5 large garlic cloves, crushed

2.5–5ml/½–1 tsp chilli powder

5ml/1 tsp salt, or to taste

22.5ml/1½ tbsp tamarind juice or
   lime juice

1 Boil the potatoes in their skins in a large pan of lightly salted boiling water for about 10 minutes, until tender. Drain, leave to cool completely, then remove the skins and cut into 2.5cm/1in cubes.

2 Heat the oil over a medium heat and add the mustard seeds. As soon as they pop, add the onion and fry, stirring regularly, until the onion is golden brown.

3 Add the garlic and cook for 2 minutes, stirring frequently.

4 Add the cooked potatoes, chilli powder and salt. Stir to mix thoroughly.

5 Add 150ml/5fl oz/½ cup warm water and cook over a medium heat for 3–4 minutes, stirring often. Stir in the tamarind juice or lime juice and remove the pan from the heat. Serve immediately.

COOK'S TIP
The potatoes can be boiled, cooled and refrigerated in advance. They are much easier to cut into neat pieces once chilled.

Per portion Energy 135kcal/568kJ; Protein 4g; Carbohydrate 29.3g, of which sugars 8.5g; Fat 1.1g, of which saturates 0.2g; Cholesterol 0mg; Calcium 45mg; Fibre 2.9g; Sodium 18mg.

Courgettes and potatoes in coconut milk

This simple but delicious Orissan dish, *Potala Rasa*, is traditionally cooked with a vegetable known as parwal, which belongs to the same family as squash and cucumber. Courgettes (zucchini) make an excellent substitute, but do take care not to overcook them or they will be mushy.

SERVES 4

450g/1lb courgettes (zucchini)
350g/12oz potatoes
60ml/4 tbsp sunflower oil or light olive oil
1 large onion, finely chopped
10ml/2 tsp ginger purée
5ml/1 tsp ground turmeric
5ml/1 tsp ground cumin
2.5–5ml/½–1 tsp chilli powder
400ml/14fl oz/1⅔ cups canned
  coconut milk
5ml/1 tsp salt, or to taste
2.5ml/½ tsp garam masala
Plain Boiled Rice (*see* page 36) or Indian
  bread, to serve

1 Trim the courgettes and halve them lengthways. Cut each half into about 2.5cm/1in chunks. Peel the potatoes and cut them into 2.5cm/1in chunks.

2 Heat half the oil in a frying pan over a medium-high heat, then add the potatoes and cook for about 3–4 minutes, until browned. Drain on kitchen paper.

3 Brown the courgettes for 2–3 minutes in the same oil, then drain on kitchen paper.

4 Reduce the heat to medium and add the remaining oil. Add the onion and fry for about 8 minutes, until the onion is soft, then add the ginger.

5 Continue to fry for 2 minutes, then add the turmeric, cumin and chilli powder.

6 Cook the spices for about 1 minute, then add the coconut milk, salt and the browned vegetables. Simmer, uncovered, for 10–12 minutes, until the vegetables are tender.

7 Stir in the garam masala and remove from the heat. Transfer to a serving dish and serve with Plain Boiled Rice or bread.

Per portion Energy 132kcal/555kJ; Protein 5g; Carbohydrate 27g, of which sugars g; Fat 1g, of which saturates 0g; Cholesterol 0mg; Calcium 88mg; Fibre 2.3g; Sodium 618mg.

Green beans with mustard, curry leaf and coconut

In Kerala, *thoren* is a very popular side dish, and it simply means stir-fried finely chopped or shredded vegetables cooked in a spice-perfumed oil. The fresh colours of the vegetables in this version, *Payaru Thoren*, along with all their nutrients, are preserved because of the quick-cooking method.

SERVES 4

450g/1lb whole green beans, fresh
  or frozen
30ml/2 tbsp sunflower oil or light olive oil
2.5ml/½ tsp black or brown mustard seeds
2.5ml/½ tsp cumin seeds
1 dried red chilli, snipped
8–10 curry leaves, fresh or dried
2.5ml/½ tsp salt, or to taste
15ml/1 tbsp desiccated (dry unsweetened
  shredded) coconut

1 Trim the beans, then blanch them in a large pan of lightly salted boiling water for 2 minutes.

2 Drain the beans, then plunge them immediately into cold water to prevent further cooking. If you are using frozen beans, it is not necessary to blanch them.

3 Heat the oil in a frying pan over a medium heat. When hot, but not smoking, add the mustard seeds.

4 As soon as the seeds start popping, add the cumin, chillies and curry leaves.

5 Allow the chillies to blacken slightly, then add the blanched beans and the salt. Stir-fry for 2–3 minutes, then cover the pan tightly and reduce the heat to low.

6 Cook the beans in their own juices for 10–12 minutes, until tender, but still firm. Stir the beans once or twice during the cooking time.

7 Add the coconut, mix well and remove from the heat. Serve immediately.

Per portion Energy 118kcal/487kJ; Protein 3g; Carbohydrate 4g, of which sugars 3g; Fat 11g, of which saturates 3g; Cholesterol 0mg; Calcium 52mg; Fibre 4.2g; Sodium 248mg.

Leeks with garlic, chilli and gram flour

Traditionally, in this recipe, *Jhunko*, a large amount of sliced onion is sautéed with garlic and chillies, and gram flour (besan) is added at the end to soak up all the juices. The mixture is then stir-fried until the gram flour releases its nutty, toasted aroma. This version uses leeks instead of onions for a more subtle flavour.

SERVES 4

60ml/4 tbsp sunflower oil or light
  olive oil
2.5ml/½ tsp black mustard seeds
5ml/1 tsp cumin seeds
450g/1lb young leeks, finely sliced
1 small red (bell) pepper, cut into
  2.5cm/1in strips
2.5ml/½ tsp ground turmeric
2.5ml/½ tsp chilli powder
2.5ml/½ tsp salt, or to taste
50g/2oz/½ cup gram flour
  (besan), sifted
any light curry, to serve

1 Heat the oil in a non-stick pan over a medium heat. When it is hot but not smoking, add the mustard and cumin seeds.

2 Add the leeks, red pepper, turmeric, chilli powder and salt. Increase the heat slightly and stir-fry the vegetables for 4–5 minutes.

3 Sprinkle the gram flour into the pan and stir-fry for 1 minute. Remove from the heat and serve with any light curry.

COOK'S TIP
Young leeks have a milder, sweeter flavour than older ones.

Per portion Energy 177kcal/738kJ; Protein 3.5g; Carbohydrate 14.3g, of which sugars 2.7g; Fat 12.2g, of which saturates 1.5g; Cholesterol 0mg; Calcium 51mg; Fibre 2.9g; Sodium 4mg.

Sweetcorn in coconut and green chilli sauce

In this popular Maharashtrian side dish, *Makki Usli*, golden corn kernels are bathed in a thick coconut sauce enhanced by the nutty taste of mustard seeds and aromatic fresh chillies. It tastes wonderful served on its own with bread, or with any simple vegetable curry.

SERVES 4

45ml/3 tbsp sunflower oil or light olive oil
2.5ml/½ tsp black or brown mustard seeds
2.5ml/½ tsp cumin seeds
1 medium onion, finely chopped
2.5ml/½ tsp ground turmeric
450g/1lb frozen sweetcorn, thawed and drained, or canned sweetcorn, drained and rinsed
5ml/1 tsp salt, or to taste
25g/1oz desiccated (dry unsweetened shredded) coconut
2 fresh green chillies, chopped
julienne strips of fresh red chilli, to garnish
Indian bread or vegetable curry, to serve

1 Heat the oil in a frying pan over a medium heat until smoking point is reached, then switch off the heat. Add the mustard seeds followed by the cumin.

2 Place the pan back over a medium heat and add the onion. Fry for 6–8 minutes, until the onion is soft, but not brown.

3 Add the turmeric, cook for 1 minute, then add the corn and the salt. Pour in 250ml/8fl oz/1 cup warm water and bring it to the boil. Simmer gently over a medium heat for 6–8 minutes.

4 Meanwhile, grind the coconut and green chillies in a coffee grinder until smooth, then add to the pan. Stir and simmer for 2–3 minutes, until the sauce has thickened. Serve garnished with the chilli strips.

Per portion Energy 258kcal/1077kJ; Protein 5g; Carbohydrate 23g, of which sugars 5g; Fat 17g, of which saturates 5g; Cholesterol 0mg; Calcium 22mg; Fibre 5.6g; Sodium 496mg.

Mung beans with ginger, chilli and lime

Mung beans (whole moong dhal) are available in many larger supermarkets and health food stores. Traditionally, they are soaked and sprouted before cooking. The sprouted beans are a good source of vitamin C. Unsprouted ones are equally delicious, and they are served raw as a snack, topped with chopped onion, Bombay Mix and a dash of lime juice or, as in this recipe *Usal*, cooked with aromatics to create a side dish.

2 Place over a high heat and bring to the boil. Reduce the heat to low, partially cover the pan and cook for 6–7 minutes, until the froth settles down.

3 Reduce the heat to low, cover and simmer for 15–17 minutes. The beans should be tender by now and most of the water will have been absorbed. Remove from the heat and keep hot.

4 Heat the oil in a frying pan over a high heat until smoking point is reached. Switch off the heat and add the mustard seeds, followed by the onion, ginger and chillies.

5 Turn the heat on to medium and fry the onion for 6–8 minutes, until it begins to colour. Add the turmeric and continue to cook for a further 1 minute.

SERVES 4

175g/6oz mung beans (whole moong dhal)
30ml/2 tbsp sunflower oil or light olive oil
2.5ml/½ tsp black or brown mustard seeds
1 large onion, finely chopped
2.5cm/1in piece of fresh root ginger, finely grated
2 fresh red chillies, sliced at an angle
5ml/1 tsp ground turmeric
2.5ml/½ tsp salt, or to taste
juice of 1 lime
a vegetable curry, to serve

1 Wash the mung beans in a sieve (strainer), then soak them in a bowl of cold water for 4–5 hours. Drain, then put them in a pan and add 300ml/½ pint/1¼ cups water.

6 Add the onion mixture to the lentils along with the salt and lime juice. Stir, transfer to a serving dish and serve with a vegetable curry.

Per portion Energy 106kcal/437kJ; Protein 2g; Carbohydrate 7g, of which sugars 8g; Fat 5g, of which saturates 1g; Cholesterol 0mg; Calcium 29mg; Fibre 3.4g; Sodium 251mg.

Split mung bean and cracked wheat kedgeree

Khichdi, along with *kadhi* (Thickened and Seasoned Yogurt, *see* page 187), is an essential part of any Gujarati meal. Different types of *khichdis* are cooked all over India, and in the 15th century one of them became the inspiration for the British dish kedgeree, which includes hard-boiled eggs and smoked fish. This recipe, *Ghau Na Phada Ni Khichdi*, is delicious as well as nutritious, offering protein, fibre, vitamins and minerals.

SERVES 4

175g/6oz skinless split mung beans
  (mung dhal)
175g/6oz cracked wheat (dalia)
50g/2oz ghee, plus 15ml/1 tbsp for tempering
5cm/2in piece of cinnamon stick, halved
5 cloves
2.5ml/½ tsp black peppercorns, crushed
1 large onion, finely sliced
10ml/2 tsp ginger purée
2–3 fresh green chillies, sliced at an angle
  (deseeded if preferred)
5ml/1 tsp ground turmeric
5ml/1 tsp chilli powder, or to taste
5ml/1 tsp salt, or to taste
200g/7oz carrots, scraped and cut like
  French Fries
150g/5oz green beans, cut into
  2.5cm/1in lengths
250g/9oz cauliflower, cut into florets
  1cm/½in in diameter
5ml/1 tsp black mustard seeds
5ml/1 tsp cumin seeds
2.5ml/½ tsp Asafoetida
Thickened and Seasoned Yogurt, to serve
  (*see* page 187)

3 Let them sizzle for 15–20 seconds, then add the onion. Fry for about 5 minutes, until the onion is soft, but not brown.

4 Add the ginger and chillies and fry for a further 4–5 minutes, until the onion is brown.

5 Drain the mung beans and the cracked wheat and add them to the pan. Add the turmeric, chilli powder and salt and cook, stirring, for 2–3 minutes.

6 Add the vegetables and pour in 900ml/1½ pints/3¾ cups hot water. Bring to the boil, reduce the heat to low, cover and cook for 20 minutes. Switch off the heat and set aside.

7 Heat the ghee for tempering over a medium-high heat. When almost smoking, add the mustard seeds, switch off the heat and add the cumin and Asafoetida. Pour over the *khichdi* and mix it gently. Serve with Thickened and Seasoned Yogurt.

1 Wash the mung beans in a sieve (strainer), then transfer to a large bowl and stir in the cracked wheat. Cover with cold water and leave to soak for 30–40 minutes.

2 In a heavy pan, heat the ghee over a medium heat and add the cinnamon stick, cloves and black peppercorns.

Per portion Energy 330kcal/1371kJ; Protein 9g; Carbohydrate 42g, of which sugars 7g; Fat 15g, of which saturates 9g; Cholesterol 35mg; Calcium 90mg; Fibre 06.1g; Sodium 523mg.

Semolina pancakes with buttermilk

Suji Ki Roti are fairly thick pancakes, which combine the fabulous flavours of finely chopped onion, green chilli, coriander (cilantro) leaves and the musky scent of root ginger. The batter is made with buttermilk or diluted yogurt, making it a healthy choice when served alongside an egg dish.

MAKES 12

300g/10½oz/scant 2 cups semolina
5ml/1 tsp salt, or to taste
2.5ml/½ tsp bicarbonate of soda
   (baking soda)
5ml/1 tsp cumin seeds
1 small onion, finely chopped
1cm/½in piece of fresh root ginger, grated
2 fresh red chillies, finely chopped
   (deseeded if preferred)
30ml/2 tbsp fresh coriander (cilantro) leaves,
   finely chopped
400ml/14fl oz/1⅔ cups buttermilk, or 150g/
   5oz/generous ½ cup natural (plain) yogurt
   blended with 300ml/½ pint/1¼ cups water
sunflower oil or light olive oil, for shallow-frying
South Indian Scrambled Eggs (*see* page 82),
   to serve (optional)

1 Place the semolina, salt, bicarbonate of soda and cumin seeds in a large mixing bowl and stir to combine.

2 Add the remaining ingredients, except the buttermilk or diluted yogurt and oil, and stir to combine thoroughly.

3 Add the buttermilk or diluted yogurt. Stir until a thick paste of a spreading consistency is formed.

4 Spread 10ml/2 tsp oil on an iron griddle or a small, heavy non-stick frying pan and heat over a medium-low heat.

5 Put one heaped tablespoon of the pancake mixture in the pan and gently spread it around to form a pancake with a diameter of 7.5cm/3in. Cover with a lid and cook for 2 minutes, until the top is set.

6 Spread 5ml/1 tsp oil on the uncooked side and turn it over with a palette knife. Cook, uncovered, for 2 minutes or until the pancake is set. Cook, tossing and turning, for a further 2–3 minutes, until browned.

7 Keep the cooked pancakes in a low oven in an open tray while you cook the remaining batter in the same way. Serve immediately on their own or with South Indian Scrambled Eggs.

Per portion Energy 341kcal/1447kJ; Protein 12g; Carbohydrate 65g, of which sugars 6g; Fat 6g, of which saturates 1g; Cholesterol 2mg; Calcium 145mg; Fibre 2.9g; Sodium 696mg.

Thickened and seasoned yogurt

Kadhi is the traditional partner for *khichdi* and there are many types of both dishes around India. This version, *Meethi Kadhi*, with a slightly sweet and sour taste, is the most popular of them all. Traditionally, palm sugar (jaggery) is used, but soft dark brown sugar is substituted in this recipe.

SERVES 4

500g/18oz/2¼ cups full-fat (whole) natural (plain) yogurt

25g/1oz/¼ cup gram flour (besan)

40g/1½oz/3 tbsp soft dark brown sugar

7.5ml/1½ tsp salt, or to taste

10ml/2 tsp finely grated fresh root ginger

15ml/1 tbsp sunflower oil or light olive oil

2.5ml/½ tsp cumin seeds

2.5cm/1in piece cinnamon stick

4 cloves

6–8 curry leaves

1.25ml/¼ tsp Asafoetida

15ml/1 tbsp fresh coriander (cilantro) leaves, chopped, plus extra, to garnish

1 Mix the yogurt and gram flour together in a bowl until smooth and creamy.

2 Add 300ml/½ pint/1¼ cups water and whisk until well blended. Add the sugar, salt and ginger and mix well.

3 Pour the mixture into a heavy pan and place over a medium-high heat.

4 Bring the mixture to the boil, reduce the heat slightly and cook, stirring, until it has thickened to the consistency of a pancake batter. Remove the pan from the heat and set aside.

5 In a small pan or a ladle, heat the oil and add the cumin seeds, cinnamon, cloves, curry leaves and Asafoetida. Pour this over the yogurt mixture and stir in the chopped coriander. Serve hot or cold.

Per portion Energy 189kcal/797kJ; Protein 9g; Carbohydrate 23g, of which sugars 20g; Fat 8g, of which saturates 3g; Cholesterol 14mg; Calcium 279mg; Fibre 0.8g; Sodium 844mg.

Crisp-fried okra in spicy yogurt dressing

Okra is a popular vegetable all over India and it is cooked in many ways. Quick-cooking it, using a stir-frying or deep-frying method, retains its glutinous nature. This recipe, *Bhindi Pachadi*, includes a yogurt dressing, but you can also serve the deep-fried okra on its own as a side dish, sprinkled with salt, chilli and cumin.

2 Remove the spices from the pan and leave to cool, then crush them finely with a mortar and pestle or a rolling pin.

3 Beat the yogurt until smooth and add the sugar. Reserve a little of the ground spices and add the remainder to the yogurt. Mix well to combine thoroughly, then cover with clear film (plastic wrap) and refrigerate until required. This can be stored for 2–3 days.

4 Mix the okra with the salt and turmeric in a small bowl. Heat the oil in a wok or other suitable pan for deep-frying until the surface starts to sizzle.

5 Add the okra to the pan in batches and fry for 2–3 minutes, until crisp and golden brown. Lift out with a slotted spoon and drain on kitchen paper. Repeat with the remaining okra.

6 Just before serving, add the fried okra to the spiced yogurt and mix well. Sprinkle the reserved spices on top and serve.

SERVES 4–6

5ml/1 tsp coriander seeds
5ml/1 tsp cumin seeds
1 dried red chilli, snipped
225g/8oz/1 cup full-fat (whole) natural (plain) yogurt
2.5ml/½ tsp sugar
225g/8oz okra, cut into discs about 3mm/⅛in thick
2.5ml/½ tsp salt, or to taste
2.5ml/½ tsp ground turmeric
sunflower oil or light olive oil, for deep-frying

1 Dry-roast the coriander, cumin and chilli for 1 minute, until they release their aroma.

Per portion Energy 106kcal/438kJ; Protein 3g; Carbohydrate 3g, of which sugars 3g; Fat 10g, of which saturates 2g; Cholesterol 5mg; Calcium 116mg; Fibre 1.7g; Sodium 184mg.

Figs in spiced yogurt

Anjeer Ka Salan is an excellent tastebud reviver with its savoury, sweet, sour and hot tastes combined in one. Dried ready-to-eat figs are easily available in supermarkets and health food shops, making this an all-year-round classic. This dish is especially good served with Saffron-scented Pilau Rice (*see* pages 156–7).

SERVES 4–5

400g/14oz dried ready-to-eat figs
250g/9oz/generous 1 cup thick natural (plain) yogurt
50g/2oz/4 tbsp ghee or unsalted butter
1 large onion, finely chopped
15ml/1 tbsp ground coriander
2.5ml/½ tsp ground turmeric
7.5ml/1½ tsp chilli powder, or to taste
5ml/1 tsp salt, or to taste
15ml/1 tbsp lemon juice
2.5ml/½ tsp garam masala

4 Add the coriander, turmeric and chilli powder and cook for about 1 minute.

5 Add the fig pieces and the salt and stir-fry for 2–3 minutes.

6 Add the yogurt, stir well, cover the pan tightly and cook for 4–5 minutes.

7 Stir in the lemon juice and garam masala. Serve hot or at room temperature.

1 Soak the figs in a bowl of salted water for 10–15 minutes, then rinse well. (*See* Cook's Tip). Slice each fig into three pieces and set aside.

2 Whisk the yogurt in a small bowl until it is smooth, then set aside.

3 Melt the ghee or butter in a frying pan over a low heat and fry the onion for 5–6 minutes, until soft and translucent.

COOK'S TIPS
• Some dried figs have added sugar in them, and soaking them in salted water eliminates this extra, unwanted, sweetness. There is no need to soak ones that have no added sugar.
• Whisking the yogurt stops it curdling during cooking.

Per portion Energy 315kcal/1352kJ; Protein 6g; Carbohydrate 47g, of which sugars 46g; Fat 13g, of which saturates 7g; Cholesterol 34mg; Calcium 304mg; Fibre 9.8g; Sodium 489mg.

Banana in spiced yogurt dressing

Banana is an unusual fruit to use in a raita, but *Paka Kela Nu Raitu* is very popular in Gujarat. Here, ripe bananas are steeped in yogurt that has a faint tinge of turmeric and the pungency of mustard powder, and the sweetness of the fruit complements both the spices in the dish and the food it accompanies.

SERVES 4

225g/8oz/1 cup full-fat (whole) natural (plain) yogurt
1.25ml/¼ tsp salt
10ml/2 tsp caster (superfine) sugar
5ml/1 tsp mustard powder
2 large ripe, firm bananas with a hint of green on their skins
15ml/1 tbsp lemon juice
1.25ml/¼ tsp chilli powder, to garnish
1.25ml/¼ tsp ground cumin, to garnish

1 Beat the yogurt until smooth. Add the salt, sugar and mustard and mix well.

2 Peel the bananas and quarter them lengthways. Chop each of these into bitesize pieces and sprinkle over the lemon juice, to prevent them discolouring.

3 Mix well, then gently fold into the yogurt mixture. Cover and chill for 1 hour.

4 Transfer the raita to a serving dish and sprinkle the chilli and cumin on top.

Per portion Energy 283kcal/1192kJ; Protein 3g; Carbohydrate 44g, of which sugars 16g; Fat 2g, of which saturates 2g; Cholesterol 0mg; Calcium 73mg; Fibre 3.7g; Sodium 620mg.

Mixed fruits with ginger, cumin and chilli

Fresh fruits, lightly dusted with spices, can be enjoyed as a side dish or after dinner instead of a dessert. Any combination of fruits will work well, depending on the season, but this recipe, *Phalon Ka Chaat*, uses three sun-kissed tropical varieties that have fantastic health benefits and are also easily available.

SERVES 4

1 ripe pomegranate
1 ripe papaya
1 small or ½ medium pineapple
175g/6oz/1½ cups seedless green grapes
175g/6oz/1½ cups seedless black grapes
2.5ml/½ tsp ground ginger
1.25ml/¼ tsp ground black pepper
2.5ml/½ tsp ground cumin
a pinch of chilli powder
2.5ml/½ tsp dried mint, or 6–8 fresh mint leaves, finely chopped
2.5ml/½ tsp sugar
2.5ml/½ tsp salt
fresh mint sprigs, to garnish

1 Using the handle of a large knife, tap the pomegranate all around to loosen the seeds, making it easier to remove them.

2 Cut the pomegranate in half and remove the seeds by peeling off the outer skin as you would an orange. Remove the white pith and skin. Reserve the seeds.

3 Peel the papaya. Cut it in half lengthwise and remove the black seeds. Scrape off the white pith under the seeds and cut the fruit into 2.5cm/1in cubes.

4 Remove the base from the pineapple, then stand it on its end and slice down the skin to remove it. Remove the eyes and cut the flesh into quarters. Remove the hard central core, then cut the remaining flesh into bitesize pieces. Halve the grapes.

5 Mix all the fruits together in a large bowl. Add the rest of the ingredients, except the salt, and stir. Cover and chill for 1–2 hours.

6 Stir in the salt and serve, garnished with the sprigs of mint.

COOK'S TIP
Papaya, or pawpaw, has a sweet, buttery taste and is reported to contain high levels of antioxidants.

Per portion Energy 167kcal/714kJ; Protein 2.2g; Carbohydrate 40.3g, of which sugars 39g; Fat 1g, of which saturates 0.1g; Cholesterol 0mg; Calcium 77mg; Fibre 5.7g; Sodium 14mg.

Pineapple salad

Golden pineapple cubes coated with coconut and yogurt and tempered with mustard, chilli and curry leaves make a delightful side dish. Although usually served as an accompaniment, *Pachadi* can be enjoyed as a wonderfully fragrant main dish when served with some boiled rice.

4 In a small, non-stick pan or a steel ladle, heat the oil over a medium heat. When the oil is hot, but not smoking, add the mustard seeds, followed by the green chilli and curry leaves. Allow the seeds to crackle for about 30 seconds.

5 Add to the pineapple mix and serve with any curry and some rice.

SERVES 4

1 small pineapple
2.5ml/½ tsp ground turmeric
5ml/1 tsp salt, or to taste
25g/1oz/2 tbsp white sugar
25g/1oz/⅓ cup desiccated (dry
  unsweetened shredded) coconut
50g/2oz/¼ cup natural (plain) yogurt
30ml/2 tbsp sunflower oil or light olive oil
2.5ml/½ tsp black mustard seeds
1 fresh green chilli, finely chopped
8–10 curry leaves, fresh or dried
curry and rice, to serve

1 Remove the base from the pineapple, then stand it on its end and slice down the skin to remove it. Remove the eyes and cut the flesh into quarters. Remove the central core, then cut the flesh into 1cm/½in wedges.

2 Put the pineapple into a pan with the turmeric, salt and sugar. Add 400ml/14fl oz/ 1½ cups water, cover and cook over a medium heat for 12–15 minutes, until the pineapple is tender. Leave to cool.

3 Grind the coconut in a coffee grinder. Add to the pineapple with the yogurt.

Per portion Energy 190kcal/796kJ; Protein 7.2g; Carbohydrate 21.3g, of which sugars 5.5g; Fat 9.3g, of which saturates 1.4g; Cholesterol 0mg; Calcium 161mg; Fibre 3.4g; Sodium 45mg.

Pear and cucumber salad

This is a delicious and unusual salad from across the north Indian border in Nepal. The Nepalese use nothing but salt, lemon juice and pepper to make *Naspati Aur Kheera Ke Salat*, but this version of the recipe includes several other ingredients to create a refreshing accompaniment.

SERVES 4

7.5ml/1½ tsp cumin seeds
3 firm William or Bartlett pears
15ml/1 tbsp lime juice
½ large cucumber
15ml/1 tbsp mayonnaise
30ml/2 tbsp Greek (US strained plain) yogurt
5ml/1 tsp wholegrain mustard
2.5ml/½ tsp salt
5ml/1 tsp sugar
2.5ml/½ tsp chilli powder

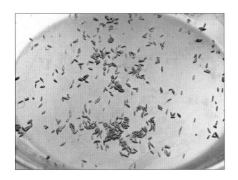

1 Preheat a small, heavy pan over a medium heat. Add the cumin seeds and stir for about 1 minute, until they are a shade darker and they release their aroma. Transfer the seeds to a plate and allow to cool.

2 Peel and core the pears, then cut them into bitesize pieces. Put them into a mixing bowl and sprinkle over the lime juice.

3 Halve the cucumber lengthways and scoop out the seeds and pulp. Chop it into pieces the same size as the pears and mix together.

4 Crush the roasted cumin seeds with a mortar and pestle or using the back of a wooden spoon.

5 Beat the mayonnaise and yogurt together in a bowl and stir in the mustard, salt, sugar, half the chilli powder and half the crushed cumin seeds.

6 Add the yogurt mixture to the pear and cucumber pieces and mix well. Transfer to a serving dish and sprinkle the remaining chilli powder and crushed cumin on top. Serve immediately.

Per portion Energy 110kcal/459kJ; Protein 2g; Carbohydrate 18g, of which sugars 17g; Fat 4g, of which saturates 1g; Cholesterol 4mg; Calcium 50mg; Fibre 0.3g; Sodium 335mg.

Sweet tamarind chutney

This sweet and tart chutney, *Amli Ni Chutney*, enlivens all kinds of fried and grilled (broiled) snacks. Use it as dip and serve with kebabs, pakoras and bhajiyas. In India, tamarind pods are soaked in water, then the seeds are removed and the flesh is pushed through a sieve (strainer) to prepare the chutney. Here, ready-to-use concentrated tamarind paste is used and dates are added to lend sweetness to the preserve.

SERVES 6–8

150g/5oz dried stoned dates
5ml/1 tsp cumin seeds
5ml/1 tsp coriander seeds
5–7.5ml/1–1½ tsp chilli powder
10ml/2 tsp concentrated tamarind paste
150ml/¼ pint/⅔ cup cold water
10ml/2 tsp soft light brown sugar
5ml/1 tsp salt

COOK'S TIP
The chutney will keep in a covered dish in the refrigerator for 1 week.

1 Put the dates in a heatproof bowl and cover with boiling water. Leave to soak for 20 minutes to rehydrate them, then drain in a colander or sieve (strainer).

2 Dry-roast the cumin and coriander seeds in a small, heavy pan for about 1 minute, until they release their aroma.

3 Remove the seeds from the pan, leave to cool, then crush with a mortar and pestle.

4 Place the dates in a blender and add the spices and the remaining ingredients. Blend until smooth, then serve at once or store in a sterilized jar (*see* Cook's Tip on page 195).

Per portion Energy 59kcal/250kJ; Protein 1g; Carbohydrate 15g, of which sugars 15g; Fat 0g, of which saturates 0g; Cholesterol 0mg; Calcium 16mg; Fibre 1.5g; Sodium 253mg.

Roasted tomato chutney

This delicious chutney recipe, *Tomato Achar*, comes from Darjeeling, with definite influences from Nepal, across the northern border. The Nepalese would roast the tomatoes over a wood fire, which imparts an unforgettable flavour. The tomatoes are then combined with chillies and spices and made into a purée. A final seasoning is added in the form of sliced garlic and fenugreek seeds.

MAKES 225G/8OZ

700g/1½lb ripe tomatoes
30ml/2 tbsp sunflower oil or light olive oil
1–2 fresh green chillies, chopped
  (deseeded if preferred)
1cm/½in piece of fresh root ginger, peeled
  and chopped
1 clove garlic, chopped
30ml/2 tbsp fresh coriander (cilantro)
  leaves, chopped
2.5ml/½ tsp salt, or to taste

1 Preheat the oven to 190ºC/375ºF/Gas 5. Halve the tomatoes widthways.

2 Put the tomato halves in a roasting pan and drizzle the oil over them. Shake to coat with the oil, then place in the centre of the oven and roast for 20 minutes, or until softened and cooked.

3 Remove the tomatoes from the oven, leave them to cool and then peel off and discard the skins.

4 Place the tomatoes in a blender or food processor along with all the remaining ingredients and purée until smooth.

5 This chutney is best eaten fresh, although it can be stored in sterilized jars (*see* Cook's Tip) in the refrigerator for up to 1 week.

COOK'S TIP
The easiest way to sterlize jars is to put them in the dishwasher. Alternatively, place washed, dried jars in an oven heated to 120ºC/250ºF/Gas ½ and bake for about 15 minutes.

Per portion Energy 334kcal/1395kJ; Protein 6.4g; Carbohydrate 23.1g, of which sugars 22.8g; Fat 24.7g, of which saturates 3.3g; Cholesterol 0mg; Calcium 149mg; Fibre 9.5g; Sodium 80mg.

Almond chutney

Almonds are very popular throughout northern India, where beautiful almond blossoms appear in the orchards of Kashmir at the onset of spring. In Indian cooking, fresh chutneys such as this tasty almond one, *Badam Ki Chutney*, are made by simply grinding all the ingredients to a smooth purée.

2 Transfer to a blender, with the water in which they were soaked. Add the remaining ingredients and blend until smooth.

3 Transfer to a serving bowl and chill. Serve with fried and grilled (broiled) snacks or use as a dip with poppadums.

VARIATION
Substitute the almonds with the same quantity of desiccated (dry unsweetened shredded) coconut.

SERVES 4–5

50g/2oz/½ cup blanched almonds

1 fresh green chilli, roughly chopped (deseeded if preferred)

1 small clove garlic

1cm/½in piece of fresh root ginger, roughly chopped

15g/½oz fresh coriander (cilantro) leaves and stalks

30ml/2 tbsp fresh mint leaves

2.5ml/½ tsp salt

5ml/1 tsp sugar

15ml/1 tbsp lemon juice

1 Soak the almonds in 175ml/6fl oz/¾ cup boiling water for 15 minutes.

Per portion Energy 79kcal/330kJ; Protein 3.1g; Carbohydrate 3.4g, of which sugars 1.3g; Fat 6.1g, of which saturates 0.5g; Cholesterol 0mg; Calcium 61mg; Fibre 0.7g; Sodium 201mg.

Coconut chutney

In traditional Tamil Nadu style, this chutney, *Thengai Thuvaiyal*, is fiery hot. Through the pungency of the heat, you can savour the wonderful flavour and mellow taste of the chillies, with the sweet undertone of coconut and the distinctive tang of tamarind. A real explosion of flavours in your mouth!

SERVES 4–5

75g/3oz/1 cup desiccated (dry unsweetened shredded) coconut
1–2 fresh green chillies, chopped (deseeded if preferred)
2.5ml/½ tsp salt, or to taste
2.5ml/½ tsp sugar
15ml/1 tbsp natural (plain) yogurt
1cm/½in piece of fresh root ginger, roughly chopped
22.5ml/1½ tbsp tamarind juice or lime juice
15ml/1 tbsp sunflower oil or light olive oil
2.5ml/½ tsp black mustard seeds
6–8 curry leaves
1 dried red chilli, chopped

3 Heat the oil in a small wok or a steel ladle over a medium heat. When hot, but not smoking, add the mustard seeds, followed by the curry leaves and red chilli.

4 Allow the seeds to crackle and the chilli to blacken slightly, then switch off the heat. Pour the entire mixture over the chutney. Mix well and serve at room temperature.

1 Put the coconut in a bowl and pour in enough boiling water to just cover it. Set aside for 15–20 minutes.

2 Transfer the coconut to a blender and add the chillies, salt, sugar, yogurt, ginger and tamarind or lime juice. Blend until the ingredients are mixed to a smooth purée, then transfer to a serving bowl.

Per portion Energy 133kcal/548kJ; Protein 1.9g; Carbohydrate 4.1g, of which sugars 2g; Fat 12.3g, of which saturates 8.4g; Cholesterol 0mg; Calcium 20mg; Fibre 2.1g; Sodium 9mg.

Bread

A staple accompaniment to many meals, bread plays a key role in the daily lives of thousands of Indians. There are infinite variations on the simple flat bread, based on a dough made with flour and water, to which spices and vegetables such as spring greens (collards) can be added. Richer doughs made with ghee or butter and milk in place of water make for softer breads, which may be flaky and stuffed, or deep-fried.

Wholesome, nutty and nutritious

Bread is an important daily food, especially in northern India, where the climate is cooler and ideal for wheat production. North Indians thrive on a daily diet of numerous kinds of bread with their curries, and these are generally made from the same three ingredients: ground grains, salt and water. Unleavened flat breads, ranging from simple, fat-free chapatis to rich, layered parathas (similar to flaky pastry), are made from wheat. Leavened breads such as naan, of which there are numerous varieties, are generally commercially made nowadays, although they are still made by local bakeries on *tandoors* in some more remote villages.

In India, especially in the rural parts, people grind their own wheat to make flour, and bake their bread on a cast-iron griddle called a *tawa*. The wheat flour, known as atta, is very fine and is made by grinding the entire wheat kernel, which is packed with essential nutrients, including a high proportion of roughage. In addition to wheat flour, breads are also made from rice flour, maize flour, gram flour (besan), ground barley, and even semolina; all of these also contain nutrients and, in the case of gram flour, vitally important protein.

The most common breads, chapatis, are simply dry-roasted, and are ideal with more complex dishes and for everyday eating. They do not keep particularly well as they tend to dry out, and are best made and consumed on the same day. Other flat breads are brushed with a small amount of oil or ghee during cooking to add moisture as well as flavour. Some types, such as Ginger and Cumin Puffed Bread, are deep-fried, creating a luxurious and tasty treat that is perfect with a simple curry that allows the bread to shine. Naan, with its soft texture and slightly sour taste from the yogurt that is used in the dough, is best cooked on a *tandoor*, which imparts a smoky flavour and cooks the bread very quickly, ensuring the desired soft finish. These can accompany practically any dish and are also fabulous on their own or with a selection of chutneys and raitas.

A wide range of spices, herbs and leafy vegetables such as spinach or spring greens (collards) can be added to the basic doughs, creating infinite variations on a theme, although the flavour of the flour used in the simpler breads is delicious without any embellishment. Cumin, ginger and fenugreek are among the favoured flavourings, depending where in the country you are. Flaky breads have a soft texture that lends itself to rich, spicy stuffings made from satisfying ingredients such as potatoes or eggs, creating all-in-one meals or light snacks that are perfect when on the go.

Plain flour flat bread

A soft dough made with strong white bread flour, ghee and warm water is what makes this Assamese flat bread, *Moidar Sukan Ruti*, so different from any other. They are dry-roasted like chapatis, but because of the fat content, they are softer and can be re-heated without drying out. They are the perfect partner for curries.

4 Cover with a damp dish towel and set aside for 30 minutes.

5 Divide the dough into 10 equal portions, then shape each into a smooth flat cakes by rotating it between your palms.

6 Place a heavy griddle or a *tawa* (the Indian cast iron griddle for making flat bread) over a medium heat.

7 Place a dough circle on the griddle and cook for 2 minutes, then turn it over with a spatula and cook for a further 2 minutes.

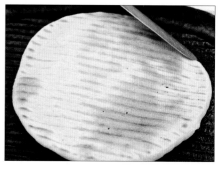

8 Press all around the edges of the bread with the spatula during cooking to encourage the bread to puff up and cook evenly.

9 Wrap each bread in a clean dish towel to keep it warm until you finish cooking the remaining dough circles. Serve immediately, or leave to cool and reheat in a moderate over for 5 minutes.

MAKES 10

400g/14oz/3⅓ strong white bread flour, plus extra for dusting
5ml/1 tsp salt
75g/3oz/6 tbsp ghee or unsalted butter, at room temperature
200ml/7fl oz/scant 1 cup warm water

1 In a large mixing bowl, mix together the flour and salt, then rub in the ghee or butter using your fingertips.

2 Gradually add the water and mix until a soft dough is formed.

3 Transfer the dough to a lightly floured surface and knead for about 10 minutes, until it is soft and smooth.

Per portion Energy 204kcal/857kJ; Protein 5g; Carbohydrate 30g, of which sugars 1g; Fat 8g, of which saturates 5g; Cholesterol 21mg; Calcium 56mg; Fibre 1.5g; Sodium 198mg.

Wholemeal flat bread

These breads from Assam, called *Ruti*, are thicker than chapatis and are griddle-cooked, with oil or ghee spread over the surface. Unlike the dough for chapatis and *Phulkas* (*see* page 205), this mixture contains a small amount of fat and warm water is used instead of cold, creating a softer, richer dough.

MAKES 8

400g/14oz/3½ cups chapati flour (atta)
or fine wholemeal (whole-wheat) flour
5ml/1 tsp salt
30ml/2 tbsp sunflower oil or light
olive oil
250ml/9fl oz/1 cup lukewarm water
a little extra flour for dusting
sunflower oil or light olive oil,
for frying

1 Mix the flour and salt together in a large mixing bowl. Add the oil and work well into the flour with your fingertips. Gradually add the water and keep stirring until a soft dough is formed.

2 Transfer the dough to a flat surface and knead it for 4–5 minutes. When all the excess moisture is absorbed by the flour, wrap the dough in clear film (plastic wrap) and let it rest for 30 minutes, until doubled in size. Alternatively, make the dough in a food processor, using a dough hook and following manufacturer's instructions.

3 Divide the dough into eight equal-size balls and make flat cakes by rotating them between the palms and pressing them down.

4 Roll out each cake on a floured surface into a 13cm/5in circle.

5 Preheat a griddle over a medium heat and place a disc on it. Cook for 2 minutes, then turn it over.

6 Spread 5ml/1 tsp oil evenly on the surface and turn it over again. Cook for 2 minutes, until browned all over. Spread 5ml/1 tsp oil on the other side, turn the bread over, and cook as above until browned.

7 Keep the cooked breads hot by wrapping them in a piece of foil lined with kitchen paper. Cook the remaining flat breads in the same way. Serve with any curry.

Per portion Energy 180kcal/761kJ; Protein 6.4g; Carbohydrate 32g, of which sugars 1.1g; Fat 3.9g, of which saturates 0.5g; Cholesterol 0mg; Calcium 19mg; Fibre 4.5g; Sodium 247mg.

Griddle-roasted wholemeal flat breads

Flat breads are a great accompaniment to vegetarian dishes. They can be served with chutneys and pickles or as part of a main meal. *Chapatis* are dry-roasted on an iron griddle (*tawa*). The dough can also be used to make *Phulkas*, which puff up like balloons under the grill and are delicious spread with melted butter.

MAKES 16
400g/14oz/3½ cups chapati flour (atta)
    or fine wholemeal (whole-wheat) flour,
    plus a little extra for dusting
5ml/1 tsp salt
250ml/9fl oz/1 cup water

1 Mix the flour and salt together in a mixing bowl. Gradually add the water.

2 Continue to mix with your fingers until a dough is formed.

3 Transfer the dough to a lightly floured surface and knead it for 4–5 minutes.

4 When all the excess moisture has been absorbed by the flour, wrap the dough in clear film (plastic wrap) and let it rest for 30 minutes. Alternatively, make the dough in a food processor, using a dough hook and following manufacturer's instructions.

5 Divide the dough into two equal parts and pinch or cut eight equal portions from each. Form the portions into balls and flatten them into neat, round cakes.

6 Dust the cakes lightly in the flour and roll each one out to a 15cm/6in circle. Keep the rest of the cakes covered with a damp dish towel while you work.

7 To make *chapatis*: preheat a heavy cast iron griddle over a medium/high heat. Place a dough circle on it, cook for about 30 seconds, then turn it over using a thin metal spatula.

8 Cook until bubbles begin to appear on the surface and turn it over again. Press the edges down gently with a clean dish towel to encourage the *chapati* to puff up (they will not always puff up, but this does not affect the taste).

9 Cook until the underneath begins to brown, then remove from the heat and keep them hot by wrapping them in foil lined with kitchen paper while you make the remaining breads in the same way.

10 For *phulkas*: preheat a grill (broiler) to high, and also preheat a heavy griddle as above. Place a dough circle on the griddle over a medium/high heat.

11 Cook for 35–40 seconds, then immediately place the pan under the grill, with the uncooked side of the bread facing up, about 13cm/5in below the heat source.

12 Let the *phulka* puff up until brown spots appear on the surface. Watch it carefully as this happens quite quickly. Remove and place the *phulka* on a piece of foil lined with kitchen paper. Repeat with the remaining dough.

VARIATION
You could add dried herbs, such as dried fenugreek leaves (kasuri methi), to the mixture if you like.

Per portion Energy 78kcal/330kJ; Protein 3.2g; Carbohydrate 16g, of which sugars 0.5g; Fat 0.6g, of which saturates 0.1g; Cholesterol 0mg; Calcium 10mg; Fibre 2.3g; Sodium 124mg.

Mung bean and wholewheat flat bread

Mah Ki Roti is traditionally made with sprouted mung beans, which can take time, but there are sprouting kits available, which make it easier. Sprouting enhances the nutritional value of the beans, but the recipe can be made without sprouting them if you wish. The delicious bread is bursting with health-giving qualities, and has a wholesome taste and unique texture.

MAKES 8

150g/5oz whole mung beans (sabut mung dhal)
5ml/1 tsp salt
1 medium onion, roughly chopped
15ml/1 tbsp fresh coriander (cilantro) leaves and stalks
30ml/2 tbsp sunflower oil or light olive oil
325g/11oz/2¾ cups strong wholemeal (whole-wheat) bread flour, plus extra for dusting
75ml–100ml/2½–3½fl oz/¼–⅓ cup water
ghee or unsalted butter, for shallow-frying

1 Wash the mung beans and soak them in a bowl of warm water. As the water cools, replace it with more warm water and leave the bowl in a warm place. During the sprouting time (*see* packet instructions), change the water 3–4 times.

2 Drain the beans and place them in a food processor.

COOK'S TIP
Some larger supermarkets and health food stores sell sprouted mung beans. If you wash and soak the beans in warm water and change the water as it gets cold, they will sprout faster. Leave it in a warm place, for 24–36 hours, and then they will be ready for use.

3 Add the salt, onion, coriander and oil to the food processor and blend until a fine, granular consistency is achieved. Add the flour and blend to combine.

4 Transfer to a bowl. Gradually add the water and mix until a soft dough is formed. Take care not to use all the water at once as the amount needed will depend on the absorbency level of the flour you are using, and you don't want the dough to be too wet.

5 Transfer the dough to a flat surface and knead it for 2–3 minutes, adding a little flour if it is too sticky. Cover with clear film (plastic wrap) and set aside to rest for 30 minutes. Alternatively, make the dough in a food processor, using a dough hook and following manufacturer's instructions.

6 Divide the dough into eight equal portions and flatten each of them into a smooth round cake. Dust each cake with a little flour.

7 Roll each portion out to a circle 13cm/5in in diameter. Keep the rest covered.

8 Place a heavy griddle over a low-medium heat and dry-roast the flat bread for 30–40 seconds on each side. Spread 5ml/1 tsp of ghee or butter on the surface and turn it over. Cook until the underside is browned.

9 Spread the surface with the ghee or butter and flip it over. Cook until browned. Wrap it in a clean dish towel until you finish cooking all the bread. Serve with any curry.

Per portion Energy 195kcal/821kJ; Protein 6g; Carbohydrate 28g, of which sugars 28g; Fat 7g, of which saturates 2g; Cholesterol 7mg; Calcium 26mg; Fibre 4.8g; Sodium 249mg.

Wholemeal flat bread with fenugreek leaves

Methi Na Thepla is a delicious spiced chapati from Gujarat where they serve it with meals, and also as a snack (*farsan*). In a Gujarati home, fresh fenugreek leaves are the obvious choice, but dried ones (kasuri methi) are more easily available elsewhere and make a lovely aromatic alternative.

MAKES 8

450g/1lb chapati flour (atta) or fine
  wholemeal (whole-wheat) flour
5ml/1 tsp salt, or to taste
30ml/2 tbsp dried fenugreek leaves
  (kasuri methi)
2.5–5ml/½–1 tsp chilli powder
2.5ml/½ tsp ground turmeric
2.5ml/½ tsp ground cumin
45ml/3 tbsp sunflower oil or light olive oil
250–300ml/9–10fl oz/generous 1 cup
  warm water
sunflower oil, for shallow-frying

1 Sift the flour into a large mixing bowl and mix in the salt, fenugreek leaves, chilli powder, turmeric and cumin.

2 Rub in the oil with your fingertips, then gradually add the water while continuing to mix. When a dough has formed, transfer it to a lightly floured surface and knead until soft and pliable. Alternatively, make the dough in a food processor.

3 Cover with a damp dish towel and let it rest for 30 minutes.

4 Divide the dough into two equal parts and cut four equal portions from each.

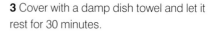

5 Form into balls and flatten each one to form a neat cake. Dust each cake lightly with flour and roll out to a 15cm/6in circle.

6 Preheat a cast iron griddle over a medium heat and place a flat bread on it. Cook for 30–35 seconds, then turn it over. Spread about 10ml/2 tsp oil over the surface of the cooked side and turn it over again. Let it cook for about 1 minute or until brown patches have appeared.

7 Spread the second side with the same amount of oil, turn it over and cook as before, until brown patches appear.

8 Transfer to a plate lined with kitchen paper. Cook all the bread in the same way. Serve on its own or with any vegetable curry.

Per portion Energy 279kcal/1171kJ; Protein 7.4g; Carbohydrate 36.6g, of which sugars 1.2g; Fat 12.5g, of which saturates 1.4g; Cholesterol 0mg; Calcium 25mg; Fibre 5.1g; Sodium 248mg.

Spiced gram flour flat bread

Besan Ki Roti is the ideal bread for anyone who needs to avoid gluten, as they are made with gram flour (besan), which is produced from ground chickpeas rather than wheat. The dough is kneaded together with grated onion, Asafoetida and chillies, then griddle-roasted, which gives a delicious aroma and a nutty taste.

MAKES 8

400g/14oz/3½ cups gram flour (besan), sifted, plus extra for dusting
5ml/1 tsp nigella seeds
2.5ml/¼ tsp Asafoetida
5ml/1 tsp salt, or to taste
1 medium onion, peeled
1 fresh green chilli, finely chopped (deseeded if preferred)
45ml/3 tbsp coriander (cilantro) leaves, finely chopped
sunflower oil, for cooking

1 Put the gram flour in a mixing bowl, then add the nigella seeds, Asafoetida and salt. Grate the onion, then add to the flour with the chilli and coriander.

2 Mix well, then gradually add 100ml/3½fl oz/ 7 tbsp water until a dough forms.

3 Transfer the dough to a flat surface and knead it for a couple of minutes with gentle pressure, turning it around frequently. If the dough sticks to your fingers, add a little oil.

4 Divide the dough into eight equal portions and flatten them into round cakes.

5 Dust each cake in the flour, then roll them out to circles of about 13cm/5in diameter with a rolling pin.

6 Preheat a griddle over a low/medium heat and place a flat bread on it.

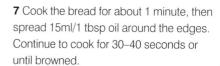

7 Cook the bread for about 1 minute, then spread 15ml/1 tbsp oil around the edges. Continue to cook for 30–40 seconds or until browned.

8 Turn the bread over and cook the second side until browned. Transfer to a plate lined with kitchen paper and keep warm while you repeat with the remaining breads.

Per portion Energy 237kcal/1002kJ; Protein 4.5g; Carbohydrate 39.2g, of which sugars 0.4g; Fat 8.1g, of which saturates 0.9g; Cholesterol 0mg; Calcium 21mg; Fibre 6g; Sodium 1mg.

Wheat-flour flat bread with spiced greens

In the state of Bihar, situated near west Bengal, this fabulous spicy wheat-flour flat bread, *Bathuway Ki Roti*, is made with locally grown greens that are difficult to get hold of anywhere else. However, you can use spinach, which makes an easy and delicious alternative. This healthy flat bread is very tasty and makes the perfect accompaniment to many Indian vegetarian dishes.

MAKES 10

250g/9oz spinach leaves
450g/1lb/4 cups chapati flour (atta) or
    fine wholemeal (whole-wheat) flour, plus
    extra for dusting
5ml/1 tsp salt
2.5ml/½ tsp aniseed
30ml/2 tbsp sunflower oil or light olive oil
sunflower oil, for shallow-frying

1 Put the spinach in a large bowl or pan and pour over boiling water to cover it completely. Leave it to soak for 2 minutes, then drain, refresh with cold water and drain again. Squeeze out as much water as possible, but make sure that the spinach remains quite moist.

2 Place the spinach in a food processor and chop it finely, but do not process it to a purée.

3 Mix the flour, salt and aniseed in a bowl. Add 15ml/1 tbsp of the oil and mix well, then stir in the spinach.

4 Gradually add 200ml/7fl oz/¾ cup water and mix until a soft dough is formed. You may not need all the water as the spinach leaves will release their own moisture into the flour, so add a little at a time.

5 Transfer to a flat surface, add the remaining oil and knead the dough for 3–4 minutes. Cover with a damp dish towel and let it rest for 15–20 minutes.

6 Divide the dough into two equal parts and pinch off or cut each half into five equal portions. Form into balls and flatten each one into a smooth, round cake.

7 Dust each cake in the flour and roll out to approximately an 18cm/7in circle.

8 Preheat a griddle over a medium heat and place a flat bread on it. Cook for 30–40 seconds, then turn it over. Spread 5ml/1 tsp of oil on the surface of the bread and turn it over again.

9 Cook until brown patches appear underneath, checking by lifting the bread with a metal spatula or a fish slice.

10 Spread 5ml/1 tsp oil on the second side, turn it over and cook until brown patches appear.

11 Repeat until all the dough circles are cooked. Serve immediately.

COOK'S TIP
Place the cooked bread on one end of a long piece of foil lined with kitchen paper. Cover with the other end to keep it hot while you cook the remaining breads. Stack the cooked breads in the foil, covering each time you add one.

Per portion Energy 166kcal/700kJ; Protein 6.4g; Carbohydrate 29.2g, of which sugars 1.3g; Fat 3.4g, of which saturates 0.4g; Cholesterol 0mg; Calcium 60mg; Fibre 4.6g; Sodium 36mg.

Spiced potato-filled flaky bread

This type of bread, known as paratha, is traditionally a rich, unleavened bread that can be plain or stuffed. This version, *Aloo Paratha*, is stuffed with spiced potatoes, and olive oil is used instead of ghee. The wholesome taste of the flour used more than makes up for the absence of ghee or butter.

MAKES 8

450g/1lb/4 cups wholemeal (whole-wheat) bread flour, plus extra for dusting
2.5ml/½ tsp salt, or to taste
30ml/2 tbsp sunflower oil or light olive oil
290ml/9fl oz/scant 1⅔ cups warm water
sunflower oil or olive oil, for shallow-frying

For the filling:
15ml/1 tbsp sunflower oil or light olive oil
2.5ml/½ tsp black or brown mustard seeds
2 shallots, finely chopped
10ml/2 tsp fresh root ginger purée
1 fresh green chilli, finely chopped (deseeded if preferred)
30ml/2 tbsp fresh coriander (cilantro) leaves, finely chopped
2.5ml/½ tsp salt, or to taste
225g/8oz potatoes, boiled in their jackets then peeled and mashed

1 Put the flour and salt in a bowl and work in the oil with your fingertips. Gradually add the water and mix until a soft dough is formed.

2 Transfer the dough to a floured surface and knead for 3–4 minutes or until all traces of stickiness disappear. Alternatively, put all the ingredients into a food processor with a dough hook and run the machine for about 5 minutes, until the dough feels soft and there is no stickiness.

3 Cover the dough with a damp dish towel and set aside for 30 minutes.

4 Meanwhile, prepare the filling. Heat the oil over a medium heat and add the mustard seeds. As soon as they start popping, add the shallots, ginger and chilli.

5 Stir-fry for 2–3 minutes, then stir in the chopped coriander and salt and remove from the heat. Transfer to a large bowl.

6 Add the mashed potato to this mixture and mix well. Divide the dough into two equal parts and make four portions out of each. Shape each portion into a ball and flatten it into a smooth cake.

7 Form the cake into a saucer shape by gently stretching, and moisten the edges with cold water. Place a portion of the filling in each, bring up the sides of the dough and seal the edges by pressing them together. Press the ball to form a flat cake.

8 Preheat a cast iron griddle or other heavy frying pan over a medium heat. Dust each of the flat cakes with the flour and, with gentle pressure, roll out to a 15cm/6in disc.

9 Place one disc on the hot griddle and cook for 1 minute, then turn it over and cook the other side for 1 minute. Spread 5ml/1 tsp oil on the cooked side, turn it over and spread oil on the other side. Flip it over again and cook the side that was oiled first for 2–3 minutes, until brown patches appear.

10 Turn it over and cook the other side for a further 2–3 minutes, until brown patches appear. Place the paratha on a piece of foil lined with kitchen paper. Cover while you cook the remaining parathas.

Per portion Energy 286kcal/1207kJ; Protein 9g; Carbohydrate 46g, of which sugars 2g; Fat 9g, of which saturates 1g; Cholesterol 0mg; Calcium 30mg; Fibre 5.1g; Sodium 252mg.

Spicy egg-filled flaky bread

This wonderful flaky bread, *Dimer Parota*, can easily steal the centre stage as it is packed full of protein, fibre and vitamins. Delicious served warm from the oven, any leftovers make an ideal accompaniment to a vegetable curry, or you could cut the bread into small pieces and serve it as an appetizer at drinks parties.

MAKES 8

275g/10oz/2½ cups wholemeal
  (whole-wheat) flour
175g/6oz/½ cup plain (all-purpose) flour,
  plus extra for dusting
2.5ml/½ tsp salt
5ml/1 tsp baking powder
30ml/2 tbsp sunflower oil or light olive oil
115g/4oz/½ cup full-fat (whole) natural
  (plain) yogurt, beaten
150ml/¼ pint/⅔ cup warm water
sunflower oil, for shallow frying

For the filling:
3 large (US extra large) eggs, beaten
1 small red onion, finely chopped
1 fresh red chilli, finely chopped
  (deseeded if preferred)
30ml/2 tbsp fresh coriander (cilantro)
  leaves, finely chopped
1.25ml/¼ tsp salt

1 Put both types of flour into a large mixing bowl and work in the salt and baking powder. Add the oil and yogurt and mix with your fingertips.

2 Gradually add the water and combine until a soft dough is formed.

> ## COOK'S TIP
> These delicious stuffed breads are ideal for a packed lunch or a snack on the go.

3 Transfer the dough to a lightly floured surface and knead it for about 10 minutes, until it is soft and pliable. Cover the dough with clear film (plastic wrap) and set aside for 30 minutes.

4 To make the filling, mix together all the ingredients and set aside.

5 Divide the dough into eight equal portions, shape into balls and flatten to round cakes. Lightly dust one cake in the flour and roll it out to a 18cm/7in circle. Keep the remaining cakes covered while you are working.

6 Preheat a heavy griddle or a non-stick frying pan over a medium heat, then place the dough circle on it and dry-roast each side of the bread for about 30 seconds.

7 Drizzle about 5ml/1 tsp oil around the edges and cook for a futher 1 minute or until brown patches appear on the underside. You can lift the bread slightly to check.

8 Turn it over and spread about 30ml/2 tbsp of the filling mixture on the cooked side. Reduce the heat slightly and drizzle 5ml/1 tsp oil around the edges.

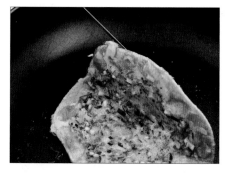

9 When the egg mixture has lightly set, and the second side of the bread has brown patches, fold the bread in half and cook until the egg has fully set. Do not worry if some egg spills out, it will soon set.

10 Keep the cooked bread wrapped in a clean dish towel while you repeat the process with all the dough balls.

Per portion Energy 291kcal/1223kJ; Protein 10g; Carbohydrate 41g, of which sugars 2g; Fat 11g, of which saturates 11g; Cholesterol 2mg; Calcium 98mg; Fibre 3.9g; Sodium 289mg.

Ginger and cumin puffed bread with spinach

This delectable bread, *Palak Puri*, from the Indore area is gently aromatic, and its flavours mingle happily with any vegetable curry. Traditionally, the dough is divided into small portions and each puri is rolled out individually, but in order to save time, you can roll out larger portions and cut them into smaller circles with a metal cutter. The crisp fried breads are divine with all manner of curries.

MAKES 20

100g/3½oz fresh spinach leaves
300g/10oz/2½ cups chapati flour (atta) or fine wholemeal (whole-wheat) flour, plus extra for dusting
2.5ml/½ tsp aniseed
2.5ml/½ tsp salt
5ml/1 tsp ginger purée
2.5ml/½ tsp chilli powder
25g/1oz butter
30ml/1fl oz/2 tbsp water
sunflower oil, for deep-frying

1 Put the spinach in a heatproof bowl and pour over enough boiling water to cover. Stir to ensure that all the leaves are immersed in the water. Leave them soaking for 2 minutes, then drain and refresh in cold water.

2 Squeeze out as much excess water as possible from the spinach and chop the leaves finely with a large knife or in a food processor, in short bursts, taking care not to reduce the spinach to a purée.

3 Put the flour in a mixing bowl and add the aniseed, salt, ginger and chilli powder. Mix well and rub in the butter.

4 Add the chopped spinach and 30ml/1fl oz/2 tbsp water, and mix until a soft dough is formed.

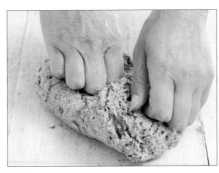

5 Transfer the dough to a flat surface and knead for 3–4 minutes.

6 Cover with a damp dish towel and set aside for 30 minutes.

7 Divide the dough into two equal parts and pinch off or cut ten equal portions from each. Form into balls and flatten to smooth, round cakes.

8 Dust the cakes lightly with flour and roll each one out to a 7.5cm/3in circle, taking care not to tear or pierce them as they will not puff up if damaged. Place them in a single layer on baking parchment and cover with another piece of parchment.

9 Heat the oil in a wok or other pan suitable for deep-frying. When the oil has a faint shimmer of rising smoke on the surface, carefully drop in one cake. As soon as it rises to the surface, gently tap round the edges to encourage puffing.

10 When it has puffed up, turn it over and fry the other side until browned. Drain on kitchen paper.

11 Keep the fried puris on a baking tray in a single layer while you cook the remaining dough. They are best eaten fresh, though they can be re-heated for 2–3 minutes in a hot oven. Serve with any curry.

COOK'S TIP
The oil should measure at least 180ºC/350ºF on a thermometer when you add the dough.

Per portion Energy 58kcal/247kJ; Protein 2.1g; Carbohydrate 9.8g, of which sugars 0.4g; Fat 1.5g, of which saturates 0.7g; Cholesterol 3mg; Calcium 15mg; Fibre 1.5g; Sodium 17mg.

Deep-fried soft puffed bread

Kumol Lusi from Assam are similar to *luchi* from east India, but they are softer and richer. They are made with plain (all-purpose) flour and the dough is enriched with ghee and hot milk, instead of water, creating a velvety soft bread. They are perfect with any vegetable curry and are also popular with egg dishes.

MAKES 16

275g/10oz/2½ cups plain (all-purpose) flour, plus a little extra for dusting

2.5ml/½ tsp salt

1.25ml/¼ tsp sugar

15ml/1 tbsp ghee or unsalted butter

175ml/6fl oz/⅔ cup lukewarm milk

sunflower oil, for deep-frying

Parsee Spiced Omelette (*see* page 83) or South-Indian Scrambled Eggs (*see* page 82), to serve

1 Sift the flour into a large bowl and add the salt, sugar and ghee or butter.

2 Mix the ingredients and gradually add the milk. Mix until a soft dough is formed.

3 Transfer the dough to a floured surface. Knead for 4–5 minutes. Alternatively, make the dough in a food processor, following manufacturer's instructions.

4 Wrap the dough in clear film (plastic wrap) and let it rest for 20–30 minutes.

5 Divide the dough into two equal parts and make eight equal-sized balls out of each. Flatten the balls into cakes by rotating and pressing them between your palms.

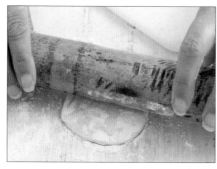

6 Dust each cake very lightly in the flour and roll them out to about 6cm/2½in circles, taking care not to tear or pierce them, as they will not puff up if damaged.

7 Place them in a single layer on a piece of baking parchment and cover with another piece of baking parchment.

8 Heat the oil in a wok or other suitable pan for deep-frying, over a medium/high heat. When the oil has a faint shimmer of rising smoke on the surface, carefully drop in one flattened dough cake. As soon as it floats, gently tap round the edges to encourage puffing.

9 When it has puffed up, turn it over and fry the other side until browned.

10 Lift out and drain on kitchen paper. Keep the fried breads on a tray in a single layer. They are best eaten fresh, although they can be reheated briefly (3–4 minutes) in a moderately hot oven.

11 Serve warm with egg dishes, such as Parsee Spiced Omelette or South-Indian Scrambled Eggs.

VARIATION

A healthier version of these breads can be made by using wholemeal (whole-wheat) flour and adding olive oil instead of ghee. This creates a wholesome taste that complements most vegetable curries, lentils, beans and peas.

Per portion Energy 72kcal/306kJ; Protein 2g; Carbohydrate 14g, of which sugars 0.9g; Fat 1.3g, of which saturates 0.6g; Cholesterol 1mg; Calcium 37mg; Fibre 0.5g; Sodium 68mg.

Deep-fried leavened bread

Bhature served with a local dish of spiced chickpeas is a Punjabi speciality. The dough for the bread is enriched with yogurt and egg, and contains a little baking powder for leavening, which results in a soft and luscious bread that is ideal served with any type of curry.

MAKES 8

350g/12oz/3 cups plain (all-purpose) flour, plus extra for dusting

2.5ml/½ tsp salt

2.5ml/½ tsp sugar

5ml/1 tsp baking powder

150g/5oz/generous ½ cup natural (plain) yogurt

1 egg

30–45ml/2–3 tbsp warm water

sunflower oil, for deep-frying

1 Sift the flour, salt, sugar and baking powder into a large bowl and mix well.

2 Beat the yogurt and egg together and add to the flour along with the warm water. Mix until a dough has formed.

3 Transfer the dough to a flat surface. Knead it for 4–5 minutes, until soft and pliable. Alternatively, use a food processor, following manufacturer's instructions.

4 Place the dough in a plastic food bag and leave to rest in a warm place for 2–3 hours, until doubled in size.

5 Divide the dough into eight equal parts and form each one into a ball, then flatten to a smooth, round cake. Dust in flour and roll out to circles about 13cm/5in across.

6 Heat the oil in a wok or other suitable pan for deep-frying over a medium heat. Check that the temperature is right by dropping a little of the dough into the oil. If it floats to the surface immediately without turning brown, then the temperature is just right.

7 Place a dough cake in the hot oil and fry for about 1 minute. When it puffs up, turn it over and fry the other side for 1 minute more or until browned. Drain on kitchen paper.

Per portion Energy 244kcal/1027kJ; Protein 5.9g; Carbohydrate 35.7g, of which sugars 2.4g; Fat 9.7g, of which saturates 1.2g; Cholesterol 24mg; Calcium 101mg; Fibre 1.4g; Sodium 149mg.

Sweet rice flour and coconut mini bread

The people of the eastern state of Orissa makes this sweetmeat, *Kakara*, for festive occasions. Roasted coconut is normally used as a filling that is enclosed in a flat bread-like dough and then deep-fried. To save time and effort, in this recipe the coconut is added to the dough instead of being used as a filling.

SERVES 6–8

150g/5oz palm sugar (jaggery) or soft dark brown sugar
5ml/1 tsp freshly ground black pepper
5ml/1 tsp fennel seeds
5ml/1 tsp ground cinnamon
2.5ml/½ tsp salt
150g/5oz/1¼ cups plain (all-purpose) flour, plus extra for dusting
150g/5oz/1¼ cups ground rice
75g/3oz desiccated (dry unsweetened shredded) coconut
sunflower oil or ghee, for deep-frying

1 Cut the palm sugar into small pieces and put these into a pan. Add 150ml/¼ pint/⅔ cup water and place over a medium heat.

2 Let the sugar dissolve, stir, then add the pepper, fennel, cinnamon and salt. Stir, then add the flour, ground rice and coconut.

3 Stir until a dough has formed, then remove from the heat. Cover with a damp dish towel and let it cool completely.

4 Knead the dough gently on a lightly floured surface for about 8 minutes, until it is smooth and pliable, then divide it into two equal pieces.

5 Roll out each half on a floured surface to a thickness of about 5mm/¼in. Stamp out rounds using a 7.5cm/3in cookie cutter. Gather up any remaining dough, roll it out and cut as before.

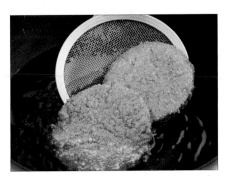

6 Heat the ghee or oil in a wok or other suitable pan for deep-frying over a medium heat and fry the bread in batches, until browned on both sides.

7 Drain on kitchen paper, leave to cool and serve as a teatime treat or with after-dinner coffee. Keep any leftover bread in an airtight container. They will keep well for 4–5 days.

Per portion Energy 325kcal/1363kJ; Protein 4g; Carbohydrate 48g, of which sugars 18g; Fat 14g, of which saturates 6g; Cholesterol 0mg; Calcium 59mg; Fibre 2.7g; Sodium 142mg.

Drinks, Desserts and Sweetmeats

Enjoyed throughout the day as well as after meals, drinks such as tea, coffee and refreshing *lassis* are popular all over India. Desserts, often made with milk and fruits, are usually reserved for special occasions, but when they are on the menu they are consumed with relish. Sweetmeats are indulged in more frequently, usually as a snack or with tea or coffee rather than as part of a meal.

Comforting, creamy and crunchy

Although both drinks and desserts are integral parts of any cuisine, they rarely feature prominently as part of a meal in India. Plain water is the most commonly consumed drink and desserts were, and still are to a large extent, reserved for special occasions. On a day to day basis, people usually opt for a piece of fresh fruit, fruit salads or some chilled, sweetened yogurt.

For those whose religion permits its consumption, alcohol is generally drunk before dinner, with chilled water being the preference during meals. However, drinking wine with food has become popular in recent years, and India produces several types that complement spicy dishes. Easy-drinking chilled whites such as Pinot Blanc and Pinot Grigio, as well as soft and fruity rosés, such as Grenache, are ideal. Generally, low-tannin red wines are best with spices, although some richer types such as Cabernet Sauvignon and Malbec are excellent.

Away from mealtimes, Indians consume vast quantities of tea and coffee, which is often flavoured with spices such as cardamom and served with a lot of milk and often some sugar. Chilled thirst-quenchers made from fruits such as lime or mango, as well as the plethora of different lassis made throughout the country, provide relief in the heat, and often contain salt to ensure proper hydration.

When the occasion calls for one, a little thought is required when deciding upon a dessert that will complement the main course. Cool, refreshing palate-cleansers such as Saffron-scented Strained Yogurt or the world-renowned classic, *kulfi*, are appropriate after a spicy meal in a hot climate, while richer warm desserts such as Cardamom-scented Coconut Dumplings or Coconut-filled Wheat Pancakes are ideal after a lighter, less heavily spiced meal.

India has a huge repertoire of sweetmeats, which tend to be rather heavy and very sugary, so they are often more suitable as a snack with tea and coffee than for a dessert. The type of sweetmeat made varies from region to region, as with the rest of the menu, and each area has its particular speciality. East India, and particularly Bengal, for instance, is famed for its dazzling range of milk-based sweets, including Milk Balls in Cardamom-scented Syrup. In western India sweetmeats come in the form of dry balls (*laddus*), which can be made of sesame seeds, rice or skinless mung beans. Indian 'fudges' also appear in many guises, depending on local ingredients, and can be made from coconut, sesame seeds or even lentils, to name but a few variations.

Sweet and salty lime drink

In Bengal this drink is known as *Lebur Sharbat* and it is very refreshing during the heat of the oppressive summer months. Many different varieties of lemon and lime are available in east India and you can use either citrus fruit, or a combination of both, according to your preference.

2 Add the lime juice to the jug and stir well to combine. Chill in the refrigerator for about 1 hour.

3 When you are ready to serve the drink, crush some ice by placing ice cubes in a clean dish towel and crushing them with a rolling pin.

4 Line individual glasses with the crushed ice and pour in the lime drink. Garnish with the slices of lime and serve immediately.

SERVES 4

30–45ml/2–3 tbsp caster (superfine) sugar
5ml/1 tsp salt
600ml/1 pint/2½ cups cold water
juice of 2 limes
ice cubes
4 slices of lime, to garnish

VARIATION

This refreshing drink would also be delicious made with freshly squeezed grapefruit juice.

1 Put the sugar, salt and water in a large jug (pitcher) and stir with a spoon until the sugar has completely dissolved.

Per portion Energy 46kcal/194kJ; Protein 50g; Carbohydrate 12g, of which sugars 12g; Fat 0g, of which saturates 0g; Cholesterol 0mg; Calcium 3mg; Fibre 0.0g; Sodium 492mg.

Cardamom- and rose-scented mango drink

Sherbat is the generic name for fruit-based drinks made with milk or water, and this one, *Amer Sherbat*, includes a touch of spice to make it extra special. Ready-to-use mango purée is sold in Indian stores, but canned mangoes that have been drained and puréed can also be used.

MAKES 1.2 LITRES/2 PINTS/5 CUPS
450g/1lb canned mango pulp or
 2 x 425g/15oz cans of sliced
 mangoes, drained
600ml/1 pint/2½ cups full-fat (whole) milk
45–60ml/3–4 tbsp sugar
5ml/1 tsp ground cardamom
30ml/2 tbsp rose water (optional)
sprigs of fresh mint, to garnish

3 Add 300ml/½ pint/1¼ cups cold water and the rose water, if using. Mix well and chill the *sherbat* in the refrigerator.

4 Pour the chilled drink into stemmed glasses, if you like, and serve garnished with the mint.

1 Put the mango pulp or slices into a food processor and add the milk, sugar and the ground cardamom.

2 Blend everything together until smooth, then transfer to a jug (pitcher).

VARIATION
For a healthier alternative, you can use skimmed or semi-skimmed (low-fat) milk if you wish.

Per portion Energy 790kcal/3344kJ; Protein 18g; Carbohydrate 147g, of which sugars 145g; Fat 19g, of which saturates 12g; Cholesterol 63mg; Calcium 595mg; Fibre 13.1g; Sodium 206mg.

Savoury yogurt drink

Lassi is made with different flavourings and it is a very welcome drink during the oppressive heat of the summer months. This version, *Namkeen Lassi*, is flavoured with black pepper and mint and is ideal as an appetizer or just as a refreshing drink, served in tall glasses lined with crushed ice.

MAKES 1.2 LITRES/2 PINTS/5 CUPS

2.5ml/½ tsp black peppercorns
2.5ml/½ tsp cumin seeds
450g/1lb/2 cups natural (plain) yogurt
10–12 fresh mint leaves
5ml/1 tsp salt, or to taste
10ml/2 tsp caster (superfine) sugar
crushed ice, to serve

COOK'S TIP
Use whole-milk yogurt, which resembles the home-made Indian version in terms of taste and texture.

1 Preheat a small, heavy pan over a medium heat and dry-roast the peppercorns and cumin seeds for about 1 minute, until they release their aroma.

2 Crush the peppercorns and cumin with a mortar and pestle. Alternatively, place them in a plastic bag and crush with a rolling pin.

3 Put the yogurt, mint, salt, sugar and the spices into a blender and add 300ml/½ pint/1¼ cups water. You could also use a bowl and stick blender. Blend until smooth.

4 Add 300ml/½ pint/1¼ cups more water and blend well. Put the crushed ice in tall glasses, pour the lassi over and serve.

Per portion Energy 396kcal/1670kJ; Protein 26g; Carbohydrate 46g, of which sugars 26g; Fat 14g, of which saturates 8g; Cholesterol 50mg; Calcium 925mg; Fibre 0.0g; Sodium 4293mg.

Sweet yogurt drink

Lassi originated in the northern state of Punjab and became a favourite drink of the nation. The people of northern India favour savoury lassi, but those in central India are partial to all things sweet, and prefer this recipe, *Meethi Lassi*. Teetotallers enjoy it, others use it as a cure for hangovers, and vegetarians thrive on it!

SERVES 4

450g/1lb/2 cups full-fat (whole) natural (plain) yogurt
75g/3oz/⅔ cup caster (superfine) sugar
30ml/2 tbsp rose water
fresh rose petals, to garnish (optional)

1 Put the yogurt and sugar into a blender and add 600ml/1 pint/2½ cups water. Blend until smooth.

2 Taste and add more sugar if necessary. Pour the lassi into a jug (pitcher) and chill in the refrigerator for several hours.

VARIATION
You can vary this sweet lassi by using other flavourings, such as vanilla extract, orange blossom water or 15ml/1 tbsp mango purée, instead of rose water.

3 Shortly before you are ready to serve the drink, place some ice cubes in a clean dish towel and crush them by hitting them with a rolling pin.

4 Stir the rose water into the lassi, and serve immediately in tall glasses lined with the crushed ice. Garnish with fresh rose petals, if you like.

Per portion Energy 137kcal/581kJ; Protein 5.8g; Carbohydrate 28g, of which sugars 28g; Fat 1.1g, of which saturates 0.6g; Cholesterol 1mg; Calcium 224mg; Fibre 0g; Sodium 95mg.

Papaya and yogurt drink

Papaya and yogurt make a very healthy combination, and this drink, *Papita Lassi*, is an ideal way to start the day or revive the body and senses in the afternoon. Rose water adds an exotic touch, but you could omit it or replace it with orange blossom water if you prefer.

2 Chop the papaya flesh roughly into small pieces, reserve a few pieces for a garnish and place the rest in a blender or large bowl.

3 Add the remaining ingredients and process in the blender, or with a stick blender, until smooth. Top with the reserved papaya chunks and serve the drink chilled.

SERVES 4
1 small ripe papaya
200g/7oz/scant 1 cup full-fat (whole)
  natural (plain) yogurt
45ml/3 tbsp sugar
250ml/8fl oz/1 cup water
15ml/1 tbsp rose water

COOK'S TIP
To make an even thicker and cooler drink, add a few ice cubes to the blender in step 3.

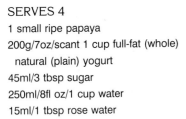

1 Cut the papaya in half lengthways, and remove the seeds and the white pith with a teaspoon.

Per portion Energy 96kcal/409kJ; Protein 3g; Carbohydrate 19g, of which sugars 19g; Fat 2g, of which saturates 1g; Cholesterol 6mg; Calcium 109mg; Fibre 0.8g; Sodium 42mg.

Spice-infused Kashmiri tea

Tea made with spices is enjoyed all over India, and the regional difference lies in the variation of the spices. During the freezing winters in this Himalayan region of Kasmir, *Qahwa* is brewed throughout the day to help keep inhabitants warm, as well as for its rehydrating and fortifying effects.

SERVES 2

450ml/16fl oz/2 cups water
1cm/½in piece of cinnamon stick
2 green cardamom pods, bruised
2 cloves
a small pinch (about 8 threads) of
   saffron, pounded
15ml/3 tsp leaf tea or 2 tea bags
milk and sugar, to taste (optional)

2 Rinse out a teapot with boiling water and put in the leaf tea or tea bags. Pour over the spiced water along with all the whole spices.

3 Brew the tea for 5 minutes, until the liquid is dark and strong, then strain the tea into individual cups. Add milk and sugar if you like, but it is also delicious without milk.

1 Bring the water to the boil in a pan and add all the spices. Simmer for 5 minutes.

> ## COOK'S TIP
> Spices such as cinnamon, cloves and cardamom are known to raise body temperature.

Per portion 15kcal/66kJ; Protein 1g; Carbohydrate 1.8g, of which sugars 0g; Fat 0.7g, of which saturates 0.1g; Cholesterol 0mg; Calcium 9mg; Fibre 0g; Sodium 2mg.

Cardamom tea

This Bengali version, *Cha*, of the much-loved spiced tea that is drunk all over the country, has the exotic aroma of cardamom, and is rich and fragrant rather than warming – perfect with a mid-morning snack or for afternoon tea. It also makes an excellent alternative to coffee after a meal.

SERVES 3–4

450ml/16fl oz/scant 2 cups water
20ml/4 tsp leaf tea, preferably Darjeeling
5–6 green cardamom pods, bruised
300ml/10fl oz/1¼ cups milk
sugar, to taste

VARIATION
If you do not have Darjeeling, you can use Assam, Ceylon or English Breakfast tea instead.

1 Put the water, tea and cardamom pods into a pan and bring to the boil.

2 Reduce the heat to low and simmer for 6–8 minutes.

3 Add the milk to the pan and increase the heat slightly. Simmer, uncovered, for 5–6 minutes, until the tea has turned a pinkish-brown colour.

4 Add more milk to taste. Strain into cups, add sugar to taste and serve.

COOK'S TIP
As well as being thirst-quenching, tea contains health-boosting antioxidants, which may help the body combat illnesses such as cancer and heart disease.

Per portion Energy 42kcal/177kJ; Protein 2.9g; Carbohydrate 4.6g, of which sugars 3.8g; Fat 1.6g, of which saturates 0.8g; Cholesterol 4mg; Calcium 95mg; Fibre 0g; Sodium 42mg.0

Milky cardamom coffee

Indian food and drink are well known for their enticing aroma and captivating flavours. Tea and coffee, flavoured with aromatic herbs and spices, are popular all over the country, although the spicing does vary from one region to another. *Elaichi Coffee* makes a delicious hot drink during the winter months.

SERVES 4
8 green cardamom pods, bruised
600ml/1 pint/2½ cups water
300ml/½ pint/1¼ cups milk
instant coffee and sugar, to taste

1 Put the cardamom pods and the water into a pan and bring to the boil.

VARIATION
This fragrant coffee is equally enjoyable served chilled in the summer, and in India it is often served in tall glasses with a scoop of vanilla ice cream as a luxurious form of iced coffee when part of afternoon tea.

2 Reduce the heat to low, cover the pan and simmer for 5–6 minutes, to allow the flavours to infuse the water.

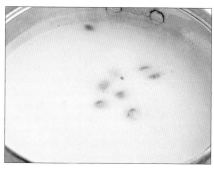

3 Add the milk and bring the liquid to the boil again.

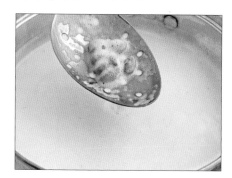

4 Remove the cardamom pods with a slotted spoon and discard them.

5 Put instant coffee and sugar to taste into individual cups and pour over the milky mixture. Stir and serve immediately.

Per portion Energy 70kcal/293kJ; Protein 3g; Carbohydrate 9g, of which sugars 9g; Fat 3g, of which saturates 2g; Cholesterol 11mg; Calcium 92mg; Fibre 0.0g; Sodium 34mg.

Saffron-scented strained yogurt

Shrikand is Maharashtra's famous signature dish. You will need a large quantity of yogurt, as it has to be strained to remove nearly all the liquid. Traditionally, *Shrikand* is served with puris, deep-fried puffed breads, but it is also good with fresh seasonal fruits as a refreshing dessert.

SERVES 4–5

3 x 425g/15oz cartons of full-fat (whole)
  natural (plain) yogurt
a pinch of saffron threads, pounded
15ml/1 tbsp hot milk
75g/3oz/⅔ cup caster (superfine) sugar
2.5ml/½ tsp ground cardamom
fresh fruits such as mango, strawberries
  or pomegranate seeds, to serve

VARIATION
This dessert can be transformed into a form of cheesecake by layering the yogurt and fruit on a base made from crushed cookies mixed with melted butter.

1 Pour the yogurt on to a large, clean muslin cloth (cheesecloth). Bring together the four corners of the cloth and tie up into a knot. Hang the muslin over the sink or in a sieve (strainer) over a bowl until all the liquid has been removed. This takes up to 6 hours, so you can leave it overnight.

2 When the yogurt is nearly ready, soak the saffron in the hot milk for 10 minutes.

3 Empty the strained yogurt solids into a mixing bowl, then beat until smooth.

4 Add the sugar, cardamom and saffron along with the soaking milk. Mix well, then chill for at least 2 hours.

5 Serve in stemmed glasses, either in alternate layers of yogurt and fruit, or topped with the fruit of your choice.

Per portion Energy 260kcal/1101kJ; Protein 14.6g; Carbohydrate 35.5g, of which sugars 35.5g; Fat 7.6g, of which saturates 4.3g; Cholesterol 28mg; Calcium 518mg; Fibre 0g; Sodium 205mg.

Ground rice in saffron-scented milk

Phirni is a luxurious dessert in which a little ground rice is cooked in milk flavoured with saffron and spices until it is reduced to the consistency of evaporated milk. In Kashmir, where it originates, the dessert is served in earthenware bowls, but stemmed glasses or glazed ramekins work just as well.

SERVES 4–5

a pinch of saffron threads, pounded
15ml/1 tbsp hot milk
300ml/10fl oz/1¼ cups full-fat (whole) milk
50g/2oz/⅓ cup ground rice
400ml/14fl oz/1½ cups canned
   evaporated milk
50g/2oz/¼ cup granulated (white) sugar
25g/1oz/¼ cup blanched, flaked
   (sliced) almonds
25g/1oz/¼ cup pistachio nuts
5ml/1 tsp ground cardamom
15ml/1 tbsp rose water
2–3 dried ready-to-eat apricots, sliced,
   to garnish

1 Soak the saffron threads in the hot milk for 10 minutes, then set aside.

2 Brush the surface of a heavy pan with a little oil, then pour in the milk.

3 Sprinkle the ground rice evenly over the milk and place the pan over a medium heat. Bring it to the boil, stirring frequently.

4 Add the evaporated milk, sugar and almonds. Reserve a few pistachio nuts, then add the remainder to the milk.

5 Continue to cook over a low heat, stirring frequently, until the mixture thickens and resembles the consistency of cooked custard, coating the back of the spoon.

6 Stir in the ground cardamom and rose water and remove from the heat. Transfer to stemmed glasses or ramekins.

7 Crush the reserved pistachio nuts and sprinkle over the top with the sliced apricots. Chill for 2 hours before serving.

Per portion portion Energy 262kcal/1096kJ; Protein 11.1g; Carbohydrate 30.2g, of which sugars 22g; Fat 11.3g, of which saturates 3.9g; Cholesterol 22mg; Calcium 308mg; Fibre 0.7g; Sodium 127mg.

Milky orange dessert

Basundi is a sweet, milky dessert that works well with most fruits, and especially tropical ones such as oranges, pineapples or mangoes. The traditional cooking method is rather time-consuming, but this quicker version uses evaporated and condensed milk as well as ground rice to speed up the thickening process.

3 Blend the ground rice with just enough water to make a paste with a pouring consistency, then add it to the milk in the pan when it comes to boiling point.

4 Cook very gently, stirring constantly, for 10–12 minutes, until the mixture has thickened to a creamy consistency.

5 Remove from the heat, cool, then chill in the refrigerator for 4–5 hours.

6 Squeeze the oranges, then stir the juice into the milk mixture with the cardamom and nutmeg. Stir in half the mandarin segments.

7 Transfer the mixture to stemmed glasses and garnish with the remaining mandarin segments and the mint sprigs.

SERVES 4–6

sunflower oil, for brushing
400g/14oz canned evaporated milk
400g/14oz canned sweetened
  condensed milk
15ml/1 tbsp ground rice
2–3 large oranges
5ml/1 tsp ground cardamom
1.25ml/¼ tsp freshly grated nutmeg
300g/10½oz canned mandarin
  segments, drained
3–4 fresh mint sprigs, to decorate

1 Grease the base of a heavy pan and pour both types of milk into it.

2 Mix the two types of milk with a whisk to combine, then place the pan over medium heat. Stir the liquid regularly as it comes to a slow simmer.

COOK'S TIP
Prepared up to the end of step 4, the dessert will keep, chilled, for 2 days.

Per portion Energy 482kcal/2032kJ; Protein 17.1g; Carbohydrate 75.8g, of which sugars 73.8g; Fat 14.2g, of which saturates 8.8g; Cholesterol 53mg; Calcium 566mg; Fibre 0.3g; Sodium 262mg.

Milky almond dessert with pistachio nuts

Doodh Pak is a luxurious dessert made from almond purée that is cooked in milk flavoured with golden saffron and fragrant cardamom. A favourite in Gujarati homes, it is eaten on its own, but is also excellent when served topped with a combination of tropical fruits such as papayas, mangoes or kiwis.

SERVES 4

150g/5oz blanched almonds
900ml/1½ pints full-fat (whole) milk
a large pinch of saffron threads, pounded
15ml/1 tbsp hot milk, for soaking
sunflower oil, for brushing
25g/1oz raw pistachio nuts, lightly crushed
75g/3oz/scant ½ cup sugar
5ml/1 tsp ground cardamom
fresh fruit and/or toasted flaked (sliced) almonds, to serve

1 Put the almonds in a heatproof bowl, cover with boiling water and soak for 20 minutes. Drain, then place in a blender.

2 Add 175ml/6fl oz/¾ cup of the milk to the almonds. Blend until it forms a fine purée.

3 Put the saffron in a small bowl with the hot milk and set aside.

4 Brush a non-stick pan with a little oil. Put the remaining milk in the pan and bring it to simmering point over a low heat.

5 Add the puréed almonds and cook until the mixture begins to bubble, stirring often. Add the saffron, pistachio nuts and sugar.

6 Continue to cook, stirring regularly to prevent sticking, for 20–25 minutes, until the mixture thickens.

7 Stir in the cardamom, remove from the heat and leave to cool.

8 Pour into the serving dishes and chill the dessert for at least 2 hours. Top with fruits and/or garnish with toasted flaked almonds, then serve.

Per portion Energy 521kcal/2168kJ; Protein 17g; Carbohydrate 33g, of which sugars 32g; Fat 36g, of which saturates 8g; Cholesterol 32mg; Calcium 371mg; Fibre 4.8g; Sodium 141mg.

Milk balls in cardamom-scented syrup

This dish, *Golap Jamun*, is traditionally made with two dairy products known as khoya (reduced solidified milk) and chenna (cottage cheese), both of which are time-consuming to make. Full-cream (whole) milk powder or skimmed milk powder mixed with single (light) cream are good, quick alternatives.

MAKES 16

5ml/1 tsp saffron threads, pounded
30ml/2 tbsp hot milk
175g/6oz/1¼ cups full-cream (whole) milk powder, or skimmed milk powder mixed with 150ml/5fl oz/½ cup single (light) cream
75g/3oz/½ cup semolina
10ml/2 tsp plain (all-purpose) flour
5ml/1 tsp ground cardamom
5ml/1 tsp baking powder
40g/1½oz/3 tbsp ghee or unsalted butter, melted
150ml/5fl oz/½ cup milk
350g/12 oz/1¾ cups granulated (white) sugar
8 green cardamom pods, bruised
900ml/1½ pints/3½ cups water
sunflower oil, for deep-frying
whipped double (heavy) cream mixed with 30ml/2 tbsp rose water, and seasonal fresh fruits, to serve

1 Soak the pounded saffron in the hot milk for 10–12 minutes.

2 In a bowl, mix together the full-cream milk powder or skimmed milk powder and cream, semolina, flour, cardamom and baking powder. Rub in the ghee or butter.

3 Add the milk and the saffron threads, including the milk in which they were soaked.

4 Mix until a soft dough is formed, then transfer to a flat surface and knead for about 5 minutes, until smooth.

5 Divide the dough into two equal parts and form eight balls out of each. Rotate them between your palms to make them as smooth as possible, without any cracks.

6 Put the sugar, cardamom pods and water in a pan and bring to the boil. Stir until the sugar has dissolved. Turn the heat down and simmer for 6–8 minutes. Remove from the heat and set aside.

7 Heat the oil in a pan over a low heat and deep-fry the balls until they are a dark brown colour. They will sink, but should start floating after a few minutes. If they do not, ease them away from the base of the pan.

8 Remove with a slotted spoon and lower into the syrup. Fry the next batch in the same way. Leave them all soaking for 2 hours before serving with the cream and fruit.

Per portion Energy 219kcal/917kJ; Protein 1.6g; Carbohydrate 28.1g, of which sugars 24.6g; Fat 11.9g, of which saturates 4.1g; Cholesterol 10mg; Calcium 58mg; Fibre 0.1g; Sodium 58mg.

Mangoes in cardamom-scented coconut cream

This dessert, *Aam Ka Rasayana*, is a delight for mango-lovers. It is easy to make and refrigerates well for a few days, so it is perfect as a make-ahead dessert for a dinner party. Unrefined palm sugar (jaggery) is traditionally used, but you could use soft dark brown sugar instead.

SERVES 4

2 large or 4 small mangoes
75g/3oz/1 cup desiccated (dry unsweetened shredded) coconut
425ml/15fl oz/1½ cups full-fat (whole) milk
5 green cardamom pods, bruised
110g/4oz palm sugar (jaggery), grated, or soft dark brown sugar
1.25ml/¼ tsp freshly grated nutmeg
strawberries or other seasonal fruit
sprigs of fresh mint, to decorate

1 Peel the mango and slice off the two large pieces on either side of the stone, then the two thinner sides. Remove the skin, then cut all the slices into bitesize pieces and set aside. Scrape off all the flesh next to the stone and reserve.

2 Put the coconut into a pan and add 300ml/10fl oz/1 cup of the milk, the cardamom and sugar. Bring to the boil, reduce the heat to low and simmer for 5 minutes.

3 Remove from the heat and cool slightly, then purée until smooth in a blender, along with the reserved mango scrapings.

COOK'S TIP
You can also prepare the mango flesh by scoring the two large side slices into cubes, then inverting the skin to make a 'hedgehog' and slicing the cubes from the skin.

4 Strain the coconut purée, pushing as much of the milk through a sieve (strainer) as possible.

5 Return the solid coconut to the blender and add the remaining milk. Blend until smooth and push it through a sieve as before. Discard the solid coconut left in the sieve.

6 Combine both the milk mixtures and add the grated nutmeg.

7 Put the chopped mango into a bowl and add the sweetened, spiced coconut milk. Mix well and chill for several hours.

8 Serve in stemmed glasses layered with sliced strawberries.

Per portion Energy 349kcal/1467kJ; Protein 5.3g; Carbohydrate 49.2g, of which sugars 48.8g; Fat 16g, of which saturates 12.7g; Cholesterol 15mg; Calcium 153mg; Fibre 5.2g; Sodium 67mg.

Rose-scented mango dessert

This dessert, *Aam Ka Mitha*, is best made with the Indian variety of mangoes known as Alphonso. They are available fresh in Indian stores during the mango season (May–August), but are also sold in cans, sliced or puréed. Canned standard mangoes from supermarkets work well, too.

2 Add the curd cheese, honey and rose water to the bowl or blender. Blitz until well blended and smooth.

3 Arrange alternate layers of kiwi cubes and pomegranate seeds in serving dishes, and top with the mango mixture.

4 Chill for at least 30 minutes, then sprinkle the ground cardamom or nutmeg on top and serve.

SERVES 4

2 x 425g/15oz cans Alphonso mangoes
225g/8oz/1 cup curd (farmer's) cheese
22.5ml/1½ tbsp honey
30ml/2 tbsp rose water
4 kiwi fruits, cut into cubes
the seeds of ½ pomegranate
1.25ml/¼ tsp ground cardamom or nutmeg

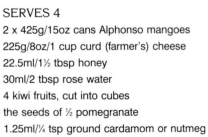

VARIATION
Low-fat curd cheese can be used, if preferred.

1 Put the mangoes along with the syrup into a food processor, or use a bowl and stick blender, and purée until smooth.

Per portion Energy 230kcal/980kJ; Protein 9g; Carbohydrate 44g, of which sugars 43g; Fat 3g, of which saturates 2g; Cholesterol 9mg; Calcium 113mg; Fibre 6.2g; Sodium 176mg.

Vermicelli dessert with dates and pistachio nuts

This popular dessert, *Sheer Khurma*, is a contribution from the Muslim community in India. The vermicelli is first sautéed in ghee, then cooked in thickened milk with a hint of spices. Chunks of dates and pistachio nuts are then added, which create a beautiful pattern and add sweetness and flavour.

SERVES 6

30ml/2 tbsp ghee or unsalted butter
25g/1oz dried vermicelli
50g/2oz/½ cup dried ready-to-eat dates,
  coarsely chopped
25g/1oz/¼ cup pistachio nuts
600ml/1 pint/2½ cups full-fat
  (whole) milk
50g/2oz/¼ cup sugar, or to taste
2.5ml/½ tsp ground cinnamon
2.5ml/½ tsp ground nutmeg
25g/1oz/¼ cup chopped pistachio nuts and
  2.5ml/½ tsp cinnamon, to garnish

1 Melt the ghee or butter in a heavy, non-stick pan over a low heat, then add the vermicelli. Cook for 3 minutes, then add the dates and pistachio nuts.

2 Stir-fry for 2–3 minutes or until the vermicelli is golden brown. Add the milk and sugar to the pan and bring it to the boil.

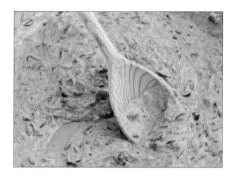

3 Reduce the heat to low and simmer gently for 20 minutes, stirring regularly to prevent sticking.

4 Stir in the spices, then remove from the heat. Garnish with chopped pistachio nuts and cinnamon and serve hot or cold.

Per portion Energy 231kcal/964kJ; Protein 5g; Carbohydrate 23g, of which sugars 19g; Fat 14g, of which saturates 7g; Cholesterol 28mg; Calcium 136mg; Fibre 0.7g; Sodium 89mg.

Coconut-stuffed parcels with cloves

The people of central India love desserts and sweetmeats. *Lavang Lata* is a pretty parcel of cardamom-scented coconut wrapped in a simple, home-made pastry with a whole clove to hold the parcel together. These delicious morsels are ideal with a cup of tea or after dinner with coffee instead of a dessert.

MAKES 12

For the pastry:
225g/8oz/2 cups plain (all-purpose) flour, plus extra for dusting
40g/1½oz/3 tbsp ghee or butter
125ml/4fl oz/½ cup cold water
12 whole cloves
sunflower oil, for deep-frying

For the filling:
50g/2oz/⅔ cup desiccated (dry unsweetened shredded) coconut
75ml/3fl oz/5 tbsp hot milk
50g/2oz seedless raisins
50g/2oz raw cashew nuts, chopped
5ml/1 tsp ground cardamom
2.5ml/½ tsp ground nutmeg

For the syrup:
175g/6oz/scant 1 cup granulated (white) sugar
5 cardamom pods, bruised
300ml/10fl oz/1¼ cups water

1 First make the pastry. Sift the flour into a mixing bowl and rub in the ghee or butter. Mix until the flour looks crumbly and has the texture of breadcrumbs.

COOK'S TIP
It is always very important to allow pastry to 'rest' for 30 minutes before rolling out and shaping, or it is likely to shrink during cooking.

2 Gradually add the water to the flour mixture and stir with a spoon until a soft dough is formed.

3 Transfer the dough to a flat surface and knead for about 1 minute, until it is smooth and pliable.

4 Cover with clear film (plastic wrap) and allow to rest for 30 minutes.

5 Meanwhile, mix all the ingredients for the filling together in a large bowl until thoroughly combined. Set aside.

6 Put all the syrup ingredients into a pan and place over a high heat. Bring to the boil, then reduce the heat to low. Simmer the mixture for 10–12 minutes, then switch off the heat.

7 Divide the dough into 12 equal parts and make a round cake out of each portion. Roll each one into a 7.5cm/3in circle.

8 Divide the filling into 12 equal parts and place one portion in the centre of each pastry circle. Enclose the filling by folding over the edges to form a square. Secure with a clove.

9 Heat the oil for deep-frying over a low/medium heat until it reaches 180°C/350°F. Fry the coconut parcels in a few batches, until they are crisp and golden brown.

10 Immerse the parcels immediately in the hot syrup (reheat the syrup gently if necessary). Spoon some of the syrup over the top and leave them immersed until you have finished frying the next batch.

11 Remove the first batch from the syrup and place them in a serving dish, then immerse the second batch in the syrup, spooning over some of the syrup as before.

12 When you have taken the last batch out of the syrup, boil the remaining syrup and reduce it by half. Spoon this syrup over the parcels and serve at room temperature.

Per portion Energy 267kcal/1118kJ; Protein 3.2g; Carbohydrate 34.1g, of which sugars 19.2g; Fat 14g, of which saturates 5g; Cholesterol 1mg; Calcium 46mg; Fibre 1.4g; Sodium 21mg.

Cardamom-scented coconut dumplings

These sweet coconut dumplings, *Narikolor Malpuwa*, are redolent with the heady aroma of crushed cardamom and make a wonderful teatime treat. They are served for breakfast in Assam, but can be enjoyed as a dessert with fresh fruits and cream, or even as wonderful sweet snacks at buffet parties.

SERVES 4–5

350ml/12fl oz/1½ cups canned
  coconut milk
110g/4oz/½ cup palm sugar (jaggery),
  grated, or soft dark brown sugar
225g/8oz/2 cups plain (all-purpose) flour
a pinch of bicarbonate of soda
  (baking soda)
5ml/1 tsp ground cardamom
1.25ml/¼ tsp ground nutmeg
5ml/1 tsp nigella seeds
25g/1oz seedless raisins
sunflower oil, for deep-frying
150ml/5fl oz/⅔ cup single (light) cream
a few pomegranate seeds or other
  seasonal fruits, to garnish

1 Put the coconut milk into a small pan and grate in the palm sugar or add the dark brown sugar. Place over a low heat and stir until the sugar is completely dissolved. Leave to cool.

2 Sift the flour into a mixing bowl and add the bicarbonate of soda, cardamom, nutmeg, nigella seeds and raisins. Mix well.

3 Add the cooled, sweetened coconut milk and mix until a thick batter is formed.

4 Heat the oil in a pan suitable for deep-frying over a low/medium heat until it reaches 180°C/350°F. Carefully drop in as many spoonfuls of the batter as the pan will hold in a single layer. Do not overcrowd the pan.

5 Fry the dumplings gently for 7–8 minutes, reducing the heat if necessary, until they are well browned. Lift out with a slotted spoon and drain on kitchen paper. Repeat until you have used all the batter.

6 Pour the cream into a pan and heat gently until just simmering. Add the dumplings and stir until they are well coated, and the cream has thickened slightly. Remove from the heat and leave to cool. Serve garnished with the pomegranate seeds.

Per portion Energy 393kcal/1657kJ; Protein 6.9g; Carbohydrate 66.3g, of which sugars 31.9g; Fat 12.9g, of which saturates 2.1g; Cholesterol 4mg; Calcium 161mg; Fibre 1.6g; Sodium 55mg.

Rice and wheat pancakes

These indulgent pancakes, *Achappam*, are enriched with coconut milk and egg. Traditionally, they are made in small metal ring moulds, but you can use large moulds instead. They are delicious on their own, or you can serve them drizzled with maple syrup and fresh fruits or with thick yogurt and clear honey.

MAKES 18

110g/4oz/1 cup plain (all-purpose) flour
110g/4oz/⅔ cup ground rice
110g/4oz/1 cup caster (superfine) sugar
5ml/1 tsp ground cardamom
22.5ml/1½ tbsp sesame seeds
2 large (US extra large) eggs
400ml/14fl oz/1½ cups canned
  coconut milk
sunflower oil, for shallow-frying

1 Sift the flour into a mixing bowl and add the ground rice, sugar, cardamom and sesame seeds. Mix well.

2 Beat the eggs and slowly add the coconut milk while beating, until well blended.

COOK'S TIP
The pancakes can be made in advance and chilled or frozen, and then reheated in a moderate oven for 6–8 minutes.

3 Pour the egg and coconut milk mixture into the flour and ground rice, and stir until you have a thick batter.

4 Pour enough oil into a large frying pan to cover the base to about 1cm/½in depth and place over a low heat. Put a 5cm/2in steel ring mould in the pan and pour in enough batter to come halfway up the mould.

5 After about 2–3 minutes, when the batter is set, carefully turn it over (the top will not be completely set at this stage) and continue to cook until it is golden brown on both sides.

6 Drain on kitchen paper while you make the remaining pancakes in the same way. Serve with a topping of your choice.

Per portion Energy 110kcal/463kJ; Protein 2.1g; Carbohydrate 17.1g, of which sugars 7.6g; Fat 4g, of which saturates 0.6g; Cholesterol 21mg; Calcium 32mg; Fibre 0.3g; Sodium 33mg.

Coconut-filled wheat pancakes

Pati Shepta is a childhood favourite that is enjoyed during the Hindu festival of lights, Diwali. Freshly grated coconut is the norm in India, but using desiccated (dry unsweetened shredded) coconut saves a fair amount of time and effort. The added cream enriches the dried coconut and tastes quite delicious.

3 Stir in the cinnamon, remove the pan from the heat and allow the mixture to cool.

4 To make the pancakes, blend all the ingredients, except the ghee or butter, in a blender. Alternatively, beat together in a large bowl. Cover and set aside for 30 minutes.

5 Brush the surface of a non-stick or cast iron frying pan with some melted ghee or butter and place it over a low heat.

6 Pour about 30ml/2 tbsp of the batter into the pan, spreading it quickly to cover the surface by tilting it. Cook for about 1 minute, until the pancake is set, then continue to cook for a further 1 minute, until brown spots appear on the underside. Carefully turn it over with a metal spatula or fish slice. Cook the other side for about 1 minute or until brown spots appear as before.

MAKES 6

For the filling:
50g/2oz/¼ cup desiccated (dry unsweetened shredded) coconut
50g/2oz/4 tbsp soft dark brown sugar
25g/1oz/1 tbsp chopped mixed nuts
250ml/8fl oz/1 cup double (heavy) cream
5ml/1 tsp ground cinnamon

For the pancakes:
2 eggs
150g/5oz/1¼ cups wholemeal (whole-wheat) flour
2.5ml/½ tsp ground cinnamon
1.25ml/¼ tsp ground clove
15ml/1 tbsp caster (superfine) sugar
200ml/7fl oz/scant 1 cup full-fat (whole) milk
melted ghee or unsalted butter, for frying
whipped cream or vanilla ice cream, to serve, (optional)

1 To make the filling, combine all the ingredients except the ground cinnamon in a small pan and place over a medium heat.

2 As soon as it begins to bubble, reduce the heat to low and let it simmer, uncovered, for 8–10 minutes, until the coconut has absorbed all the liquid. Stir regularly during the cooking time.

7 Spread about 15ml/1 tbsp of the filling on one side of the pancake and roll it up. Make the rest of the pancakes the same way.

Per portion Energy 452kcal/1879kJ; Protein 9g; Carbohydrate 30g, of which sugars 15g; Fat 34g, of which saturates 20g; Cholesterol 139mg; Calcium 102mg; Fibre 4.2g; Sodium 71mg.

Wheat pancakes with black peppercorns

Many varieties of *Malpuas* are made all over the sub-continent. This central Indian version, with sweetness from palm sugar (jaggery) and spiciness from crushed black pepper, offers a different taste sensation from other versions. Serve on their own with after-dinner coffee or as a dessert topped with cream and fruits.

MAKES 12
115g/4oz/⅔ cup semolina
115g/4oz/1 cup self-raising (self-rising) flour
5ml/1 tsp freshly ground black pepper
2.5ml/½ tsp ground cardamom
2.5ml½ tsp freshly grated nutmeg
75g/3oz/⅓ cup full-fat (whole) natural
   (plain) yogurt
250ml/8fl oz/1 cup milk
110g/4oz palm sugar (jaggery) or soft
   dark brown sugar
75ml/2½fl oz/⅓ cup water
sunflower or light olive oil, for
   shallow-frying
whipped cream and seasonal fresh fruit,
   to serve

1 Dry-roast the semolina in a heavy pan for about 10 minutes, until it is golden brown, stirring constantly.

2 Transfer the semolina to a mixing bowl then add the flour, ground black pepper, cardamom and nutmeg. Mix well, then add the yogurt and stir to combine.

3 Put the milk in a non-stick pan and place over a medium heat. Cut the palm sugar into small pieces, add it or the brown sugar to the milk and stir until dissolved.

4 Add the sweetened milk to the semolina mixture, then add the water. Mix with a spoon until a smooth batter is formed.

5 In a frying pan, heat enough oil to cover the surface to a depth of about 2.5cm/1in over a medium heat.

6 Spread a generous tablespoon of the batter in a circular motion to form a pancake about 7.5cm/3in in diameter.

7 Fry the pancake until golden brown on both sides, then remove with a slotted spoon and drain on kitchen paper. Use the remaining batter to make more pancakes in the same way.

8 Serve warm, with whipped cream and fresh fruit.

Per portion Energy 155kcal/653kJ; Protein 3g; Carbohydrate 25g, of which sugars 10g; Fat 6g, of which saturates 1g; Cholesterol 4mg; Calcium 82mg; Fibre 0.9g; Sodium 57mg.

Cardamom-scented banana fudge with coconut

Halwa is the generic Indian name for any sweetmeat cooked with sugar and a hint of spice to a soft fudge consistency. When made with freshly grated coconut and mashed banana, this *Balehannu Halwa* is divine. It is quicker to use desiccated (dry unsweetened shredded) coconut, lightly cooked in milk, than fresh coconut.

SERVES 4–5

110g/4oz/1⅓ cups desiccated (dry
 unsweetened shredded) coconut
200ml/7fl oz/¾ cup full-fat (whole) milk
4–5 semi-ripe bananas
75g/3oz/6 tbsp ghee or unsalted butter
25g/1oz seedless raisins
50g/2oz raw cashew nuts, chopped (optional)
110g/4oz/1 cup granulated (white) sugar
5ml/1 tsp ground cardamom
2.5ml/½ tsp freshly grated nutmeg
25g/1oz pistachio nuts, crushed (optional)
15ml/1 tbsp toasted coconut flakes

1 Place the coconut and milk in a pan and stir over a medium heat until the coconut has absorbed all the milk. Remove from the heat and set aside.

2 Mash the bananas in a large bowl with a potato masher or fork.

3 Melt the ghee or butter in a frying pan over a low heat, then add the mashed banana and coconut. Stir and cook for 4–5 minutes.

4 Add the raisins, cashew nuts and sugar, and increase the heat to medium. Continue to cook, stirring all the time, for 15–17 minutes until the mixture reaches a soft fudge-like consistency.

5 Add the cardamom and grated nutmeg, and mix well.

6 Brush a 30cm/12in plate with some melted butter and spread the fudge on it, shaping it into a 15cm/6in square. Sprinkle the pistachio nuts and coconut flakes on the surface and press them down firmly.

7 Allow to cool, then chill for 2–3 hours. Cut into squares or diamonds and serve.

> ## VARIATIONS
> • Ripe mango can be used instead of banana in this recipe.
> • Toasted sunflower seeds make a good alternative to nuts.

Per portion Energy 572kcal/2386kJ; Protein 6.9g; Carbohydrate 53.2g, of which sugars 49.4g; Fat 38.3g, of which saturates 21.2g; Cholesterol 6mg; Calcium 79mg; Fibre 4.8g; Sodium 89mg.

Soft mango fudge

This fruity sweetmeat is a recreation of a very old recipe by a prominent Assamese housewife called Dhanada Kumari Saikia. This version, *Aamor Haluwa*, produces a wonderfully sweet and flavoursome fudge studded with crunchy nuts, which makes the ideal end to a spicy meal.

SERVES 4–6

125g/4¼oz/scant ¾ cup caster (superfine) sugar
a good pinch of saffron threads, pounded
115g/4oz/½ cup ghee or unsalted butter
115g/4oz/⅔ cup semolina
50g/2oz/½ cup raw cashew nuts, chopped
115g/4oz/½ cup ground almonds
300ml/½ pint/1¼ cups sweetened mango purée or 2 x 400g/14oz cans of sliced mango, drained and puréed
30ml/2 tbsp rose water
22.5ml/1½ tbsp shelled pistachio nuts, lightly roasted and crushed

1 Put the sugar into a pan and add 300ml/ ½ pint/1¼ cups water. Place over a high heat and stir until the sugar has dissolved. Stir in the saffron and set aside.

2 In a heavy pan, melt the ghee or butter over a low heat, then add the semolina and cashew nuts. Cook for 5–6 minutes, stirring frequently.

3 Add the ground almonds and continue to cook, stirring, for 3–4 minutes or until the mixture is light brown and a toasted aroma is released.

4 Mix the mango purée and rose water together and add to the sugar syrup. Pour the mixture into the semolina and stir over a low heat for 3–4 minutes or until it thickens and stops sticking to the bottom and sides of the pan.

5 Grease a 30cm x 18cm/12in x 7in baking tin (pan).

6 Using a metal spoon, spread the fudge mixture into the tin. Press down firmly to level the surface.

7 Sprinkle the pistachio nuts on top and gently but firmly press them in. Leave to cool, then cut into 4cm/1½in squares. Serve at room temperature.

Per portion Energy 525kcal/2193kJ; Protein 8g; Carbohydrate 47g, of which sugars 30g; Fat 35g, of which saturates 14g; Cholesterol 54mg; Calcium 62mg; Fibre 4.6g; Sodium 18mg.

Black sesame seed fudge

Sesame seeds grow throughout India and they come in all shades from pale ivory to brown and black. The ivory ones are used to enrich and thicken curries, while the black seeds are used mainly in the north-east to make sweetmeats. If black seeds prove difficult to find, ivory ones can be used in this recipe, *Tilor Borfi*.

3 Add the ground sesame seeds. Stir over a medium heat for 5–6 minutes, until the mixture stops sticking to the bottom and sides of the pan.

4 Brush a 30cm/12in plate with a little oil and spread the sesame mixture on it. Push the sides in with the back of a metal spoon to make a rough square about 1cm/½in thick.

5 Rub the peanuts with a clean cloth to remove some of the salt, then split them into halves.

6 Press them gently on to the surface of the fudge, leave to cool, then chill for an hour or two before cutting into squares or diamonds and serving.

SERVES 6
350g/12oz/generous 2 cups black
  sesame seeds
5 cardamom pods, bruised
150g/5oz/⅔ cup palm sugar (jaggery),
  grated, or soft dark brown sugar
200ml/7fl oz/¾ cup water
25g/1oz roasted peanuts

1 Dry-roast the black sesame seeds and the cardamom pods in a heavy pan over a medium heat, stirring constantly, for 7–8 minutes. Transfer them to a large plate and let them cool. When cold, grind them in a food processor or coffee grinder.

2 Put the sugar into a heavy pan and add 200ml/7fl oz/¾ cup water. Place over a medium heat and bring to the boil. Cook for about 2 minutes.

COOK'S TIP
Any leftover fudge can be stored in the refrigerator for 4–5 days.

Per portion Energy 471kcal/1959kJ; Protein 11.8g; Carbohydrate 27.2g, of which sugars 26.6g; Fat 35.8g, of which saturates 5.2g; Cholesterol 0mg; Calcium 407mg; Fibre 4.9g; Sodium 13mg.

Soft lentil fudge with cardamom and saffron

Lentils provide the necessary protein for the vast majority of the vegetarian population in India. This fudge, *Mung Dhal Halva*, is an example of how many different ways lentils can be cooked. Here, yellow split lentils (moong or mung dhal) are cooked in milk and sugar until the mixture reaches a soft fudge consistency.

SERVES 4–6

250g/9oz yellow split lentils (moong or mung dhal)
115g/4oz/½ cup ghee or unsalted butter
600ml/1 pint/2½ cups full-fat (whole) milk
115g/4oz/generous ½ cup sugar
a good pinch of saffron threads, pounded
150ml/¼ pint/⅔ cup double (heavy) cream
5ml/1 tsp ground cardamom or other flavourings such as nutmeg or cinnamon
30ml/2 tbsp roasted unsalted pistachio nuts, crushed, to garnish

1 Wash the lentils in several changes of water, then soak in a bowl of cold water for 2–3 hours.

2 Drain well and grind to a fine paste in a food processor without adding any water.

3 In a large non-stick pan frying pan, melt the ghee or butter over a low heat and add the lentil paste. Stir and cook for 10–12 minutes, until the lentil paste is dry and crumbly.

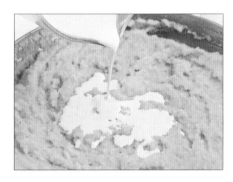

4 Add the milk, sugar and pounded saffron. Increase the heat slightly and let it come to the simmering point.

5 Reduce the heat to low and beat the mixture in order to break up any lumps.

6 Continue cooking, stirring regularly, for 10–12 minutes. Add the cream and continue to cook, stirring, for a further 8–10 minutes.

7 Add the cardamom or other flavourings and cook until the mixture stops sticking to the bottom and sides of the pan.

8 Remove from the heat and spread in a buttered 25 x 25cm/10 x 10in square tin (pan).

9 Smooth the top and sprinkle with the pistachio nuts. Press them down gently and leave the fudge to cool completely. Cut into squares and serve.

Per portion Energy 586kcal/2444kJ; Protein 13g; Carbohydrate 50g, of which sugars 26g; Fat 39g, of which saturates 24g; Cholesterol 102mg; Calcium 149mg; Fibre 4.5g; Sodium 76mg.

Index

PICTURE ACKNOWLEDGEMENTS:
The publisher would like to thank Jon
Whitaker for his stunning photography
throughout the book, apart from the
following images:
Alamy pages 6, 7, 8, 9bl, 9br, 10, 11, 12, 14t,
14bl, 15, 16, 17, 18, 19, 20, 21, 22br, 23, 26bl,
26br, 27t; **Corbis** page 13b; **Graham Walker**
author image on jacket; **iStockphoto** pages
9t, 14br, 28b, 32b, 35b, 37t, 39b.